Prezi™

FOR

DUMMIES®

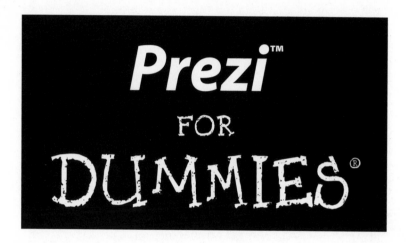

by **Stephanie Diamond**

WILEY

Wiley Publishing, Inc.

Prezi™ For Dummies®

Published by
Wiley Publishing, Inc.
111 River Street
Hoboken, NJ 07030-5774

www.wiley.com

Copyright © 2010 by Wiley Publishing, Inc., Indianapolis, Indiana

Published by Wiley Publishing, Inc., Indianapolis, Indiana

Published simultaneously in Canada

For general information on our other products and services, please contact our Customer Care Department within the U.S. at 877-762-2974, outside the U.S. at 317-572-3993, or fax 317-572-4002.

For technical support, please visit www.wiley.com/techsupport.

Wiley also publishes its books in a variety of electronic formats. Some content that appears in print may not be available in electronic books.

Library of Congress Control Number: 2010933473

ISBN: 978-0-470-62586-6

Manufactured in the United States of America

10 9 8 7 6 5 4 3 2 1

WILEY

About the Author

Stephanie Diamond is a thought leader and management marketing professional with 20+ years of experience building profits in over 75 different industries. She has worked with solopreneurs, small business owners, and multibillion dollar corporations.

She worked for eight years as a marketing director at AOL. When she joined, there were less than 1 million subscribers. When she left in 2002, there were 36 million. While at AOL, she developed a highly successful line of multimedia products that brought in an annual $40 million dollars in incremental revenue.

In 2002, she founded Digital Media Works, Inc. (http://digmediaworks.com), an online marketing company that helps business owners discover the hidden profits in their business. She's passionate about guiding online companies to successfully generate more revenue and find their company's real value.

As a strategic thinker, Stephanie uses all the current visual thinking techniques and brain research to help companies get to the essence of their brand. In the Marketing Message blog (www.marketingmessageblog.com), she shares her perspective about how companies can improve their marketing by understanding and communicating their value using stories.

Stephanie received a BA in Psychology from Hofstra University and an MSW and MPH from the University of Hawaii. She lives in New York with her husband and 14-year-old Maltese named Tyler.

Dedication

To Barry, who makes all things possible.

To my family for their encouragement and love.

Author's Acknowledgments

It is my great privilege to write this book. I want to offer great thanks to Wiley Publishing, Inc. for letting me introduce *Prezi For Dummies*. Specifically, I want to thank the wonderfully creative group — Acquisitions Editor Amy Fandrei, Project Editor Chris W. Morris, Copy Editor Virginia Sanders, and Editorial Manager Leah Cameron for sharing their talents and support.

I want to thank the folks at Prezi for letting me share their great accomplishment with a waiting audience. Thanks to Adam Somlai-Fischer, Angelie Argawal, Zoli Radnai, and Patrick Wenger for their help and enthusiasm.

Thanks to Matt Wagner, my agent at Fresh Books, for his continued work on my behalf.

Finally, thanks to you for choosing this book to learn about Prezi. I wish you enormous joy on your exciting journey.

Publisher's Acknowledgments

We're proud of this book; please send us your comments through our online registration form located at http://dummies.custhelp.com. For other comments, please contact our Customer Care Department within the U.S. at 877-762-2974, outside the U.S. at 317-572-3993, or fax 317-572-4002.

Some of the people who helped bring this book to market include the following:

Acquisitions and Editorial

Senior Project Editor: Christopher Morris

Acquisitions Editor: Amy Fandrei

Copy Editor: Virginia Sanders

Technical Editor: Angelie Agarwal

Editorial Manager: Kevin Kirschner

Editorial Assistant: Amanda Graham

Sr. Editorial Assistant: Cherie Case

Cartoons: Rich Tennant (www.the5thwave.com)

Composition Services

Project Coordinator: Patrick Redmond

Layout and Graphics: Amy Hassos, Joyce Haughey, Ronald G. Terry

Proofreaders: ConText Editorial Services, Inc.

Indexer: Infodex Indexing Services, Inc.

Publishing and Editorial for Technology Dummies

   Richard Swadley, Vice President and Executive Group Publisher

   Andy Cummings, Vice President and Publisher

   Mary Bednarek, Executive Acquisitions Director

   Mary C. Corder, Editorial Director

Publishing for Consumer Dummies

   Diane Graves Steele, Vice President and Publisher

Composition Services

   Debbie Stailey, Director of Composition Services

Contents at a Glance

Table of Contents

Introduction

Welcome to *Prezi For Dummies*. You're entering the magical world of digital storytelling. I'm honored to introduce Prezi to you in this book. It will change your thinking about how presentations are created and delivered.

The developers of Prezi started with the notion that slides were the wrong medium for making persuasive arguments. Instead, they dreamed of an unlimited whiteboard as a powerful starting point. With Prezi, you now have the chance to create presentations of all kinds without limitations.

Like most people who begin to explore a new application, you may be approaching it with some trepidation. You ask yourself: "Will it be quick and easy to learn?" "Are there things that I won't understand?" Be assured, as you begin working with Prezi, you should feel anticipation, not fear — it's easy and fun! My advice to you is just to charge in and start playing with the digital canvas. Think back to a time when a blank slate was an opportunity to explore and create without fear. Prezi gives you the tools. You supply the creativity.

If you follow the steps I've detailed in this book to plan and get content on the canvas. you'll feel a weight lifting from your shoulders. No more shoe-horning charts, numbers, and words to fit on a single slide. No more counting bullets or wedging images together to represent a great idea.

Your prezis can start a whole new line of thinking, tell a persuasive story, or get you that raise you deserve. It's all in the execution. So get started now!

About This Book

Because Prezi is such a unique and flexible application, I've made sure to highlight how to get up and running fast by covering the most important topics.

These topics include the following:

- ✓ Using the main Bubble menu
- ✓ Picking the right subscription plan to suit your needs
- ✓ Planning in analog to jump-start your presentation
- ✓ Setting up your storyline using the Path function

- Working with the Smart Zooming feature to display the big picture and the details of each presentation
- Uploading a variety of digital media to make your prezi stand out
- Using the Transformation Zebra tool to make editing easy
- Developing your story to sell your ideas
- Navigating the Prezi canvas to work smarter
- Mind Mapping to brainstorm using Prezi
- Sharing your prezis with colleagues and friends
- Presenting with a projector and remote clicker
- Interacting with the Prezi Community
- Using Prezi for more than business applications

Foolish Assumptions

As I wrote this book, I tried to cover all the different situations you would come up against when creating new presentations using Prezi.

I have a picture of you in my mind and make the following assumptions about you:

- You're not a professional presenter.
- You've used other presentation software in the past and are looking for something with greater flexibility.
- You're willing to spend time finding out about using visual persuasion and storytelling to deliver your message.
- You're comfortable using your browser to view online software.
- You want to use presentations to give yourself a competitive advantage.

Conventions Used in This Book

To make sure instructions are clear and easy, I follow these conventions:

- When you need to take a specific action in a step list, they are printed in **bold**.
- When you see something printed this way — http://prezi.com — you're looking at a Web address (URL).

How This Book Is Organized

In this book, I cover what you need to know about Prezi to make the most of its powerful features. This book consists of five parts that show you how to use Prezi to develop amazing presentations. I've also brought together information about visual thinking and storytelling that will make your use of Prezi more effective. The chapters are modular so that you can skip around and focus on topics as they become pertinent to the current stage of your presentation.

Part 1: Establishing a Prezi Mindset

In Part I, you start with the basics. First you look at what goes into creating a Prezi mindset. When you begin working with Prezi, you realize that it's not going to fit into an old-style presentation mold. I introduce you to a new way of thinking about presentations. Chapter 1 covers how you can develop a mindset that makes your presentations more powerful. In Chapter 2, you find out how to create your first prezi from start to finish. You get to see the freedom a no-slide medium can deliver.

Part II: Exploring the Prezi Universe

Part II is an exploration of how the main interface — the Bubble menu — is used. In Chapter 3, you see how you navigate the open digital canvas and what the main functions are used for. Chapter 4 covers the use of the Desktop version of Prezi, which is available for Prezi Pro subscribers. Chapter 5 gives you an overview of the Prezi home base you set up online and shows you how to set up and collaborate with workgroups. Sharing prezis with friends and family is built right into the interface. Chapter 6 gives you a tour of the active Prezi community and how to find reusable content for your own prezis.

Part III: Creating Show-Stopping Prezis

In Part III, you discover how visuals impact your ability to persuade. Chapter 7 walks you through the complete planning process. You see how to create a structure, tell interesting stories, and deliver a memorable presentation. In Chapter 8, you look at the use of graphics to increase the value of your message. Chapter 9 covers what designers can do with Prezi to show off their custom work.

Part IV: Using Prezi beyond Presentations

Part IV introduces you to other uses for Prezi beyond the business presentation. In Chapter 10, you get an in-depth look at brainstorming for new ideas. You see how you can use Mind Mapping and new research about the brain to deliver more powerful messages. Chapter 11 shows you how to use Prezi to develop a business plan that sells your ideas. Chapter 12 introduces you to the use of Prezi in the classroom. Prezi has created a special education license that makes it affordable for teachers and students. In Chapter 13, you tour the wonderful world of Prezi for scrapbooks, collections, recipes, and much more.

Part V: Part of Tens

Part V is the popular Part of Tens section found in all *For Dummies* books. This is the section where you find all sorts of useful information in groups of ten. In this section are ten ways to fill a blank screen, ten things that you should know about visual thinking, ten tips for Mind Mapping with Prezi, and the ten worst things to do with Prezi.

Icons Used in This Book

To make sure that you are alerted to specific information, I use the following icons:

When you see this Tip icon, it means I want to share some information that will make things easier or quicker for you.

If this icon pops up on the page, it's there to point out the information you need to store in your memory bank to use when you're working with Prezi.

Pay special attention when you see this warning icon. Hopefully, it will prevent you from making a big mistake or having to backtrack.

Appendix: Resources for Presenters

The appendix includes resources that help round out your knowledge of presenting in a digital environment. I include some Web sites and books that you may find helpful in taking a deeper dive into specific topics.

Where to Go from Here

I hope this book helps you to use Prezi in ways you hadn't thought of before. There's so much you can do. Using this book, you can create presentations with a whole new attitude. As the application expands and Prezi incorporates new ideas, I expect it will become a staple of presenters around the world.

I'd love to get your feedback about how you're using the book and what new things you're doing with Prezi. Feel free to leave comments for me on my blog at www.marketingmessageblog.com.

Part I
Establishing a Prezi Mindset

The 5th Wave   By Rich Tennant

"No, it's not a pie chart, it's just a corn chip that got scanned into the document."

In this part . . .

Welcome to the No-Slide Zone. You're entering a world where presentations are not all alike. Your audience will be delighted that you can entertain as well as inform them. That's a potent combination. But what makes this application so different from other presentation applications? And what do you need to do to dazzle your audiences with Prezi? The answers to these questions follow.

In Chapter 1, you see what you need to do to develop a Prezi mindset. You find out why Prezi is so different and how you can use it in a number of different ways. In Chapter 2, you create your first prezi and see what all the fuss is about. Fasten your seatbelt!

Chapter 1

Getting Started with Prezi

Welcome to a new way of presenting. Hopefully Prezi can inspire you to think differently about your next presentation. Prezi can take your slide-driven talks in a whole new direction. Part of the appeal of Prezi is its totally unique way of presenting ideas. But it's more than that: It's a way to free yourself from the boundaries of time and space. Does that sound magical? I hope so. Your journey into Prezi will be exciting.

Unlike more conventional presentation applications, Prezi gives you the tools to work in several dimensions at once to wow a formerly bored audience. When you see how to traverse layers and zoom around, you'll see what I mean.

In this chapter, I introduce you to a new presentation paradigm. And the price is right. You can start with the free version and decide where to go from there. Prezi is also hosted online so everything is just a little bit easier. The key to getting comfortable with Prezi is to jump right in and experiment.

Evolving Presentations

If you were unlucky enough to attend a business presentation before the mid-1980s, you saw a person standing in the front of the room, clicking through 35mm slides in a carousel or you saw a person slapping transparencies on an overhead projector.

Unfortunately, these presentations usually required a darkened room, which was a recipe for disaster. When the lights came back on, you'd see a bunch of bleary-eyed colleagues pretending they were awake the whole time. Of course, no one was fooled — or persuaded.

When computers came on the scene, there was some relief. Professional-looking graphics could be created without a camera or an extensive art department. People could show presentations as they had before, but now the slides were digital.

For 20 years, this method has prevailed. Some people are very comfortable with it and don't plan to try anything new. Others, though, see room for alternatives. They want something that adds a more visual way of telling a story.

Enter Prezi. It provides something that the other presentation software applications don't: movement. When you watch a prezi for the first time, you're struck by the fact that your screen has layers. You can zoom into them and out again to explore the canvas. And you can put it on Autoplay and let it roll. That's when the fun begins.

Finding Out Just What Prezi Is

Prezi describes itself as a digital storytelling tool. This is a deceptively simple description. To understand the difference between Prezi and other presentation tools, you need to look at the difference between a process and its content.

Most slide programs dictate a process. They're set up to organize material for a presenter to talk about in a linear fashion, which is great for the presenter but not always great for the audience. Prezi, on the other hand, uses content to create a story line. With Prezi, the organization of the material doesn't dictate a particular process — the story does.

Just like any tool, you have to figure out how to make Prezi work for you. It's easy to use, however, and when you get rolling, you'll probably prefer it to other presentation software. But you'll have to open your mind to a different way of thinking about what goes into presenting.

First and foremost, Prezi helps you tell a persuasive story that can change people's minds. With Prezi, your only limitation is the amount of time you have to spend on creating something unique.

Breaking the slide barrier

Can you imagine creating a presentation that doesn't include slides? Up until now, you likely couldn't. Breaking your addiction to information in rectangular bullet lists is going to be key to using Prezi. If you think I'm kidding, I'm not. When you first try Prezi, your impulse may be to try to put all your information into the built-in Frame tool (brackets, circles, and rectangles) and show them one by one like a slide show. Resist this urge!

What if directors had taken the new medium of TV as an opportunity to show people reading radio scripts at a microphone? At first, this might have been acceptable, but eventually people would have started to balk, because this approach didn't take advantage of the visual medium that television is. The medium of television meant that storytellers no longer had to just tell, they had to show as well. That's what Prezi lets you do.

With Prezi, you need to use the visual medium and the ability to zoom in and out — not make it fit an old paradigm. You need to think differently about how things are displayed and discussed. When you get comfortable with it, though, this new paradigm will spur your creativity. Don't be afraid to put anything on the canvas and play with it. Your results will be better, and your audience will thank you for it.

One of the best ways to retrain your eye is to look in the Prezi Explore tab and see what others have done. You'll begin to notice how some people try to experiment with new ideas and others just try to re-create a slide motif. When you recognize this, you'll be able to avoid it.

Getting to know the Prezi menu

The Prezi Bubble menu is the heart of the application. In keeping with Prezi's uniqueness, it doesn't look like the ordinary Windows-style menu. It's called a *Bubble menu* because each menu choice is a circle that looks something like a bubble. The main menu consists of one major center bubble with five smaller bubbles around it. (See Figure 1-1.)

All the action takes place here. Using these command bubbles, you can create anything you can imagine. In Chapter 3, the menu is presented in complete detail. Here I list the main bubbles and their functions.

The menu consists of the following bubbles:

- **Write bubble:** This is where you can add and format text.
- **Transformation Zebra:** Located in the Write bubble. It allows you to move, resize, and rotate any object you upload to the canvas.
- **Insert bubble:** The submenu includes Load Files and Shapes bubbles.
- **Frame bubble:** The submenu offers you Bracket, Circle, Rectangle, and Hidden Frame bubbles.
- **Path bubble:** Here you find the 1-2-3 Add, Capture View, and Delete All bubbles.
- **Colors and Fonts bubble:** Here you select the style for your prezi. It includes several choices of colors and fonts.

✔ **Show bubble:** This is the mode from which you present. When the prezi is in Show mode, the Bubble menu recedes, and the canvas lines are removed. From here you can set timing intervals and Autoplay, manually zoom in and zoom out and expand to use the full screen.

It doesn't take long to understand how to use the menu. Just dive right in and experiment. You can't break anything. Nothing is irreversible. All you need to do is click the Undo link in the upper-right corner if you don't like something.

Publishing online

Prezi wants to make it easy for you to distinguish between *Prezi*, which is the company name, and *prezi*, which is a presentation created with Prezi. This capitalization convention is used throughout the book. Prezi is hosted online, so publishing your prezi is very easy. Your options are dependent upon which license you have. If you have the Free license, your prezi is automatically published (made public) and appears in the Explore tab.

If you have the Enjoy or Pro license, you can decide when or whether you want to make your prezi public. To put it in the Explore tab to share with others, you must make it public. (See Figure 1-2.)

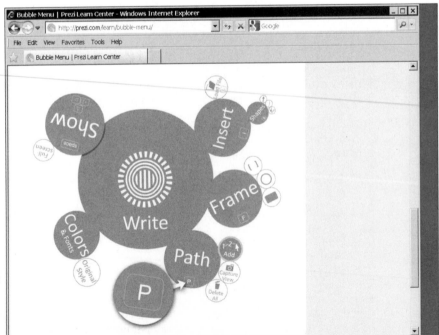

Figure 1-1:
Prezi Bubble
menu.

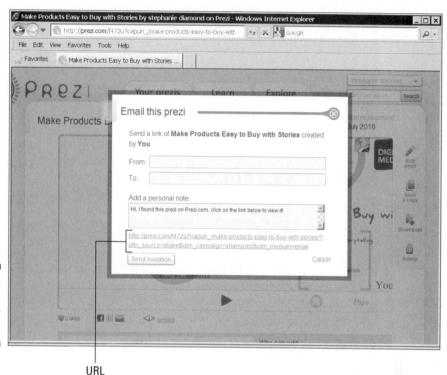

Figure 1-2:
A public
URL for your
prezi.

URL

Working offline with Prezi Desktop

With Prezi Desktop, you can work on your desktop without worrying about staying connected. No Internet today? No problem. (See Figure 1-3.)

Using the Desktop software offers you several benefits, including the following:

- ✔ You can work offline anywhere without an Internet connection.
- ✔ You aren't limited by the designated online space for your account. You're only limited by your hard disk.
- ✔ It provides an extra layer of security because you can work offline and then upload your Prezi online or do the opposite, so that you have a duplicate in another place.

The Prezi Desktop is available to subscribers with Pro or Edu Pro licenses. The Bubble menu works exactly like the online application, so there's no learning curve. After you download the application to your desktop, you can quickly get started. At the opening screen, you can see both your online and offline prezis on the desktop if you log in. If not, you only see the prezis you have on your hard drive. The available prezis look like sticky notes. When you open one by clicking it, you see the familiar Bubble menu.

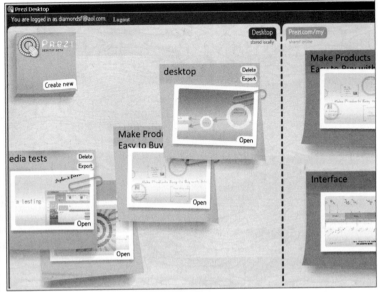

Figure 1-3:
The Prezi
Desktop
before you
open a
prezi.

Understanding what Prezi is not

Because Prezi looks different and changes well-worn presentation paths, some people may have some misconceptions about using it.

Before you get started, you should be aware that Prezi is *not* the following:

- ✔ **A way to reuse slide presentations as-is:** You can take a slide presentation and just convert it to a prezi, but the end result is just boring. Some have tried, all have failed.

- ✔ **A program that requires design skills:** There's no need for design skills. You can use any kind of graphics that suit your presentation, and you can show the big picture and the details at the same time. Prezi offers a Smart Zooming feature so that the best way to zoom is predetermined. No algorithms need to be harmed in the process of creating your prezi.

- ✔ **Like any other presentation software:** Because Prezi developers threw out the slide motif on day one, you need to rethink how you present. Don't worry; it will be fun. It will spur your creative thinking.

- ✔ **A way to make weak art look good:** No software program is going to make that smiling-bear-holding-a-sign clipart look right in your presentation. On the other hand, if you have good visuals, you can use them in ways you haven't done before.

- ✔ **Only for presentations:** There are lots of other uses for Prezi, including Mind Mapping, note-taking, and sharing information such as photos and recipes. When you see what Prezi can do, you'll find your own favorites.

Signing Up and Picking the Right Plan for You

Prezi offers five subscriber options, so you can pick the one that works for you: Free, Enjoy, Pro, Edu Enjoy, and Edu Pro. All the plans allow you to create a Prezi online and download it to present offline. If you're just experimenting, the free 30-day trial may be the right choice to start. When you see how much online storage space you think you'll need and how you'll use it, you can choose either the Enjoy or Pro plans. The available plans are as follows (see Figure 1-4):

- ✔ **The Free plan:** The Free plan allows you to create and edit prezis online. You get 100MB of free storage space and you can present a downloaded prezi offline. On the flip side, you can't make content private or remove the Prezi watermark. If you don't have the need for large storage or private prezis, then this might be the choice for you.

- ✔ **Enjoy:** Cost $59 annual fee; 30-day free trial. The Enjoy plan gives you 500MB of online storage space to use for your prezis. When you present, you don't see the Prezi watermark on the left side of the screen like you would if you had the Free plan. Your prezis remain private unless you make them public.

   You can share a public or private prezi. Using the Get link or Share downward arrow, you can send an e-mail via Prezi with a link to the prezi.

- ✔ **Pro:** Cost $159 annual fee; 30-day free trial. The Pro plan gives you 2,000MB of online storage space. When you present, you don't see the Prezi watermark. With this plan, your prezis remain private unless you make them public.

- ✔ **Edu Enjoy and Edu Pro:** Prezi is becoming hugely popular in the classroom. Teachers want to be able to use the software and have their students use it as well. Prezi recognized that educators were not able to afford the program for themselves and their students, so Prezi created separate educational plans. Teachers and students who request and qualify have the option of using the Edu Enjoy Plan (500MB of online storage) for free or the Edu Pro plan (2,000MB of online storage) for $59 annually. Nonprofits that request and qualify for the Edu Enjoy plan may also access the Edu plans.

If you choose to cancel your account, you'll be able to show the prezis you've already created if you leave your account open. This means that you won't lose the work you've completed. But you won't be able to create or edit new ones unless you sign up for a new free account.

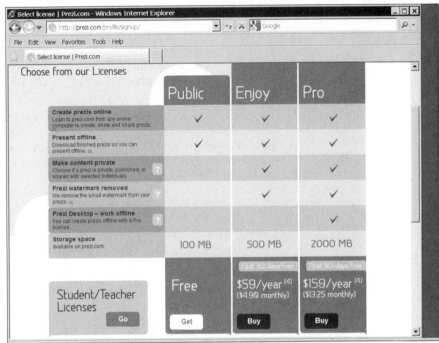

Figure 1-4:
Prezi plans.

Technical requirements

To use Prezi, your computer must have the following:

- ✔ **Adobe Flash Player 9 or higher:** You don't need a Flash Player installed on your computer, but you do need to be able to run it online.
- ✔ **Minimum 1GB memory.**
- ✔ **A mouse or touchpad.**

You must have one of the following operating systems to use Prezi Desktop or Prezi.com:

- ✔ **Windows:** XP, Vista, 7
- ✔ **Mac:** OS X

Meeting Prezi's public face

When you go to Prezi.com (http://prezi.com), you find three tabs in the upper-left corner of the site. They are Your Prezis, Learn, and Explore. Before you sign up, the Home tab shows you the features and benefits of Prezi. After you sign up, the Home tab changes to the Your Prezis tab

The following content is found on each of the tabs (see Figure 1-5):

- ✔ **Your Prezis:** After you sign up, the Home tab becomes the Your Prezis tab, and this is where you access all the prezis you create. In this tab you see all your prezis laid out for you. You can also sort your prezis by title or by last opened. You can display this sort by all, those owned by you, or those shared with you.

- ✔ **Learn:** There are three columns on this page where all the e-learning content is located. In the first column, you see the Prezi Academy where you can find Basic, Advanced, and Expert lessons. Next you see the Live from Prezi Universe column where you find tips, ideas, and updates from Prezi. The third column is where you find a link to the manual and links to the different Prezi tech support sites.

- ✔ **Explore:** This area is a great resource. Here you can find all the prezis that have been created by those with Free licenses. You can also find prezis that have been made public for the purpose of sharing them with others. People may also designate their prezis as Reusable so that you can use them as a foundation to build your own prezi. The Explore area is searchable by topic and whether or not it is reusable.

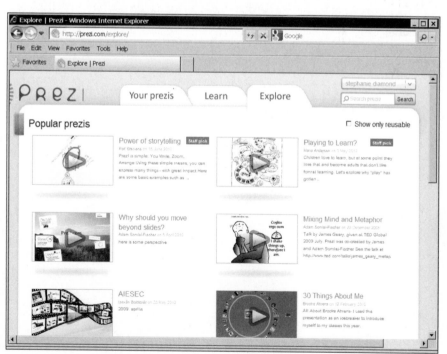

Figure 1-5:
Prezi con-
tent tabs.

Changing the Way You Present with Prezi

If you're comfortable with a presentation process that can't be varied, then Prezi is not for you. Prezi gives you options. Options can be scary, but only until you try out a few. Then they can be liberating.

Comparing Prezi to traditional, slide-based programs is like comparing a large digital whiteboard to a deck of cards. On the whiteboard everything is laid out before you. No content is hidden. With the deck of cards you need to go card by card to see the content.

Imagine starting a slide presentation with slide number five and then zipping back to one and then out to ten. The audience would be frustrated for two reasons: first because the information is out of order, and second because moving back and forth seamlessly is clumsy and awkward. I'm sure you've seen a presenter scanning back and forth, frantically trying to find information on a slide near the beginning. It's not pretty.

With Prezi, you avoid this problem completely. All your data is available to you on one canvas. If you want to speak about something, you can access your presentation content like you would on a whiteboard: You point at it. It's all there to see at once. If you want to tell the story in a different way to each audience, you don't need to reorder anything. You just follow the story in a different way.

Telling your story

Fiction writers have it much easier than business writers when they want to plot a story, or so some people think. They can make up anything they want and let the story take them anywhere they want to go. When it comes to telling a business story, however, there are constraints based on facts, figures, and outcomes. But is this really such a limiting factor?

Actually, it's not, if you think about it differently. You aren't trying to make up a story. Your job is to tell one that already exists. Your job is different. You need to take the ideas you want to convey and weave them into a story that people can understand and relate to. This is covered more thoroughly in Chapter 8.

Take the following actions as you construct your story:

✔ **Look at the plots.** You don't need to get too complicated with your plotting for a business presentation. Luckily, you know how it turns out before you begin your presentation so that you can pace it effectively.

✔ **Decide who the hero is.** Even in a business presentation, the hero is still important. You need to make the audience care about the outcome. That's what the hero does. Remember, in this case the hero doesn't have to be a person. It does have to resonate with the audience.

✔ **Figure out the hook.** Every story needs a *hook* — the thing that makes people sit up and pay attention instead of texting their friends or looking for a great sushi restaurant in the neighborhood. If you don't supply one, don't wonder why your audience can't seem to settle down and listen at the beginning.

✔ **Figure out the sequence of events.** Prezi gives you the opportunity to create a story line and set a Path to follow. Creating a story line makes your presentation stronger. You can also ensure that people can see the content in the order you intended if you're not present by having them set specific timing intervals you suggest.

Planning differently

Even if you're a die-hard keyboard user, I recommend that you plan your first prezi using a pencil and paper or other sketching medium. Prezi presents you with options that require you to think in ways you haven't before. To do this effectively, you need to think and draw first.

For example, your first prezi might include the following planning sequence:

1. After your story is created as described in the preceding section, decide what you'll use as your key phrases and text content.

2. Find and assemble the visuals that support your ideas. You determine what visuals you already have, what you need to create, or what you need to purchase.

3. Figure out how to place these visuals on the digital canvas in a way that provides meaning just by looking at it. Should you use a metaphor? What about using a familiar pattern that relates to the content?

   Because you want to show both the big picture and the details, a random arrangement without grouping will be inefficient.

4. Figure out what order you want the content to be viewed in and how to zoom in and out to reach that content.

You can see how planning on paper would support this process more easily. When you get the hang of it, you may want to work directly online.

Thinking visually

When you creating a prezi, you translate some of your ideas and concepts into visuals. Thankfully, prezis don't lend themselves to heavy text passages and ponderous bullet lists. There are built-in design tools that Prezi provides to help you break down the text into more easily digested pieces.

Throughout this book, I also talk about how to use visuals that you create with other software programs or find from outside sources. I list the acceptable formats in the next section.

The visuals themselves might include the following:

- Story illustrations
- Word art
- Custom designed keywords and phrases
- Metaphors
- Mind Maps
- Flow charts, graphs, statistics
- Maps and timelines
- Personas
- Photos and stock images
- Hand-drawn images (see Figure 1-6)
- Animation, video with audio
- Scrapbooking material

Representing movement using layering

When you lay your elements on the Prezi canvas, you can focus on it using three built-in movements: You can zoom in, zoom out, and rotate it. Think about how different this is than just placing a static image on the screen. (See Figure 1-7.)

When you view a slide, you look at it head on. If you're speaking to a particular element of the slide, you can't zoom in and focus on it unless you take a slice of it and make that your next slide. Looking at content in Prezi mimics a natural process. If you want to see it up close, you can click it or create a preset to zoom in on it.

This zooming opens up your ability to show things in all sorts of new ways. The perception is that you have actual movement. In addition, when you add timing to the equation, your audience perceives the material as using time and space as part of the show.

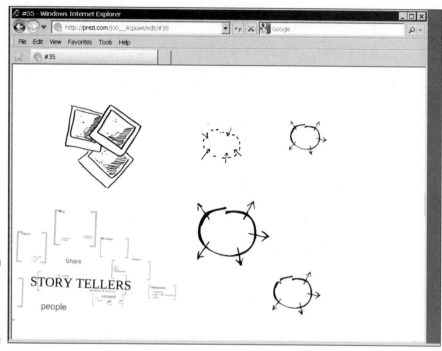

Figure 1-6:
A prezi with
hand-drawn
graphics.

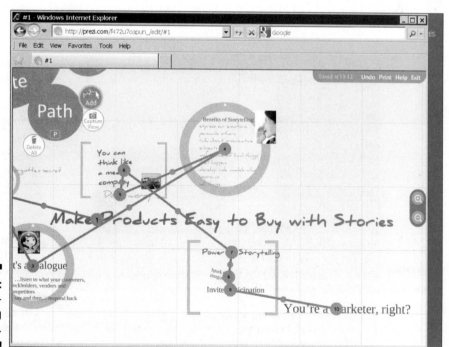

Figure 1-7:
Demon-
strating
movement.

Exploring the big picture and details at the same time

One of the best ways to explain the meaning of something is to show how it fits into a larger context. That concept is known as seeing how a detail fits into the big picture. In his book *Visual Explanations*, Edward Tufte recommends using a method called *PGP* to explain complex ideas or data. PGP refers to explaining things by using a Particular point, a General point, and then another Particular point.

So, for example, if you were explaining a graphic showing sales figures in Prezi, you would first point to a particular number and speak to it and then pull out to a more general point that shows the greater context. Then you would move back in again and discuss another particular point that enhances the original argument you made. In Figure 1-8 you see the total big picture of the presentation (Presenting with Multimedia) and the way it's broken out into the details (grouped by graphic formats.)

Surprisingly, Prezi is set up to do exactly that with no additional work on your part. To use the PGP method, you would use Smart Zooming to zoom in to a data point on the Prezi canvas, then zoom out to show the bigger picture, and then zoom back in to enhance that point. That's how prezis are meant to be used. They're created to help you explain things in the easiest way possible. If you remember this method when you are planning your prezis, you can make complex ideas seem simpler.

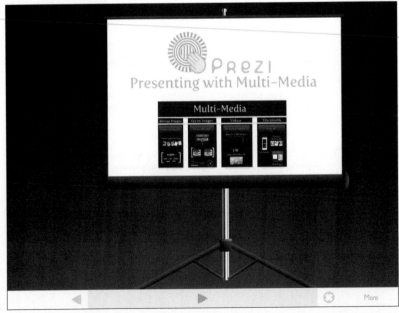

Figure 1-8:
Looking at
the big
picture and
the details.

Getting Ready to Present

Prezis provide you with a unique opportunity to develop and follow a story line supported by just the right text and images. To support this, whether you're presenting online or offline, you need to remember to do two things before you present.

The two things are as follows:

✔ **Set a Path:** Determine which chunk of information the audience will see each time you advance the screen. This determination is based on how you've constructed the story line and the sequence of events.

Don't forget that you can also present without a Path if you want to encourage a dialogue with your audience. Freeform presentations in Prezi foster interaction by allowing the audience to steer the conversation. You won't have to scroll back and forth to find the slides under discussion. Just click it with your cursor and you're there.

✔ **Determine timing intervals:** *Timing intervals* refer to the amount of time that elapses between Path screens when you are using Autoplay. You can choose 4, 10, or 20 seconds. They're critical. After you set up an interval, watch it several times to make sure you've made the correct choice.

Remember to watch your prezi like an audience member. If the material goes by too fast or too slow, the impact will be lost. I've seen prezis that have lots of text on the screen (which is not a good idea) and have the screens going by at 4 seconds each. This is frustrating for your audience members, who will quickly give up.

Presenting online or offline

When you have everything set up, prezis can be presented both online from a browser window or offline from your hard drive, CD, or USB drive. When choosing a method, you need to know the following:

✔ **Online:** Prezis are hosted online, so if you want to present from a browser, it's very easy. All you need to do is log in to your account and play your prezi from there. If you have a Free license, your prezi is published, and the URL is visible. If you have the Enjoy or Pro account, you can present from a private prezi or make your prezi public. The choice is yours. Your main concern when presenting online is always your Internet connection. If it fails during the presentation, you're in trouble.

✔ **Offline:** If you download your prezi to a hard drive or other device like a CD or USB drive, you have more insurance that your prezi will be available when you want it. You can very easily download your prezi using the online controls. Just remember that you can't create a prezi offline without an Pro account that gives you access to Prezi Desktop.

Remember that you can't edit your offline prezi after you've downloaded it unless you have a Pro account. To edit it, you need to edit the online version and redownload it.

Working with Collaborators

Collaboration on the Internet is critical. Prezi makes it very easy for you to invite others to work with you . To make working in teams a snap, you'll use the coeditor link on the Your Prezis page. (See Figure 1-9.) Collaboration is covered in more depth in Chapter 5.

Figure 1-9: Inviting a coeditor.

Displaying Your Prezis

Prezis can be shared in a variety of ways. Don't hesitate to give it wide exposure. See Chapter 5 for more information about sharing your prezis.

Aside from sharing in e-mails, you can display your Prezi in the following ways:

✔ Embed on a Web page

✔ Publish to a social media site

✔ Share on your blog

✔ Put in the Prezi Explore tab (with or without Reuse rights)

Developing a Presentation Partnership

The one thing that separates a good presenter from a bad one is her ability to focus on the audience. As a good presenter, you must establish a partnership between yourself and the audience. You're in this together. The time you spend together will either be a worthwhile experience or it won't. If you start planning your presentation by focusing on what you know about the people watching and how you need to communicate your message, you're way ahead of the game.

The only way to fail in this respect is to be wrong about who the audience members are and how you need to communicate with them. Following are some of the things you need to consider at the beginning of the planning phase:

✔ **Context:** What is this audience's view of the world in relation to this topic? Before you develop conclusions, make sure you've done some research on the audience first.

✔ **Trust:** Understand that before people believe a word you say, they need to trust your motives. If they think you have a hidden agenda or aren't completely truthful, you'll have a hard time convincing them of anything.

✔ **WIIFM (What's In It For Me?):** When you decided to make this presentation, you made a calculation. You thought about what you would gain by making it. Rest assured, your audience members will make the same calculation about watching it. Make sure you make it worth their while.

✔ **Learning styles:** Your audience is made up of visual, auditory, and kinesthetic learners. Vary the content to appeal to everyone.

✔ **Physical limits:** Your audience is subject to the usual factors: hunger, thirst, sleepiness, and so on. Try to do what you can to mitigate these factors.

✔ **Need for simplicity:** Simplicity makes complex ideas seem easier to grasp. Don't try to show that you know everything about a subject. Curate the material and pick out only the most relevant.

Interacting with the Prezi Community

You'll be happy to know that Prezi has a very robust community. Prezi users share their presentations online and actively provide the opportunity to "like" and comments on well-done prezis. There are social networks, online tutorials, and tech support areas.

The Prezi community includes the following:

✔ **Prezis Explore tab** (`http://prezi.com/explore`): Prezi subscribers display their prezis in this area. There are great examples of all kinds of prezis for you to comment on and copy for your reuse.

✔ **Prezi Learn Center** (`http://prezi.com/learn`): Here you'll find an online manual, tutorials, and information about how to use Prezi's features.

✔ **The company Twitter account** (`http://twitter.com/Prezi`): At the company account you'll see information about updates, new ideas, and examples shared by the community. (See Figure 1-10.)

✔ **The tech support Twitter account** (`http://twitter.com/Prezisupport`): Users tweet about real-time questions and issues they are having. You can get quick answers to many of your questions here.

✔ **Prezi "Get Satisfaction" tech support site** (`http://community.prezi.com/prezi`): This site is very robust and provides a place for you to ask complex questions that can't be handled with a quick answer.

✔ **Prezi Blog** (`http://blog.prezi.com`): Prezi has a lively blog where you can find the latest information about who is using Prezi and innovations people have created.

Figure 1-10:
Prezi on
Twitter.

Seeing That Prezis Aren't Limited to Presentations

Because Prezi is a storytelling tool, think of using it when you want to communicate something to others. That means that when you want to introduce a new product or service, or solve a problem, you can use Prezi to deliver your message. But you can also use it for nonbusiness applications. There's nothing inherently business-oriented about the tool. It all depends on how you use it.

Problem solving and brainstorming

There are lots of different problem-solving methods that you can employ using Prezi. My favorite is a Mind Map, which I cover in Chapters 10 and 16. But you can also use it to create other diagrams and flowcharts that help with problem solving.

For inspiration on other visual methods you can use, you might want to check out the "Periodic Table of Visual Methods for Management" created by Ralph Lengler and Martin Eppler. Just like the periodic table of elements that you learned about in science class, this is a chart of visual elements. It is broken into six categories via color coding: data visualization, information visualization, concept visualization, strategy visualization, metaphor visualization, and compound visualization.

When you roll over one of the elements with your cursor, an image pops up showing you what it looks like. This chart helps you familiarize yourself with a variety of different methods and perhaps find one for the task at hand. It's available on the Visual Literacy site. (See Figure 1-11.) Here's the direct link to it: www.visual-literacy.org/periodic_table/periodic_table.html

Business plans and other business uses

When you're selling ideas and need to persuade for commercial reasons, you'll want to turn to visuals. Your goal is to have your story strike an emotional chord with the viewer and then have them explain that resonance to themselves with facts and figures. People buy on emotion but justify their purchase with logic. With Prezi, you're already halfway there because you have all the tools at your fingertips.

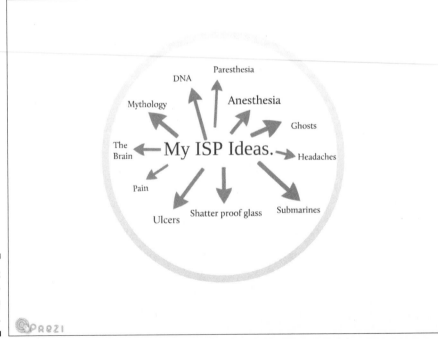

Figure 1-11:
Brain-
storming
with Prezi.

Because of the popularity of social media networks, people in business are jumping on the notion that persuasion is best done through stories. Stories are easily told in a social media environment. That's why many venture capitalists have started focusing on the story a business can tell online. Some have adopted the credo that you need to describe your business in 30 seconds or less to get an appointment to show them your plan.. If you follow up your description with a prezi, you'll at least have the chance to mesmerize them with your story. (See Figure 1-12.) Chapter 11 discusses using Prezi for business plans in depth.

Scrapbooks, recipes, hobbies, and so on

When you start to think about Prezi as a way to display your favorite collection, demonstrate a recipe, or create a party invitation, you'll be excited to see how far you can push the tools. (See Figure 1-13.)

You can embed video, audio, and animation in your prezi. These options take you much farther than a digital scrapbook or other illustration tool that's flat and static. Remember that Prezi has *layers,* which means that you can zoom in and out and rotate your materials. You can also pace your prezi so that it's fast, slow, or moves to the beat.

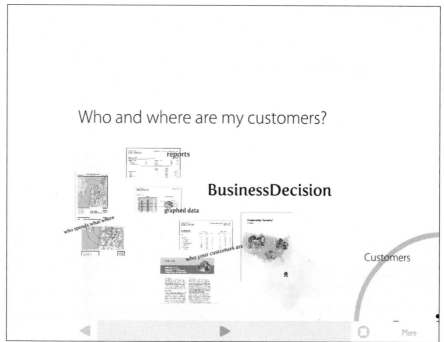

Figure 1-12: Presenting a business plan.

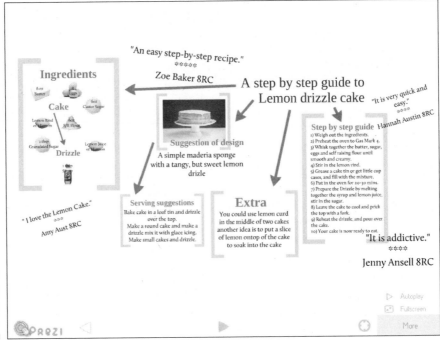

Figure 1-13:
A recipe in
Prezi.

Understanding How Professionals Can Use Prezi

If you're a professional designer, you'll want to take a look at Prezi. It provides you with a great tool to do either of the following:

- ✔ **Show off your entire portfolio.** With Prezi you can create a stand-alone portfolio file. You can upload your current graphics and add text to educate the client about your work. You can set the Path so that you can tell a story line about your career.

- ✔ **Create custom graphics for others.** Prezis are a visual medium. If you have some great graphics to offer storytellers, you'll want to contact them.

Educating with Prezi

Prezi has received a great deal of attention from the educational community. Both students and teachers are interested in using Prezi to show as well as tell. For this reason, Prezi has created a special license for educators and their students. (See Chapter 12 for more on the Edu license.)

Chapter 2

Preparing for Your First Prezi

. . . .

. . . .

Creating your first prezi is an exciting experience. You'll feel the freedom that breaking out of a slide motif can offer. Some people may also feel nervous about the lack of boundaries. This is expected. With any new experience, people try to find the edges and sneak back to the center where it's comfortable.

Prezi makes it easy to explore without much risk. You can do everything you normally do to create a presentation and a whole lot you haven't tried before. That's where the fun comes in.

In this chapter, I introduce you to some of the best ways to plan your first prezi. The tips and shortcuts you find here make it a fun experience from the beginning. Dive right in and explore!

Gathering Your Ideas in Analog

Many people have trained themselves to turn to a computer whenever a knowledge job needs doing. Users know from experience that typing into a computer makes everything legible and easy to revise. It's really a joy when you can move an entire paragraph of text with the click of a mouse. But what about brainstorming and storyboarding? Might a pencil and paper be more effective when you need to craft a full-blown presentation from scratch?

There's some debate around this question. Some people find that they can't contemplate letting go of their keyboards even for a minute. If you're one of these people, you can plan your prezi totally onscreen. But, because you're new to this process and you need to carefully consider Prezi's unique dimensions, I recommend that you develop your first prezi offline until you decide what media and text you'll be using for it.

Suggested tools to use

Pens, markers, paper, chalkboards, Etch A Sketch — everyone has preferences. Use whatever helps you do your best thinking. Pick a set of tools that feels comfortable to you and make sure you have a way to erase or scratch out and start again.

At this point, revising is a good way to explore all the possibilities Prezi has to offer. You'll be using the tools mentioned in this section to think through the presentation from the highest level. Prezi allows you to work in several dimensions at once, so working "in analog" lets you sketch freely without being encumbered by anything.

Here are a few tools to consider:

- **Sketching:** Colored pencils, drawing pens and pencils, markers, chalk
- **Surfaces:** A variety of paper sizes and thicknesses, notebooks, journals, whiteboard, cork board, sticky notes, blackboard
- **Reference material:** Magazines, design books, photos, online stock photo sites, original content you created on paper or with other graphic software

Presentation planning basics

Starting with the planning basics gives you a firm foundation for the presentation. The planning basics are the decisions and details that go into creating most presentations. It's a good idea to start your planning by answering questions rather than starting with a blank sheet. Staring at a large white space can cause the proverbial brain freeze in otherwise healthy planners. It's okay to type the answers to the following questions into a word processor document if you want, but after this, it's analog.

Here are the questions you need to consider at the outset:

- ✔ **Who is the audience?** The key to a great presentation revolves around how well you understand and deliver on your audience's expectations. So that you can deliver on those expectations more effectively, list what you know about your audience. Is it a business gathering? What are the demographics? If you know someone who's knowledgeable about the group members, interview that person and learn about the members' needs. Figure out what sort of knowledge level the audience members are likely to have. Is your topic new to them? If it is, you'll want to supply any information that must be known before you move into a more complex discussion.

- ✔ **What is the appropriate tone?** You need to decide what the tone of your presentation will be. Is this a serious presentation with far-reaching implications? Ask yourself how humor can be used effectively. A business presentation will have a much different tone from that of a school club or convention. Don't overdo the humor if you're unsure about your audience. People can easily be offended when they don't understand the joke.

- ✔ **How long will it be?** The length of the presentation dictates how much content you need and the extent to which you can entertain questions. Build in some question time at the end so you can be flexible.

- ✔ **What is the venue?** What is the environment in which you will give your presentation? Is it a large room? Will you be standing at a podium or dais? The whole tenor of the presentation is affected by the size of the room and the seating arrangement. If you're in a small gathering, people will feel more comfortable asking questions.

- ✔ **What contact information do I need?** It's a good idea to get cell numbers or e-mail/Twitter addresses from people you'll need to stay in contact with. You want to know the contact info for the host of the event, the conference or hotel manager, and the tech support person in charge. Find out what their preferred method of contact is ahead of time. It will save time later.

- ✔ **What equipment is needed?** This is critical. Plan to bring your own laptop and other accessories and discuss what you need ahead of time with the designated technical person. Don't rely on what managers say if they haven't used the equipment themselves. I've been very thankful when I've arrived with all the cables and equipment I need and found that none of them was available onsite. Don't find yourself frantically hopping in a cab on the way to a computer store at 8 in the morning!

- ✔ **Do I need any additional logistics information related to the presentation?** This is for any related items or information that doesn't fit into the other categories.

It's a good idea to keep all this information together in one place with a copy of your prezi so that you can come back and repeat the presentation. You'll be able to update and review what you were thinking and make changes with regard to the audience or presentation style. Although it's fresh in your mind right after a presentation, your memory will fade, and you don't want to lose valuable thoughts.

Things that make planning with Prezi unique

In addition to the basics, there are dimensions that using Prezi introduces that make your presentation completely unique. Prezi introduces new ways to handle the following:

- ✔ **Movement:** With most presentation software, you move one slide forward and one slide back; there's not much to consider. With Prezi, you can zoom in and out and rotate. As you plan, you'll want to keep this in mind to add focus and drama.

- ✔ **Key messages, concepts, and keywords:** Prezi lets you put particular emphasis on words and phrases so that their meaning, the way they look, and the order in which you present them can be manipulated to great effect.

- ✔ **Media:** There's almost no limit on the type of media you can use with Prezi. Even in cases where you can't use a media type in its native format, you can convert it to a PDF and use that. You can use common formats for images such as JPG, PNG, and GIF. File formats for video like FLV or FLV are supported. You can also place the media anywhere on the canvas. This makes it even more unusual and memorable.

- ✔ **Pacing:** You decide how fast or slow the presentation moves along by setting up a unique Path. The screens can zoom in and out and rotate to set a rhythm that matches your content. (See the section "Creating a Path of Ideas," later in this chapter, for more details.)

  You can also affect pacing by presenting without a Path. Create a free-form prezi and let the flow of ideas be steered by the conversation. You can zoom to a particular object, pan across the canvas, and zoom out for an overview. Let the audience dictate the order and pace of the presentation.

- ✔ **Presenter attended or Autoplay:** Using timing intervals that Autoplay, you can display a prezi that automatically plays the presentation. You can set up specific timing intervals by which the screens are viewed, ensuring the exact viewing experience you want. If you won't be present when the prezi is viewed, you can instruct the viewer to set the timing interval to your specifications and then it will Autoplay. (See the section on discovering the Show mode in Chapter 3 for more details.)

Developing Your Story

The creation and development of your story is the most critical step in the planning process. It sets the stage for everything that follows it. You can find more information about developing your story in Chapter 7.

When people think of stories, they don't necessarily relate them to a business setting. But all business problems have a narrative. Ideas, events, and emotions all make up the description of the problem. To have an effective presentation, you need to relay this story to your audience. You want to make it easy for the audience to understand what the issues are and imagine along with you how they might be solved. Without a story, your presentation has no real meaning to the audience.

To begin the brainstorming process, I recommend using a Mind Map that you create on paper or another suitable writing surface. If you strongly prefer, you can work your map online in the future. Information about creating a Prezi Mind Map is available in Chapters 10 and 16.

A *Mind Map* is a visual thinking tool that allows you to get your ideas out where you can see and manipulate them. It's easier to work with ideas when they're visible to you. You're then free to brainstorm and add new ideas without having to hold everything in your mind at once. When you put your thoughts on paper or canvas, your mind begins to see patterns and make associations you would never find without the visual input.

At this point, I would stay analog and keep the focus on the story, not the tools. When you're more familiar with Prezi and all its dimensions, you can work directly online from the start. If you have a preferred brainstorming method, use whatever you're comfortable with for this phase. You want to keep focus on the brainstorming process and not get distracted.

Defining your selling direction

The first thing you want to consider when you start planning your presentation is your *selling direction*. This term, coined by Chic Thompson in his book, *What A Great Idea 2.0*, refers to the ways in which you consider who you're selling your ideas to. When you're clear about the type of selling message required, you'll have a better idea about how to make it happen.

The possible directions are

- ✔ **Selling in:** This is about selling yourself on your vision, feelings, and commitment to the ideas in your presentation. If you feel lukewarm, your feelings will come through loud and clear to your audience. It's easy to spot someone who doesn't believe in what he's saying. There's no enthusiasm or life-changing fervor. Not every presentation can have earth-shaking ideas in them, but all ideas can have an advocate.

- ✔ **Selling up:** If you work in an organization, a group, or are a consultant, you'll find that there are times when you have to sell to the managers of that group. You have to convince the people you work for that your ideas or plans are worthy of implementation. In this type of presentation, you need to consider your audience members' constraints. You need to demonstrate that the ideas in your presentation will bring them success.

- ✔ **Selling down:** This refers to situations where you're in a management role and have to show your staff or constituents reasons why your ideas will make things easier and better for them. In this type of presentation, it's a good idea to think about what changes might occur if your ideas came to fruition. Will you be unsettling people? Will people fear losing their jobs? If so, you need to be prepared to deal with that.

- ✔ **Selling out:** Oops, this isn't what it sounds like. Remember, I'm talking about sales direction. This refers to presentations you give to an external audience to sell your ideas. You need to understand the needs of your audience, but you also need to shake people from their autopilot state. This is where the dramatic capabilities of a prezi shine. Don't be surprised if people come up to you after watching a prezi to ask about the tool itself. If done right, it shakes the cobwebs out of complacent viewers and makes them think.

Finding your key messages

At this point, you've chosen some working tools, put together the information you need to start your presentation, and determined your selling direction. Now you need to uncover the key messages, ideas, and concepts that will become the basis of your prezi.

It's time to brainstorm ideas by creating your offline Mind Map. This map acts as the underpinning of the story you want to create.

To create a Mind Map for your presentation, take your drawing tools and do as follows:

1. **Draw a circle and simply print your title in the center of a horizontal sheet of paper or other writing surface.**

2. **In the center circle, also print your selling direction. (See "Defining your selling direction," earlier in this chapter.)**

3. **Like the spokes of a wheel, use lines radiating out for each of the thoughts that occur to you. Put down all the ideas you can think of. (See Figure 2-1.)**

4. **Make connections and don't worry about the hierarchy at this point.**

   As you go more in depth later in the planning process, you can add and revise the map to suit your needs. Right now, you're looking for patterns and ways to group content together.

5. **Work on the map until you're satisfied that you've scoped out everything you need.**

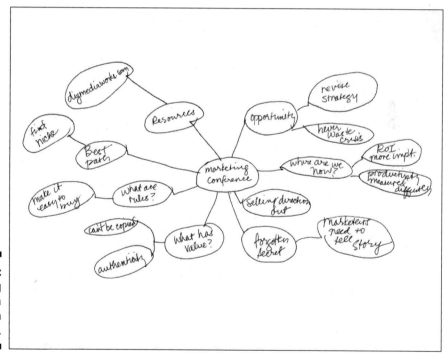

Figure 2-1:
Starting point for of a hand-drawn Mind Map.

Communicating with design

With the advent of graphical interfaces, design has taken center stage in the 21st century. Web designers live or die by their ability to communicate a brand or sell a product based on single design. This is also true of major bricks and mortar stores like IKEA and Target who have built their reputations by creating unique designs for everyday items.

Prezi now joins this movement by providing the nondesigner with the ability to create show-stopping presentations without special artistic skills. This levels the playing field for people who want to produce a special presentation but don't have the budget to hire a professional. When planning your prezi, it's important to take advantage of all the bells and whistles at your fingertips.

It's well known that the human brain responds to novelty. When you create a prezi, it's likely that you've created something that your audience has never seen before. Your prezi is totally unique because no one else has presented the movement of the objects and the use of the canvas in exactly the same way you have.

With this in mind, you want to embrace the novelty and carefully plan to make it a focus. Don't be afraid to experiment with the design. At the top-right of every prezi canvas is a handy Undo link that can be used to instantly remove the evidence of your unsuccessful attempt at greatness.

Creating your story design

In addition to all the other ways Prezi communicates your message, it allows you to show meaning with the story as a design element. This means that your audience will be able to get meaning as you zoom in and then out again. They see how the big picture and the details fit together and form shapes and tell a story.

To see what's possible, you can look at how other people have handled this concept by clicking the Explore tab at the top of the main page at Prezi.com. Look at other prezis and see what catches your eye based on the big picture shape you see. There are lots of ways to treat the design as a significant part of the message.

One way to accomplish this is to use metaphors. For example, you could make the canvas a cork board and pin notes to it that hold information. This way the audience receives the notes as information from a larger message board. Figure 2-2 shows a school prospectus that uses a desk and envelopes as a metaphor.

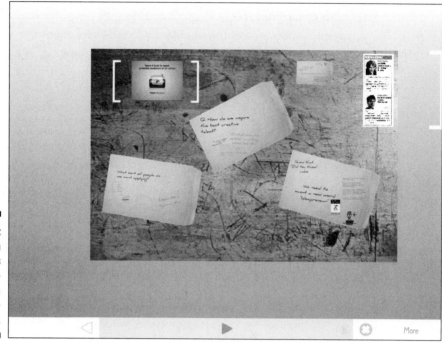

Figure 2-2:
A desk with envelopes as the metaphor for a school prospectus.

Or, if it makes sense for your message, you can simply create a shape with other objects fitting into it. If this is a good idea for you, make sure to begin thinking about this parameter as soon as you have constructed your key messages. It's part of the big picture message you convey.

When your Mind Map is done, take a new sheet of paper (or blank surface) to begin creating the design of your presentation.

To build the story design take the following steps:

1. **Look at the big picture of your ideas and start to think about how to break them into keywords and categories that support them.**

   The key here is to be able to see how you can tell a story about the whole and then break it into parts.

2. **Explore and draw a shape or series of shapes that might make up the presentation message.**

   You can create a metaphor that fits your ideas or you can put all your ideas in one big circle and build the canvas that way. You can scatter the main ideas randomly and then create order with the frames you put around them. Spend some time on this so that you get a feel for how it will look when you zoom out and then back in.

3. **When you've created a tentative order or organization to your ideas, use this drawing as your** *design outline* **and return to it when you've completed the rest of the planning phase in this chapter.**

   After you've selected graphics, art, and text, you'll have a better idea of how your presentation can be put together.

Incubating your ideas

An important part of any planning process is the incubation period. This is where the exhortation to "sleep on it" comes from. Throughout the ages, creative thinkers, musicians, and artists have stepped away from their work to return with a renewed sense of vigor.

Current brain research shows that much of human thinking and connecting is done when people are not directly focusing on a problem. That's why some people say they get their best ideas when they're exercising or taking a shower. Take advantage of this tip when you're developing your prezi and you'll find that your ideas strengthen over time.

You can use a tactic that Beethoven used to develop his music. He kept a series of notebooks with ideas that progressed from one level of complexity to the next. He would jot down an idea in a notebook and let it incubate. At a later date, he would return to that notebook and add new thinking to the idea and put it in a new notebook to repeat the process. By looking at his notebooks over time, he could see how his idea progressed and what influenced his thinking. If you have the time, develop the ideas for your prezi and return to them at a later date to see how your thinking has evolved. Redo your draft prezi with your latest thinking and so on. You can also do this with prezis that you've previously presented. Go back and redo them with fresh eyes and document the progress of your ideas. The key is to capture how you arrived at your idea as well as the actual idea itself. Doing so can help you understand the genesis of your ideas and propel them forward.

Testing your ideas

In his book *Rocket Surgery Made Easy*, Steve Krug talks about testing your *napkin sketches* as early as possible. His work is related to usability of online interfaces. He suggests you ask people you meet in coffee shops and grocery store lines what they think when you show them something that you're working on. If they get it without any previous knowledge, you're on the right track.

Your presentation may or may not lend itself to this type of engagement, but I would recommend that you talk to friends or colleagues about specific ideas and how you've grouped them together for meaning and clarity. This is key for presentation planning. If you're met with blank stares or polite nods, you know your ideas aren't commanding any interest, and it's back to the drawing board! Don't work without some kind of audience feedback. It can be eye-opening when you show your work to others.

Reviewing before moving to the next phase

Before you start the next phase of working directly in Prezi, it's a good idea to review everything you've done up to this point. This can be a quick check to make sure that you've covered all your bases before you move to the next phase.

Did you remember to do the following?

- Collect all the basic information about your presentation, including logistics.
- Consider the unique dimensions Prezi provides and how to use them in your design.
- Pick a selling direction and work at making that your focus
- Develop all key messages to your satisfaction.
- Incubate your ideas for a period of time.
- Test your ideas in the real world by getting feedback.

Opening Your First Prezi

With your tentative plan firmly in hand, it's time to start a new prezi. You can add content while you're still in the planning stages to support your effort. This means you can upload graphics, links, and documents as placeholders until you decide exactly how you'd like to present them. Your prezi will act as your collection point.

The content you think you'll use can be uploaded and waiting off to the side of the canvas for you to position as you see fit. If you have very large files, don't feel you have to upload everything. But there will be certain items you know you'll use, and you can save time by uploading them. Be flexible when you're starting out and see what process works best for you.

To create your first prezi, do the following:

1. **Go to http://prezi.com/your.**

   The Your Prezis tab is the page where all your prezis can be found. In the upper-left corner of the page, you see two other tabs: Learn and Explore. On the Learn tab, you can find Help information and an online manual. On the Explore tab, you can find prezis created by other users that can give you great ideas. If the prezis are designated for reuse, you have an opportunity to use them as templates for your own presentation.

2. **Click the New Prezi button at the top left.**

3. **Type a title for your new prezi in the text box and type in a description where prompted.**

   Think carefully about the title you will use. Choosing a title is important because the search function for displaying prezis in the Explore tab is based on information in the title. You want to make your prezi easy to find so place good keywords in your title.

4. **Click the New Prezi button. (See Figure 2-3.)**

   A new prezi is created for you to start editing.

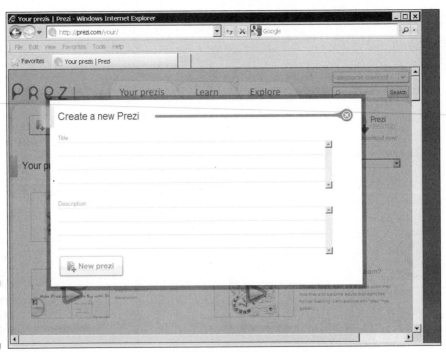

Figure 2-3:
Creating a
new prezi.

Exploring Styles

When beginning a new prezi, you can start by picking a style. There are preset style groups to choose from. Styles in Prezi refer to the particular colors, fonts, and background you will use for your presentation. Each one has its own mood and feeling.

Deciding which style to use can be a fun experience if you approach it from the right point of view. You're going to be choosing elements that affect the way your prezi communicates your message. But at this point you may not be completely sure what you want. Just react to the styles and see if they have the right mood and feel for this presentation As you become more familiar with the styles, you'll develop favorites. For now, pick one that resonates with you.

To pick your style, follow these steps:

1. **Open a prezi you've created.**

2. **Click the Colors & Fonts bubble.**

   The available styles appear. (See Figure 2-4.) Pick a style by clicking it. Each style offers different background colors and type faces.

3. **Explore each of the styles by clicking them.**

   When you click a style, you see a new prezi open with the background color you chose. If this looks good, you can add in some type to see the fonts. If not, proceed to click another one until you find one you like.

4. **In the style of your choice, type in some text by clicking the Write bubble and then double-clicking the canvas.**

   The text box opens, and you can type in a few words or phrases. Then, by clicking the words Title or Body below the text, you can see the way the words look in the available fonts. To experiment further, you can also add a bullet or change the paragraph alignment by clicking the icons located to the upper left of the prompt box.

 Pick the style that seems most appropriate at this time. Don't worry too much if you're unsure about your chosen style at the very beginning. As you get into the process, you'll be able to easily change to another style. But, remember that when you change the style, all the fonts and backgrounds change as well. The positioning and mood change, too. These changes are artistically significant even though they can be done with just the click of a mouse. So, if you change very late in the game, you might be creating a lot more work for yourself than you intended. It's best to settle on a theme before you create your final text designs.

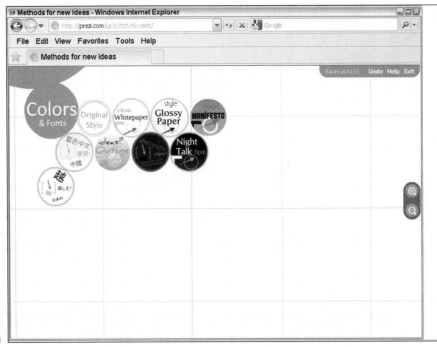

Collecting and Creating Images, Text, and Graphics

To create a really dynamic prezi, think carefully about all the different text and graphic sources you can draw from. Your sources are almost limitless. Here are some categories for you to consider:

- ✔ **Text styles from within Prezi:** You can choose these from the Colors and Fonts Bubble menu.

- ✔ **Text styles you copy from other design programs:** You can cut and paste them into a text box from the Write Bubble.

- ✔ **Any image in JPG, PNG, or GIF format:** Maximum size for an uploaded image is 2,880 x 2,880.

- ✔ **Video:** File formats in Flash FLV or F4V are supported.

- ✔ **Sounds:** You need to convert your audio file into an FLV format.

- ✔ **Images, charts, spreadsheets, graphs, and any content that can be converted to a PDF and uploaded to Prezi:** For example, you can take an Excel spreadsheet and convert it to a PDF and upload it.

✔ **Digital images from stock photo sites, your own personal photos, and other photo sites:** XXX. The Web is chock-full of images that can be used to spice up a presentation and bring clarity to a collection of keywords.

✔ **Graphics and images you created from drawing software like Adobe Photoshop:** Just convert them to a PDF.

✔ **YouTube videos:** Cut and paste the URL of the video into a text box from the Write Bubble and the video will play within Prezi.

Collecting digital objects for presentation

Because there are so many potential sources of great objects to upload, you need a process to collect and manage them if you're using more than just a few. I like to upload all the potential content I'm thinking of using into my prezi at once. At the same time, to capture all the pertinent details, I create a spreadsheet or word processor document with four columns.

The suggested columns are as follows:

✔ **Title for the graphic:** This is so you can identify the graphic on the screen and refer to it.

✔ **A brief description of the content:** For example, video, sound, and so on.

✔ **Who created it:** To recognize copyright and permission if needed.

✔ **Source or online link:** Where the object can be found if you want to go back and revise it.

After you have completed the preceding list, load your potential media into your prezi and place them off to the side of the canvas until you need them. Keep the documentation sheet handy. (See section on inserting with the Insert bubble in Chapter 3 for detailed information on uploading your media into your prezi.) As you go through your prezi, selecting the final graphics and deleting the rest, also delete them from your sheet. You end up with a final record of the objects that make up your presentation. This way, you can return to the presentation at a later date and know exactly what you used and where you got it.

Developing text elements

The ability to communicate with text is one of the places where Prezi really excels. Using the Transformation Zebra tool, you can move, resize, or rotate any text on the canvas. You can find complete information about using the Zebra tool in Chapter 3, but you'll want to experiment with text to convey your ideas as soon as possible.

To put some text on the canvas to experiment, use the following steps:

1. **Open the prezi you created from the Your Prezis tab (`http://prezi.com/your`).**

2. **Click the Edit Prezi button.**

   The Prezi canvas opens in Edit mode. Based on the style you chose, several fonts and colors are available to you.

3. **Double-click anywhere on the canvas to open a text box.**

4. **Choose one of the three font types available below the text box and click it.**

5. **Type some text on the canvas and click OK.**

   The text box disappears, and the text you typed appears.

6. **Click the text, and the Transformation Zebra tool appears over the text.**

The Zebra tool (see Figure 2-5) is made up of three concentric circles. By moving one of the circles, you can direct the action.

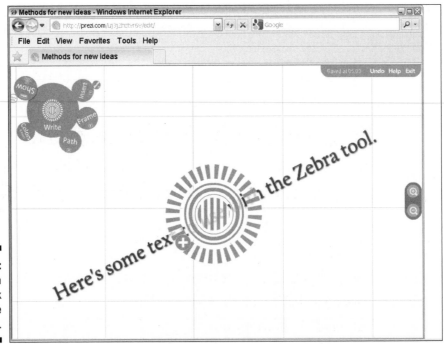

Figure 2-5:
The Zebra tool at work on some text.

To explore what the Zebra tool can do with text, try the following:

- **Move:** Place your cursor on the center circle and drag it wherever you'd like to place it on the canvas.

- **Resize:** Place your cursor on the second inside ring and drag it up or down to increase or decrease the text.

- **Rotate:** Place your cursor on the outer ring and swing it up and down.

- **Color code:** Try using one color for one category of idea and a different one for another. Grouping by color will communicate a message.

- **Size comparisons:** Make one word in a sentence much larger than the rest to stand out.

- **Symbols:** Cut and paste symbols from a design program and upload them using the Insert bubble. Then use the Zebra to stylize them.

- **Add emphasis with Shapes tool:** Take the text you created and click the Insert⇨Shapes bubble from the Write Menu. Click the highlight option to highlight the text. Click the arrow shape and point an arrow toward or away from the text.

- **Group items with Frames tool:** Click the Frame bubble from the Write Menu. Click the bracket option to put a bracket around the text to set it apart or to group similar items or topics. Click the circle and put one around the text. You can choose the rectangle to put your text inside the rectangle to separate it from the other text.

- **Zoom:** Don't forget that you'll also be able to zoom in and out of the text to emphasize it during the presentation.

Using content from other programs

Prezis can accept many different media formats. In addition to copyrighted content from others, you can use graphics and content you've created on your own. This gives you the opportunity to use existing objects created for other purposes. It also allows you to freely imagine and create something specifically for your presentation.

Some popular design programs you might use are

- Adobe: Photoshop, Illustrator, Acrobat, Flash
- Smart Draw
- CorelDraw Graphics Suite

As long as you have an acceptable native format for images, video, or sound or can convert something you have to a PDF, you can use it. You can find more information about this in Chapter 9.

Don't forget that you can use hand-drawn items by scanning them into your computer in a PDF format and uploading them to your presentation.

Framing and Positioning Ideas

The Frames tool is very unique. It allows you to put a border around content to group it together or provide emphasis. It provides structure for your presentation. By navigating within a container and then outside of it, your frame can tell a story about how ideas fit together. (See also the section on choosing frames as information containers in Chapter 8.)

One useful way to determine whether you're grouping your information effectively is to use the *squint test*. This test, created by Dr. Andrew Abela, suggests that you look at the information group and squint at it. If you can see how the information fits together from that vantage point, you're using your Frames tool effectively to lay out your content. (You can read more about Dr. Abela's work in the appendix.)

To use Frames to structure your content, follow these steps:

1. **Open the prezi you created from the Your Prezis tab (`http://prezi.com/your`).**

2. **Click the Edit Prezi button.**

   Your prezi is now in Edit mode.

3. **From the Write Menu, click Frame.**

   Four choices of borders — a bracket, a circle, a rectangle, and a hidden frame — appear.

4. **To try out a Frame, click the Bracket.**

   Place your cursor near a graphic, group of text, or other object and drag it so that the brackets appear around the objects.

5. **If you click on the object again the Zebra tool appears.**

   Us the Zebra tool as outlined earlier in the "Developing text elements" section to move, size, or rotate the objects.

   Now when you set up the Path, you can zoom in and out of these objects to provide the audience with a perspective on the big picture and the details of your presentation. (See Figure 2-6.)

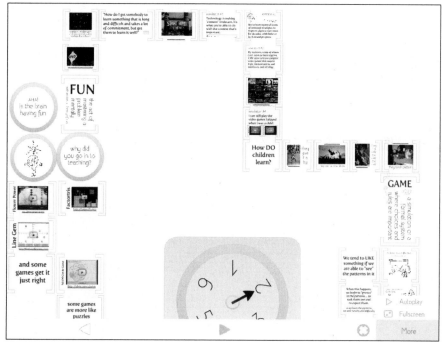

Figure 2-6:
Using the
Frames tool
to create a
game board.

The display of a game board is a clever way to move the user progressively through the content. You get the most from the Frames tool when the layout itself communicates information. For example, if you were to create a graphic of a flight of stairs and put each step of information on a literal step, you would be using the layout to explain the movement. Frames communicate groups of information. By using that as a guideline, you're helping the viewer understand the content.

Once you create a Frame with content inside it, you'll find it's useful to be able to move the Frame and the content as one entity. To do this, create a finished object with a Frame, and then hold the Shift key and drag your cursor around it. When you release, there will be a Zebra tool over the content, and everything in the space you selected with your cursor will move together.

To size the Frames correctly for projectors, hold down the Shift key while dragging your cursor around your object. You will produce a 4:3 aspect ratio, which is a standard for projectors. The aspect ratio is the ratio of the width of an image in relation to its height.

Creating a Path of Ideas

One of the unique features of Prezi is that you can set up what is called a *Path*. The Path tool allows you to show the presentation in the order you want and with the focus you want. Most slide presentations are static — you can move from slide to slide, but nothing breaks up the monotony. With Prezi, you can zoom and create drama with movement.

Following a unique order

Because you have the ability to jump from text to graphics and back again, you have the freedom to tell your story in any order you like. You can use repetition to emphasize an important concept. You can choose to construct a list of steps or not. By making a choice about how the order flows, you communicate a stronger message than if you always go from point A to point B. Your presentation isn't linear in any way, thus providing much needed variety.

To set up a Path, use the following steps:

1. **Go to the Your Prezis tab (`http://prezi.com/your`) and click a prezi to open it.**

2. **Click the Edit Prezi button on the right side of the screen.**

3. **Click the Path bubble from the Prezi menu.**

   Three smaller bubbles open: 1-2-3 Add, Capture View, and Delete All.

4. **To set up your Path, click the 1-2-3 Add bubble.**

   To start the Path, click the object or text you want to show first. It will likely be the title you created. After you click it, you see the number 1 in a circle where you clicked. This represents the first area of the screen that will be shown.

5. **To set up the next area you want it to move to, click that object.**

   A circle with a 2 in it will be placed on that area. Notice that a line connects you from number 1 to number 2. Continue clicking objects until you have the Path set up the way you want it. (See Figure 2-7.)

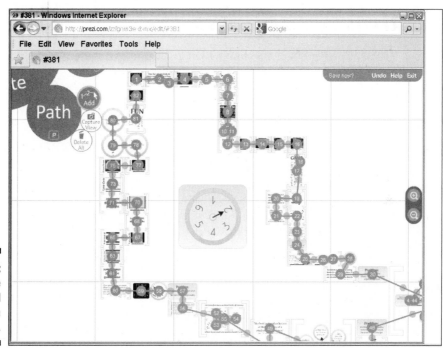

Figure 2-7:
Using the
Path tool
to create a
game board.

Creating a definite focus

With the Path tool, you can zoom in to focus on something or zoom out and see the big picture. This is where your story design really matters. When planning your first prezi, you'll want to experiment with setting up your Path to shift focus.

After you set up a Path, as described in the preceding section, experiment with the Path focus by taking the following steps:

1. **Go to some text you've created and put a circle around it by clicking the Frame bubble.**

2. **Click the bubble with the circle and drag your cursor to place a circle around the chosen text.**

3. **Go to the Path bubble. Click in the center of the circle you just created, and the number 1 is placed in it.**

   By placing it in the center of the object you will get a view of the circle with the text in it.

4. **Follow up by clicking the text itself, and the number 2 is placed on it.**

   This causes the Path to zoom in on the word itself.

5. **To view what this looks like, go to the Write menu and click Show.**

6. **Click the right-facing arrow in the bottom-left corner of the screen.**

   The resulting screen shows the circle and the text together.

7. **Click the right-facing arrow again to zoom in on the text you set up.**

   If you continue to do this with several different object and graphics on the screen, you'll see how to show the big picture and the details of your presentation.

Iterating until You're Ready to Present

People who create presentations are familiar with the impulse to iterate until the moment they're standing up, facing a crowd, remote clicker in hand. Revision is desirable up to a point. Obsessing about finding the exactly right word isn't.

After your graphics are completed, when you work with slides, your focus is usually on massaging the text. Because Prezi gives you additional dimensions on which to revise, you may find that your desire to change is self-limiting. Because each change impacts so many other variables, you quickly begin to weigh whether a change in one tiny place really improves the whole.

This is particularly helpful because prezis require you to think about the whole and the parts very early on. You'll feel less insecure about whether you've covered everything sooner in the iteration process. Confidence in your presentation goes a long way to making it successful.

Proofing your presentation

Every presentation should be proofread. There's nothing worse than seeing misspelled words or other content zooming and rotating sky high on a screen. Your credibility can go right out the window.

Prezi doesn't have a spell checker. The expectation is that you won't be writing reams of copy. But, you will still have keywords and text that need to be checked. You'll also want to make sure the sequence of ideas is in the right order. Sometimes after looking at something for too long, you cease to be able to actually see what it says. This is where the Invite Editors link comes in handy. You can ask someone to edit your work.

If you're creating text with some other creation program and then uploading it to Prezi, you can always run it through a spell checker first, import it into that program once corrected, and then load it into Prezi.

If you'd like to let someone edit your presentation, follow these steps:

1. **Click to open the prezi you want proofed from the Your Prezis tab (http://prezi.com/your).**

   The main Prezi screen opens.

2. **In the center of the prezi screen on the lower right in the grey box, click the Invite Editors link.**

   A screen pops up with a link to your editable prezi.

3. **Highlight the link with your cursor and press Ctrl+C.**

   If you want to revoke the share link you sent previously and generate a new one, you can click the Reset share link button below the URL presented to you.

4. **Close the pop-up screen by clicking the X in the upper-right corner.**

5. **Open your e-mail program or other sharing program and press Ctrl+V to paste it into the message box.**

   Send it as you normally would. When your collaborator receives the e-mail and clicks the link, he will be added as a coeditor and be able to edit your prezi.

Practicing until you feel confident

Feeling confident about presenting is a very personal thing. Some people practice a presentation once or twice and feel ready. Others can practice daily for a month and still not feel prepared. There's no actual rule about how much is enough. After I've practiced for a while, I do a test check by visualizing myself presenting. If I feel anxious or ill-prepared, I go back and practice until I'm ready.

Here are some tips for practicing your presentation:

✔ **Record audio of yourself.** It's really helpful to hear how you sound. Use a recording device or call a free conference call line to record yourself. I use an online service that provides a way to record from your computer or a phone line. Lots of these services exist online, and there are several software programs that also record your voice.

✔ **Time yourself with a stop watch.** If you have a stop watch of your own or even a clock nearby, practice your presentation for timing and pace. Don't try to wing it and expect the timing to end up perfect. If you go too far over (or under) time, you'll certainly disrupt a program of speakers.

✔ **Time yourself with an online counter.** There are lots of free online services like Online Stopwatch (`http://online-stopwatch.com`) that give you the ability to count up (or down) to time your presentation.

✔ **Present to a colleague or friend.** If you have someone you trust to give you honest feedback, do the presentation for him. This is a great way to find out if you're delivering a coherent, interesting message.

Part II
Exploring the Prezi Universe

In this part . . .

Creating presentations has never been considered a fun activity. You start with fear and end with anxiety. But it doesn't have to be that way. Presentations can take on a whole new level of pleasure for everyone. When using Prezi, you can interact with your content by zooming in and out to make everything more memorable. You'll emerge triumphant, and your audience will thank you.

In this part, you look in detail at the interface, called the Bubble menu, and see what makes it so easy. You see how to set up a group to collaborate online with colleagues and friends. Also, I take a spin around the online Prezi community and show you how to share presentation ideas and reuse some really great Prezi content created by others.

Chapter 3

Getting Familiar with the Online Interface

*E*verything about Prezi is unique. The interface takes the form of a group of round *bubbles* rather than linear menu bars. This should signal to you that the online program isn't bound by typical conventions. You're presented with an unlimited digital canvas upon which you can create dynamic presentations. The good news is that's it's easy to understand and use. And it works with all sorts of other program formats like Acrobat and Flash, so you can use media you've created in other programs to enhance your prezi.

This chapter acts as an introduction to the Prezi menu and shows you how to navigate using the built-in tools like the Transformation Zebra tool. Seeing a presentation created with Prezi is all the coaxing you'll need to dive right in and get started.

Introducing Prezi Components

To get started with Prezi, try out the main Bubble menu that sits on the upper left of your Prezi Edit screen. Remember that you'll be able to do things in Prezi that you can't with slide programs, so be prepared to try new ideas.

Prezi has two modes: Show and Edit. When you open and revise a prezi you are automatically in Edit mode. You will stay in that mode until you are ready to finalize your presentation. To move to Show mode you click the Show bubble. Show mode has lots of tools for you to enhance your presentation, so look at both in detail.

You can toggle between Edit and Show modes by clicking the grey Show bubble. That handy little Show bubble allows you to make revisions up until the time you present. But don't get carried away, making changes at the last moment and then forgetting what you did. Doing so ruins the flow of your presentation.

The available quick keyboard shortcuts for Edit and Show modes on a Mac or PC appear in Table 3-1.

Table 3-1	Keyboard Shortcuts for Edit and Show Modes
To Do This	**Use This Shortcut**
Open an edit text box	Double-click on the canvas
Toggle between Edit and Show modes	Press the spacebar
Go forward and back in the Path from Show mode	Use the left- and right-arrow keys
Zoom in and back out from Show mode	Use the up- and down-arrow keys
Save	Press Ctrl+S
Undo	Press Ctrl+Z
Escape from full screen in Show mode	Press Escape

Viewing Edit mode

Edit mode (see Figure 3-1) is for adding text and graphics, designing your movement, and creating a Path for your prezi to follow. When you open a prezi, the default is Edit mode. You don't need to do anything to get into that mode. All your creation activities are done here.

From this mode, you can use the following Bubble menus:

✔ **Write:** From this bubble, you type in text, add Web links, access the Transformation Zebra, and choose your styles and font colors.

✔ **Insert:** Using this bubble, you can upload media files and add shapes — an arrow, a free line, and a highlighter.

✔ **Frame:** From this bubble, you can add *containers* around your content to group it or help emphasize it. The available containers are a bracket, a circle, a rectangle, and a hidden frame.

✔ **Path:** Setting up a Path is the way you create navigation for your finished prezi. From the Path, you can set up the views one by one, capture a specific broad view within a Frame (container), and delete your entire Path and start over.

✔ **Colors & Fonts:** There are several styles from which to choose. Each style has fonts and colors within them. You can experiment with each of them to suit the current prezi you're working on.

Figure 3-1:
Prezi in Edit
mode.

Discovering Show mode

When you are in Show mode (see Figure 3-2) you can either set up the timing intervals or you can just go right into presenting using the arrow buttons or Autoplay. In this mode the grid background and Bubble menu disappear. When you're presenting, your prezi is always in Show mode. Whenever you click the Show bubble you automatically go into Show mode.

From this mode, you can do the following:

✔ **Go into Full Screen mode:** To accommodate a projector or for wider screen viewing.

✔ **Set the timing intervals for your prezi.** Prezi automatically advances to the next Frame depending on the selected time interval. There are settings for 4, 10, and 20 seconds between screens.

✔ **Zoom in and out by clicking objects:** If you want to respond to the audience or go back to something, you can click and zoom in on it.

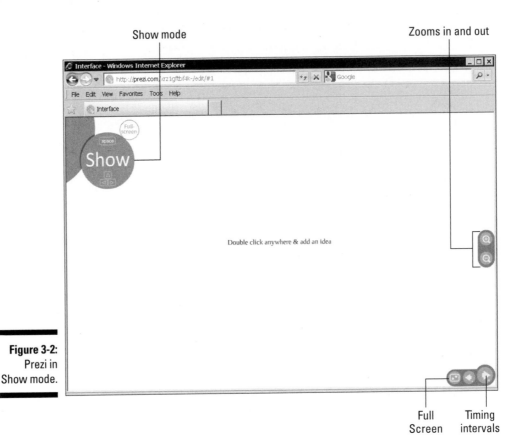

Show mode

Zooms in and out

Double click anywhere & add an idea

Figure 3-2:
Prezi in
Show mode.

Full
Screen

Timing
intervals

To set up timing intervals, do the following:

1. **Go to the Your Prezis tab (`http://prezi.com/your`) and click a prezi to open it.**

2. **Click the Edit button on the right side of the screen.**

3. **From the Bubble menu, click Show.**

   In Show mode, a right-arrow button appears on the bottom-right side of the screen.

4. **Hold down the right-arrow button.**

   The timing interval choices pop up. (See Figure 3-3.) The choices are 4 seconds, 10 seconds, or 20 seconds. These seconds refer to the amount of seconds each screen displays before moving to the next screen when you Autoplay it.

5. **Click to choose the timing interval you prefer.**

   After you choose your interval, the prezi begins Autoplaying. If you need to stop the presentation at any point, click Previous, which is the arrow facing left; or click Next, the arrow facing right.

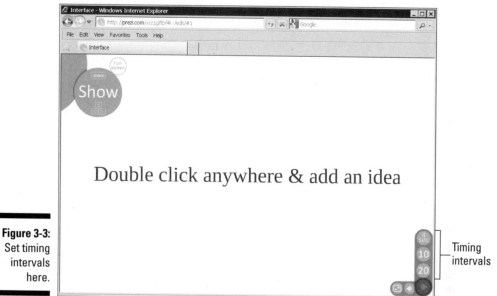

Figure 3-3: Set timing intervals here.

Timing intervals

Navigating the Canvas

The canvas is the digital work surface upon which you create your prezi. (See Figure 3-4.) It has a grid background and is unlimited in size. You can imagine and create anything from this space. There are no boundaries except the ones you establish when you develop your prezi.

The canvas has the following elements:

✔ **Editable, unlimited screen:** There is no limit to the screen space available to develop your prezi. You can move left or right, and up or down without constraints. Your only question is how to use the space to effectively communicate your message.

✔ **Bubble menu:** You do all your editing and revising from the Bubble menu in the upper left. When you click a submenu (the bubbles that surround the Write bubble), you will see additional choices presented to you. For example, when you click the Frame bubble, four choices appear — Bracket, Circle, Rectangle, or Hidden Frame. This is the case for all the other submenus as well.

✓ **Save, Undo, Print, Help, and Exit links:** While your prezi is in Edit mode, you can see these links in the upper-right corner of the canvas:

- *The Save link:* Automatically saves your prezi in short intervals.

- *The Undo link:* Deletes what you have just put on the canvas.

- *The Print link:* Saves your prezi as a PDF so that you can print each individual Path screen.

- *The Help link:* Brings up a Quick Help menu.

- *The Exit link:* Saves and exits your current prezi.

✓ **Zoom buttons:** The Zoom In button is the + (plus sign), and the Zoom Out button is the – (minus sign) you see on the middle right. Use these when you want to move manually around the canvas.

Even though your prezi is automatically saved in short intervals, remember to click this link now and then just to be safe.

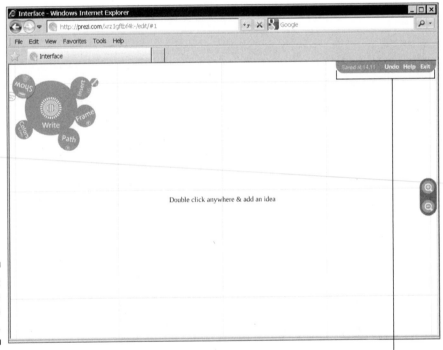

Figure 3-4:
This is the editable canvas.

Action links for Save, Help, Undo, and Exit

Interacting with the Bubble Menu

The Bubble menu in the upper-left corner of the Prezi canvas is the menu from which you create your prezi. The menu is very streamlined and easy to understand. Each individual component is labeled, and navigating the menu is intuitive. The following sections take a closer look at the various parts of the Bubble menu.

Using the Write bubble

The Write bubble is the central control from which you add and style text; put in Web links; and move, resize, rotate, and zoom objects. It's very easy to add text to your presentation from the text editor.

Double-click anywhere on the canvas, and the text box appears. (See Figure 3-5.) Type in some text and try the following:

Figure 3-5:
Write text functions.

✔ **To create bullets, click the bullet icon type in your text and click OK.** The text appears as wide as the space in the box, so use the right and left arrows at the end of the box to make it smaller or bigger.

✔ **To justify text, type in some text and then click one of the justify icons to make it left-, center-, or right-aligned and click OK.**

✔ **To vary the fonts, type in some text and then click Title 1, Title 2, or Body.** The theme you have chosen determines the available fonts and colors. To change from one style to another, simply click one of the choices and type in some text. You can only have one font in a text box at a time, so create the text you want in one font and then start a new box with a different font.

✔ **To resize the text once you have it on the canvas, click it once, and the Transformation Zebra appears over it.** From the Zebra, you can rotate the center ring to resize it. To move it around, use the inside ring, and to rotate it, use the outer ring. A more complete description of how to use the Transformation Zebra is available in the section "Moving around using the Transformation Zebra," later in this chapter.

> ✔ **To introduce text with a different font and color than those available in the Colors & Fonts Bubble menu, you need to use a graphics or other design program to create it.** Then save it as a PDF, JPG, or other media format, and choose Insert Bubble⇨Upload File to add the text to the canvas. After you place it on the canvas, you can use the Transformation Zebra to move, resize, and rotate the text as you would any other object.

Embedding Web links in your presentation

From within the text editor, you can add active Web links to your prezi. This is very useful because it allows you to go right to a place on the Web from within the presentation.

For example, if you're doing a presentation for some investors and you want to show them the Web site you've created for your future business, you can click the URL right on the Prezi canvas and you're seamlessly taken there. No fumbling or mistyping your address. The flow is professional.

When you've concluded discussing your Web site, you can close the Web page and return to your presentation where you left off. If you're online while presenting, you can go anywhere on the Internet within your presentation with embedded URL links. Don't forget this feature; it's very handy.

To add a Web link, take the following steps:

1. **Double-click anywhere on the canvas.**

   The text box appears.

2. **Type the URL into the box and click OK. (See Figure 3-6.)**

   Don't forget to include the entire address starting with `http://` or the link won't work.

3. **To make the link active, save and exit your prezi by clicking the links in the upper-right corner.**

4. **Reopen that prezi, and the link is now active.**

   It has a line under it denoting an active link. To confirm that it's working, click it as you would any other Web link and watch it go to the URL. Now during a presentation, you can go right to any Web page from Prezi and then come back to your spot in the presentation.

Figure 3-6:
Embedding
a Web link.

Inserting with the Insert bubble

The Insert tool has two functions. Via the submenu of Bubbles, it lets you upload media to be used in your presentation and it lets you add shapes to enhance your presentation.

When you click the Insert bubble, your screen should look like the one in Figure 3-7. The submenu bubbles offer the following two choices:

- ✔ **Load File:** Allows you to upload all your media
- ✔ **Shapes:** Offers three line tools to enhance your presentation

Figure 3-7:
The Insert
bubble
brings two
tools
forward.

Loading files with Load File

From the Insert bubble, you can go to the Load File function. This is your gateway to uploading an exciting collection of objects for your presentation.

You can upload the following types of media:

- ✔ **Text with a different font and color:** Create text using a graphics program and upload it to Prezi.
- ✔ **Any image in a Vector, JPG, PNG, or GIF format:** The maximum size for an uploaded image is 2,880 x 2,880.
- ✔ **Video:** File formats in FlashFLV or F4V are supported.
- ✔ **Audio:** To use this, you must first convert your audio file into an FLV format.
- ✔ **Images, charts, spreadsheets, graphs, and any content that can be converted to a PDF and uploaded to Prezi:** For example, you can take an Excel spreadsheet and convert it to a PDF and upload it.
- ✔ **Digital images from stock photo sites, your own personal photos, and other photo sites:** You can use any photo you like by making sure to convert it to one of the acceptable formats above. This could run the gamut from product shots to vacation photos.
- ✔ **Graphics and images you created from drawing software like Adobe Photoshop:** Just convert them to a PDF.

The maximum file size that you can upload online is 50MB. If you're using Prezi Desktop, your file size isn't limited, but if you decide to upload the file online, remember that the restriction applies.

To use the Load File function, take the following steps:

1. **Go to the Your Prezis tab (`http://prezi.com/your`) and click a prezi to open it.**

2. **Click the Edit button on the right side of the screen.**

3. **From the Bubble menu, click Insert.**

   Two smaller bubbles present themselves.

4. **Click the Load File bubble.**

   A Windows file screen opens, asking you to select the file(s) to upload by Prezi.com.

5. **Pick the file you want and click the Open button.**

   You see a message that says `Downloading Media` on the canvas and then your image appears. (See Figure 3-8.) You can now move it and work with it as you would any other object on the canvas.

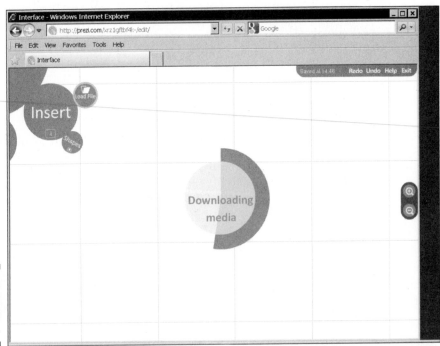

Figure 3-8:
Adding media to the canvas.

Drawing with Shapes

When creating a presentation it is helpful to have professional-looking drawing tools to augment your designs. Prezi has provided three that enhance text and add clarity. If you think about the kinds of lines you make to annotate your work, you would probably include an arrow to point out something important, a free-form line, and a highlighter for emphasis. Those same tools are available to you on your prezi canvas. To use the Shapes tool, take the following steps:

1. **From the Bubble menu, click Insert.**

   Two smaller bubbles present themselves.

2. **Click the Shapes bubble.**

   Submenu bubbles appear, offering the following three drawing tools:

   - *Arrow:* A ready-made arrow that can be resized and placed anywhere on the canvas.

   - *Line:* A free-form line that you can use to draw with.

   - *Highlighter:* A line that resembles a highlighter with which you can draw over something to give it emphasis.

To experiment with these tools, try any of the following (see Figure 3-9):

- **To create an arrow:** Click the Arrow bubble and place your cursor on the canvas and drag it to create an arrow and then let it go. Click the arrow so the Transformation Zebra appears. Now you can move and adjust it to suit your prezi.

- **To draw a free-form line:** Click the Line bubble and drag it across the canvas. You see a line that you can use as you would a pen to draw with.

- **To draw a line using the Highlighter:** Click the Highlighter bubble and drag it across some text or other object on the canvas. You see a transparent line whose color is determined by the style you chose from the Colors & Fonts bubble. If the highlighter plays an important part in your presentation, experiment with the styles in the Colors & Fonts bubble to see what works best. It's different in each of the styles.

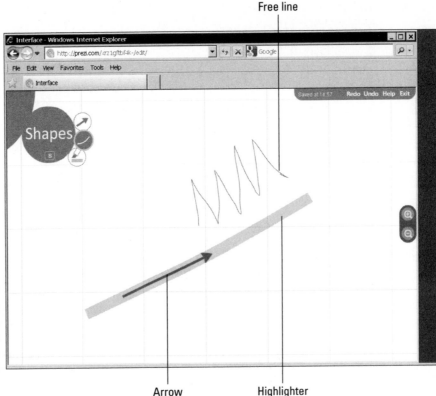

Free line

Arrow   Highlighter

Figure 3-9:
Lines drawn
with the
Shapes tool.

Grouping with the Frame bubble

The Frame bubble not only provides four stylish *containers* for your content, but it also allows you to group things to provide meaning. Grouping objects in this way can help you tell your story or help make clearer the point you're trying to make.

The Frame choices (see Figure 3-10) are as follows:

Figure 3-10:
Clicking the
Frame bub-
ble brings
four tools
forward.

✔ **Bracket:** *Brackets* are marks that appear around text or numbers to set them apart in some way. Designers use brackets as a stylish way to separate graphic elements or text. That is how they are used in prezis. You can group information and convey meaning by adding brackets around content.

To try the Bracket tool, take the following steps.

1. **From the Bubble menu, click Frame.**

   Four smaller bubbles present themselves.

2. **Click the Bracket bubble and drag your cursor around the outside of an object or some text.**

   A Bracket is positioned around the object or text. If you're satisfied with the positioning, let go of the cursor. (See Figure 3-11.)

3. **If you want to delete the Bracket while it is still live, click the Undo link in the upper-right corner of the screen.**

   Don't worry if the Bracket isn't positioned exactly as you want it. You can use the Transformation Zebra tool to enlarge it or move it later. This also lets you revise the use of that Bracket if you change the contents within it.

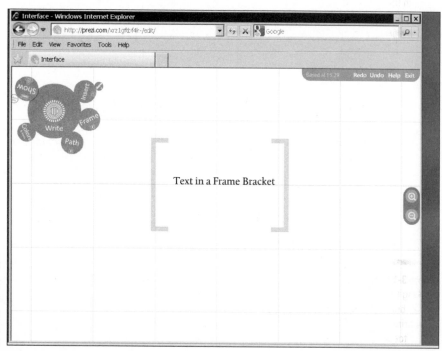

Figure 3-11:
Text in
a Frame
Bracket.

✔ **Circle:** The Circle is a very popular Frame because it's very easy for people to understand the meaning of this type of grouping. If you look in the Explore tab, you can see a lot of community members using multiple circles to communicate meaning.

It's easy to tell when the Rectangle and Bracket Frames are rotated left or right. Not so with a Circle. The top of the Circle Frame has an indicator that lets you know its position. It's a small arrow indicator. If you use the Zebra tool to rotate the circle left or right the arrow moves accordingly. This is important to know because it dictates the amount of rotation of all elements inside the circle.

To use the Circle tool, take the following steps:

1. **From the Bubble menu, click Frame.**

   Four smaller bubbles present themselves.

2. **Click the Circle bubble and then click and drag on the prezi around some text or objects.**

   Let the cursor go if you're satisfied with its placement. (See Figure 3-12.) You can move it using the Transformation Zebra.

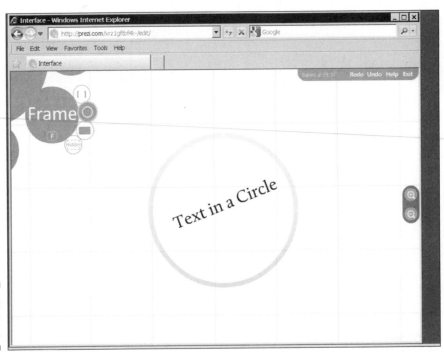

Figure 3-12:
Text in a Circle.

✔ **Rectangle:** Depending on which style you choose from the Colors & Fonts bubble, your Rectangle can be a solid darker color or very light. You can choose the shade that suits your purpose by creating a Rectangle and then clicking through the styles. Pick the one that suits your current presentation.

Some uses for the Rectangle are as follows:

- Topic heading
- Caption under photo
- Defined background for a group of elements
- A blank shape that represents a box

To use the Rectangle tool, take the following steps.

1. **From the Bubble menu, click Frame.**

    Four bubbles present themselves.

2. **Click the Rectangle bubble and then click and drag on the prezi to make a Rectangle of the size you want, either around something or on its own.**

    If you double-click the Rectangle, the text editor allows you to place text right on it. (See Figure 3-13.) Then you can use the Transformation Zebra to move it, resize it, or rotate it.

Figure 3-13: A Rectangle with text.

TIP

To size the Rectangle Frame correctly for projectors, hold down the Shift key while dragging your cursor around your object. You will produce a 4:3 aspect ratio, which is a standard for projectors. The aspect ratio is the ratio of the width of an image in relation to its height.

✔ **Hidden:** This Frame is called Hidden because it isn't visible after you go into Show mode. Its purpose is to group items without having the container be seen. It may be counterintuitive to want to hide a Frame, but this tool gives you visual control that is very helpful. For example, if you show a large graphic and want to point to a specific detail, you can put a Hidden Frame around that detail and zoom right to it without interfering with the image as a whole. It would look weird to put a visible Bracket around a small detail, but a Hidden Frame does the trick.

To use the Hidden tool, take the following steps:

1. **From the Bubble menu, click Frame.**

   Four bubbles present themselves.

2. **Click the Hidden bubble and then click and drag around a group of elements. (See Figure 3-14.)**

3. **Click the Write bubble to bring the entire menu back into view and then click Show.**

   The Hidden Frame disappears, and you can now select the elements as one unit.

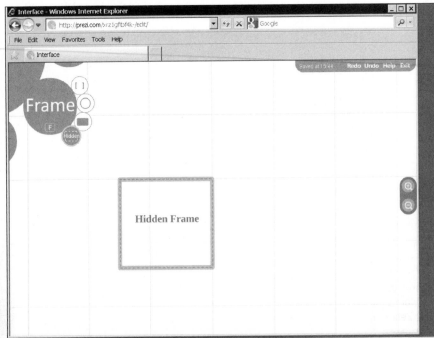

Figure 3-14:
A Hidden Frame with text.

Positioning your Frames

It's important to understand that each of the Frames tools can actually have two different positions on the screen. They can be forward (on top) and be more prominent or back (below) and faded-looking. When you place a Frame on an object or text already on the screen, it is in the *forward* position. If you want to bring an object forward and move the Frame back, do the following:

1. **Go to the Your Prezis tab (`http://prezi.com/your`) and click a prezi to open it.**

2. **Click the Edit button on the right side of the screen.**

3. **From the menu, click the Write bubble.**

4. **For this example, click the Circle bubble and drag it around some text or objects already on the canvas.**

   It's now in the forward position and the text is behind.

5. **To place the objects in the forward position to make them more visible, click the Transformation Zebra on top of the text.**

6. **Click the + sign on the outer ring of the Circle.**

   This brings up a menu of options. (See Figure 3-15.)

7. **Click the Send Backward link.**

   The text appears brighter because it now holds the forward position.

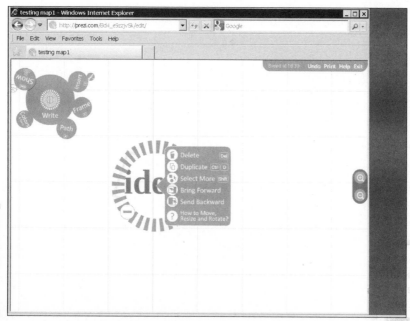

Figure 3-15:
Bringing text forward with the Transformation Zebra.

Creating your story line with the Path bubble

The Path bubble has a very unique and valuable function in your presentation. It's the tool that allows you to create your story line. This tool sets Prezi apart from other presentation programs.

When you're creating a slide show, you go from one slide to the next, to the next, and then to the next — until you're done. If you want to back up or go ahead to a particular slide, you need to traverse the others. With the Prezi Path tool, however, you can skip that unwieldy navigation. You can create a narrative for your presentation by designating a series of steps using Path numbers. This means that you can jump from place to place in your presentation without having to go over everything before it. You take a direct route.

Clicking the Path bubble brings three tools forward (see Figure 3-16):

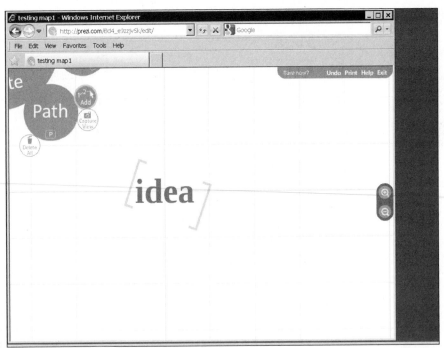

Figure 3-16:
The Path bubble tools.

✔ **1-2-3 Add:** The 1-2-3 Add tool helps you to set up Path numbers that allow you to move from element to element regardless of proximity. You can create a Path and iterate until you're certain that you've told your story in the most powerful way.

To use the Path tool, take the following steps:

1. **Click the Path bubble from the Prezi menu.**

   Three smaller bubbles open that say 1-2-3 Add, Capture View, and Delete All.

2. **To set up your Path, click the 1-2-3 Add bubble.**

3. **To start the Path, click some text or a graphic you want to show first. It might be the title you created.**

   When you click it, you see the number 1 in a circle on top of the element you clicked. This represents the first area of the screen that will be shown.

4. **To set up the next area in your presentation that you want to move to, click that object.**

   A circle with a 2 in it will be placed on top of that area. Also notice that a line connects you from number 1 to number 2 so you can follow it.

5. **Continue clicking objects until you have the Path set up the way you want it.(See Figure 3-17.)**

   If you want the view to be the center of a grouping of objects, click the center of the Frame.

After the Path is set, you can revise it by dragging the numbers to different objects on the screen with your mouse. Experiment by setting up a sequence and then testing whether you like it. You can revise until you're satisfied with it. The Path screens will each be printed if you choose the Print link.

✔ **Capture View:** The Capture View allows you to pick a group of elements and make them a screen view in your Path. That way you can show individual elements and then zoom out for a precise look at the group.

To use the Capture View tool, do the following:

1. **Click the Path bubble from the Prezi menu.**

   Your presentation shows the Path numbers you've already created, along with three smaller bubbles that say 1-2-3 Add, Capture View, and Delete All. Position the view as you want it to display.

2. **Click the Capture View bubble.**

   You see that a square has captured that entire view. (See Figure 3-18.) Now you can put a Path number on that view as a separate screen.

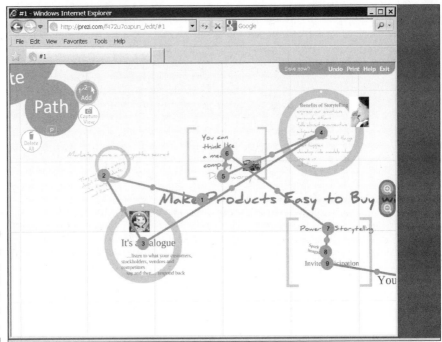

Figure 3-17:
Using the
1-2-3 Add
bubble to
create the
Path.

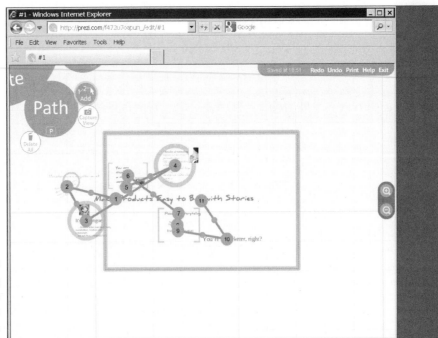

Figure 3-18:
The Capture
View in a
Path.

🖊 **Delete All:** When you create a Path, you can revise it and move things until it seems right. If after watching it in Show mode you decide that it isn't right and that you want to start over, use the Delete All tool. It's quick and easy.

To use the Delete All Path tool, take the following steps:

1. **Click the Path bubble from the Prezi menu.**

   Your presentation shows the Path numbers you've already created along with three smaller bubbles that say 1-2-3 Add, Capture View, and Delete All.

2. **Click the Delete All bubble.**

   You now see that the entire Path set up has been deleted. You can now begin again or save and close your prezi.

If you delete the Path and go to print your prezi, you have only one screen printed. The Path screens correspond to the number of pages that will be printed.

Here are some tips about using the Path:

🖊 To remove a Path number once selected, drag it off to the background.

🖊 From the Path tool, select the Capture View bubble to take a snapshot of that view and add it to the numbered Path.

🖊 When in the Path tool, use the Delete All button to remove the entire Path to start again.

🖊 To revise the Path, drag the large numbered circle you want to move from its current location and drag it to the location you want and release it.

Styling with the Colors & Fonts bubble

When you click the Colors & Fonts bubble, you're accessing the design formats that are included with Prezi. The available styles (see Figure 3-19) have a different background and three fonts associated with each. These styles are accessed from the Write text editor. When Prezi is in Edit mode, double-click the canvas, which opens the text editor and displays the choices that correspond to that design style.

You can freely change from one style to another by clicking the respective bubble. You're limited by the number of available built-in styles. But you can add your own customs fonts and colors by creating them in another design program and simply uploading them to the Prezi canvas.

Each style has its own personality. If you open a new prezi and type some words on the canvas, you can then experiment to see which ones suit you best.

Figure 3-20 shows an example of the Glossy Paper style.

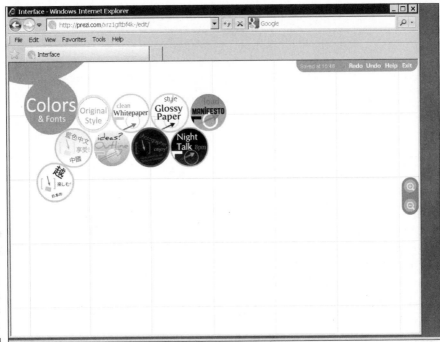

Figure 3-19:
The available styles in the Colors & Fonts bubble.

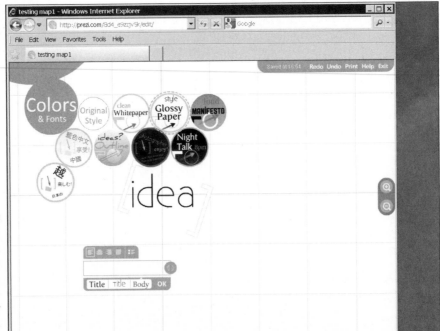

Figure 3-20:
The colors and fonts associated with the Glossy Paper style.

Moving around using the Transformation Zebra

The Transformation Zebra is an integral part of the menu and appears when Prezi is in Write mode and you click an object. With this one tool, you can move, resize, and rotate all your elements. Exploring this function helps you become a master of the canvas in short order.

To access the Transformation Zebra tool, here's what you do:

1. **Make sure Prezi is in Write mode.**

   To get into Write mode, click the Write bubble in the center of the main Bubble menu.

2. **Click an element on the canvas.**

   The Transformation Zebra appears on top of the element. (See Figure 3-21.) You can now use it to move, resize, and rotate anything you have in your presentation.

Move

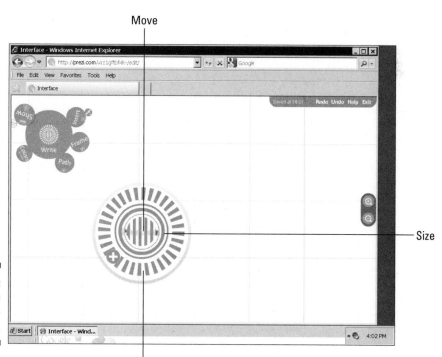

Size

Rotate

Figure 3-21: Rings of the Transformation Zebra.

To explore what the Zebra tool can do with objects, try any of the following from the Write bubble where you access the Transformation Zebra:

- **Move:** Click an object and drag it wherever you'd like to place it on the canvas.

- **Resize:** Place your cursor on the second inside ring and drag it up or down to increase or decrease the text.

- **Rotate:** Place your cursor on the outer ring and swing it up and down.

- **Size comparisons:** Make one word in a sentence much larger than the rest to stand out.

- **Symbols:** Cut and paste symbols from a design program and use the Zebra to resize and rotate them.

- **Bring out another menu of options:** Click the + (plus sign) you see in the lower-left portion of the outer circle. From the additional menu that appears, you can delete items, duplicate them, bring them forward or send them back, and select several objects one after another. If you want to see a demo of how the rings work, click the ? (question mark) that says, `How to Move, Resize and Rotate?`

Taking Advantage of Smart Zooming

Smart Zooming is a feature that really causes your audience to sit up and take notice. Most presentation software has no movement capabilities, unless you count moving from slide to slide. Prezi audiences are drawn to the unique activity up on the screen.

Using Smart Zooming, you can communicate your message more effectively by emphasizing things as you talk about them. This function works in Show mode because it's used in real time. When you want to move about the canvas without using a Path, use Smart Zooming. It gives you the ability to make a point or answer a question by jumping back and zooming in to the point under discussion.

To understand how it works, try the following:

- **Zoom in:** In Show mode, click an element on your screen. Notice that Prezi zooms in, and the element gets larger. This zoom-in movement is determined for you based on how you have placed your item. You don't have to worry about how to zoom in or center it. If you've rotated an object, the software shows that rotation and presents the element to you right side up. It's all part of the program. You can also use the +

(plus sign) button on the mid-right side of your canvas to zoom in and center the entire canvas.

✔ **Zoom out:** Again in Show mode, after you've clicked an object, you can click anywhere else on the canvas and the object will zoom out. Using the – (minus sign) button, you can zoom out and center the entire canvas. This function allows you to show the big picture of the elements by going from the details out to the larger view.

Printing Your Prezi

Printing your prezi is a great way for you and your audience or work group to have a record of the presentation. There are several benefits to printing your prezi, including the following:

✔ **Your prezi is saved as a PDF file.**

✔ **The number of pages that prints is determined by the number of items you have set up in your Path.** Each screen you print is a screen that you have set up to be viewed as an individual Path number.

✔ **You can carry your prezi-in-progress with you.** That way you can make notes on it when you can't use a computer to access your prezi.

✔ **You can send a printed version to audiences without an Internet connection.** It won't have the same impact, but it will give them a good idea of what you have in mind.

✔ **You can print out some of the screen as part of a handout.** You can select a few pages from Prezi Acrobat and create a file from them for your audience.

To print your prezi in PDF format, take the following steps:

1. **Go to the Your Prezis tab (`http://prezi.com/your`) and click a prezi to open it.**

2. **Click the Edit button on the right side of the screen.**

3. **From the links menu in the upper right of your Prezi canvas, click Print. (See Figure 3-22.)**

   When you click this link, a message pops out below it that says, `Starting`. This message shows you the number of pages that will print based on the Path numbers you have set up. If you don't have a Path set up, Prezi prints the one main screen.

4. Click the Click to Save PDF link.

The Save File window pops up and asks which location you want to save it to. Name a location, and it will be saved there. Then go to the document and print it out as you normally would print a PDF. If you want to, you can readjust the Path based on how the PDF prints and then reprint it.

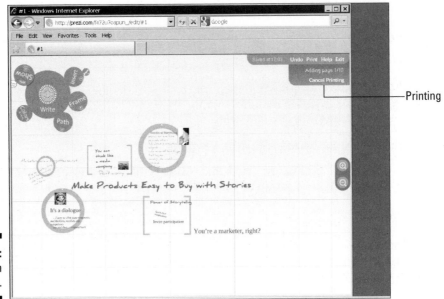

Printing

Figure 3-22:
Printing in
Prezi.

Chapter 4

Discovering the Prezi Desktop

A s valuable as Prezi is as an online application, there may be times when working offline on your computer makes sense. When you're traveling or working from a remote location, you don't always have Internet access. With Prezi Desktop, you can still work on your presentation offline when the mood strikes.

After you've downloaded and installed Prezi Desktop, you can do all the same things you could do online except one: You can't publish your prezi. For that, you still have to go online.

In this chapter, you find out how to download Prezi Desktop and set it up to use offline.

Downloading the Offline Editor

One of the great benefits of working from your computer is that you're not restricted by the size of the files you want to upload. This means that video or other large files in your presentation aren't limited by the amount of space you have in your online account. You're limited only by your own hard drive space.

Prezi Desktop is available only to users with a Pro or Edu Pro license. You can try Prezi Desktop if you opt for the free 30-day trial version, so you can decide whether you want to purchase the Pro version after the trial is up.

Your Pro or Edu Pro account allows you to download Prezi Desktop to three of your computers. This should be sufficient for most users. The application works with Windows, Mac, or Linux, and you can choose to keep presentations on your hard drive or upload them to your Prezi account online.

Before you download the offline Prezi Desktop Editor, you must have Administrator privileges set up. These privileges are automatically set up for you when you sign up for your Pro or Edu Pro license, so you don't need to worry about it. If you were to change your own privileges for some reason, you'd need to restore it to Administrator to proceed with downloading.

Putting Prezi on your desktop

Prezi makes downloading to the desktop really easy. To download the offline editor to your desktop, follow these steps:

1. **On the Your Prezis page (`http://prezi.com/your`), click the Download Now! link in the upper-right corner to download the Prezi Desktop.**

   A new page opens that displays several links related to the desktop version and a video introducing the Prezi Desktop.

2. **Click the Download and Install link.**

   The Download and Install Prezi Desktop screen appears. On this screen is a graphic box near the top that shows the current version of Prezi and, farther down on the page, instructions on how to install. (See Figure 4-1.)

3. **Click the Install Now button in the box, and the install process begins.**

   A screen pops up to ask `Would you like to open or save this file?`

4. **Click the Open button.**

   The Getting Ready to Install This Application screen appears, and you see the files loading. The next screen asks, `Are you sure you want to install this application to your computer?`

5. **Click Install.**

   A new screen pops up with the default installation preferences selected. The preferences install Adobe Air, add a shortcut to the desktop, start the application after installation, and install it to your Program files folder.

6. **If you agree with these settings, click Continue.**

   A screen from Adobe asks whether you want to allow changes to your computer.

7. **Click Yes, and the application installs.**

   The Prezi Desktop application opens on your desktop.

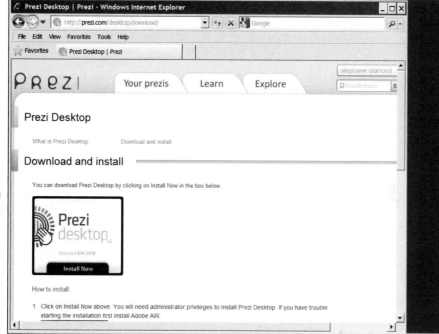

Figure 4-1:
The graphic
box with
the Install
Now button
for install-
ing Prezi
Desktop.

Installing Adobe Air

When you use Prezi online you can easily use the tools to navigate the work-space. In order for you to be able to do all the exciting zooming and editing offline you need to download one additional application — Adobe Air.

Adobe Air is a software application written by Adobe Inc. to work with Windows, Mac, and Linux operating systems. It allows developers to transfer the same kind of advanced functions they use online to the desktop. After you download it, you don't need to think about it again. The application takes care of running it.

To download Adobe Air, follow these steps:

1. **On the Your Prezis page (`http://prezi.com/your`), click the Download Now! link for the Prezi Desktop.**

   A new page opens that displays several links related to the desktop ver-sion and a video introducing the Prezi Desktop.

2. **Click the Get Adobe Air button.**

   This step takes you to Adobe.com, where a new screen pops up, asking whether you want to download the latest version of Adobe Air.

3. **Click the Download Now button. (See Figure 4-2.)**

   A Thank You screen pops up, telling you that your download will start automatically.

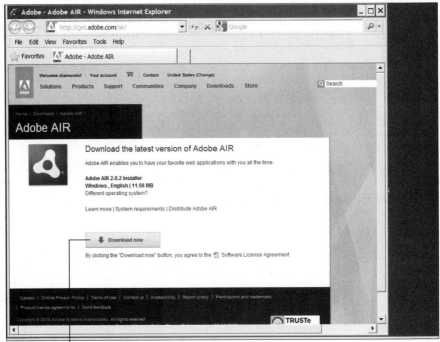

Download Now button

4. **When the download screen appears, click Run.**

   The files begin downloading. It's a large file, so depending on the speed of your connection, don't be surprised if it takes a few minutes. After the files have downloaded, you're told that you've successfully downloaded the file.

5. **Click the Finish button.**

Getting the manual for the Desktop

When you're working offline, it's a good idea to have the manual downloaded to your computer. Make sure you have it downloaded to each computer that has Prezi Desktop on it. (You're allowed to install Prezi Desktop on up to three computers.) That way you can quickly reference something you're working on without have to connect to the Internet.

To get the manual to refer to offline, do the following:

1. **From the Your Prezis page (http://prezi.com/your), click the Download Now! link for the Prezi Desktop.**

   On the new page opens, you see several links related to the desktop version.

2. **Under the video in the bottom left of the screen is a link that says Prezi Desktop Guide (PDF format) — click that link.**

   A screen pops up asking whether you want to save or open the file.

3. **Click the open button, and the PDF of the manual opens.**

4. **Save it to your desktop if you want it to be handy.**

   Now when you are working offline you can quickly refer to the guide.

Using the Desktop

Prezi Desktop works just like the online version. You see all the same menus and commands.

Activating Prezi Desktop the first time

Before you use the Prezi Desktop for the first time, you must activate it. To access Prezi Desktop, go to the Start Menu in Windows or the Applications folder on a Mac, or double-click the Prezi Desktop icon if you chose that default.

A welcome screen pops up. (See Figure 4-3.) You see this screen only once. Type in the log in where prompted and your software is activated via Prezi.com.

After you have activated your software, you don't need to get online unless you want to download a prezi not currently on your local desktop, upload a presentation from your desktop, or look at one of the online presentations in the Explore tab.

Editing your offline prezi

Open the Prezi Desktop application and you'll see the same functions that are available in the online version, so you can proceed to edit exactly the same way. (See Figure 4-4.) Double-click on the canvas to begin adding text and choose Bubble menu items as you normally do.

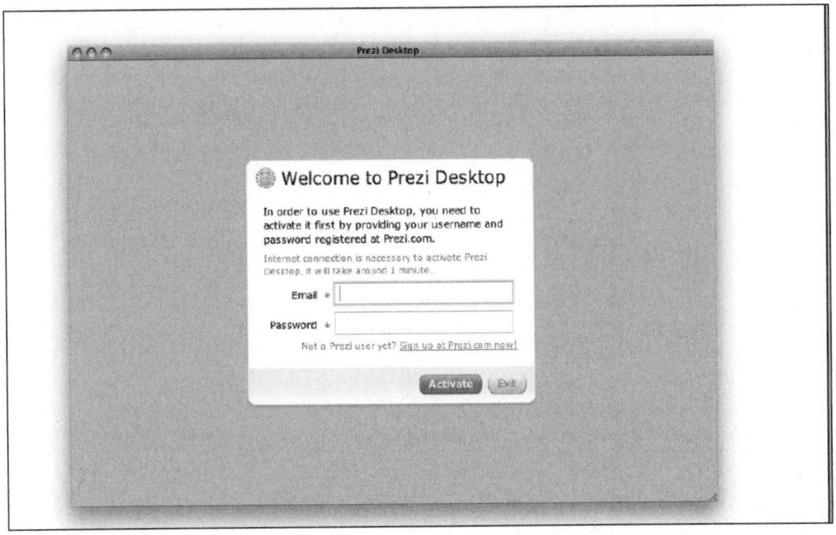

Figure 4-3:
Activation
screen
for Prezi
Desktop.

Figure 4-4:
Editing
the Prezi
Desktop.

Using Prezi Desktop commands

Prezi has made it super easy to coordinate Prezi Desktop with your online account. If you can access a file menu, you're an expert.

The default file extension for prezis is `.pez`. That should be easy to remember.

To access commands, use the following menu options (see Figure 4-5):

- ✔ **New:** Opens a new offline prezi.
- ✔ **Open:** Opens a prezi already in progress.
- ✔ **Export as a portable prezi:** Downloads your prezi for use offline for a presentation.
- ✔ **Print:** Prints the file as a PDF.
- ✔ **Upload to Prezi.com:** Saves your offline Desktop prezi to your online account.

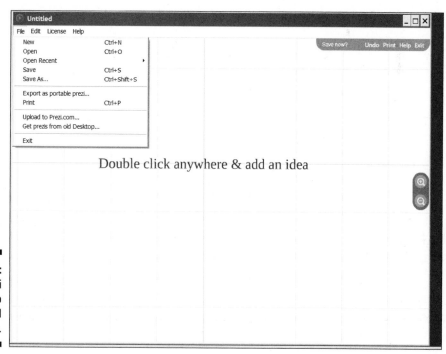

Figure 4-5: Prezi Desktop command options.

It's a good idea to copy your offline prezi to your online account, and vice versa, if you want to have secured backup copies of each. By doing so, you have duplicates of all your prezis in case something happens to one of the files. If you do this, remember to keep them both up-to-date.

Chapter 5

Navigating the "Your Prezis" Page

*T*he Internet gives people around the world the ability to collaborate in exciting new ways. Because Prezi is hosted online, you don't have to worry about securing space on a server or finding compatible ways to interact with your colleagues online. Prezi does it for you.

Using applications online makes creating and managing information easy. You always know where your work is stored, and the software is always up-to-date. Using the Your Prezis tab within Prezi as your home base for all the presentations you create is a step up from offline applications that require you to buy upgrades and hunt around for account and support information. You can spend your valuable time dreaming up show-stopping prezis. You'll be able to create multiple iterations and polish your presentation until it shines.

In this chapter, you explore how to get around online within the Your Prezis tab. All your presentations can be found here, and new examples by the Prezi community are constantly being displayed in the Explore tab for you to see and reuse. In this chapter, I show you how to use commands from the Your Prezis tab.

Also in this chapter, you discover the options you have for sharing and collaborating with others as you work with Prezi. You'll be able to accommodate your various work teams by inviting coeditors. How you want to share your presentations is up to you. You can e-mail a private prezi, embed it on a Web site or a blog, or send a public Prezi via e-mail.

You also explore the fun of using social networks such as Twitter and Facebook to spread your best ideas. Prezi makes it easy to communicate with your followers and friends on these networks. If you want to share your opinions online about your favorite presentations, you can rate public prezis, add your comments, and engage others in the community.

Managing the "Your Prezis" Page with Commands

The Prezi interface is very clear and straightforward. It includes large visible buttons for most of the major commands and also online tips when needed. The following sections describe each of the buttons and links in detail.

Open

When you opened your Prezi account, you set up your login information. To open a presentation from the Your Prezis tab, do the following:

1. **Go to the Your Prezis tab (`http://prezi.com/your`) and open a prezi by clicking it. Log in if you haven't done so already.**

   This is the home base where all your prezis can be found.

2. **Click the Edit Prezi button. (See Figure 5-1.)**

   Your editing screen opens, and you can begin revising your prezi.

Download

The value of being able to download a prezi to your hard drive is that you can keep it stored offline and available. If you have a Pro or Edu Pro license, you can also use Prezi Desktop to edit offline without an Internet connection. This frees you up to work whenever inspiration strikes.

If you have a Public or Enjoy license, a portable prezi isn't editable after you download it. You can share it, but if you want to edit it, you must go back to the online copy, revise it, and then download it again. If you have Prezi Desktop, you can edit it after you download it.

Edit Prezi button

Figure 5-1:
Click the
Edit Prezi
button to
launch a
prezi.

To download a prezi, follow these steps:

1. **Go to the Your Prezis tab (`http://prezi.com/your`).**

2. **Find the prezi you want to download and click to open it.**

3. **Click the Download button to the right of the Prezi screen.**

   A screen opens that gives you the option to download as a Portable prezi. Or if you're using Prezi Desktop, you can select the Download for Prezi desktop option so that you can edit the prezi after downloading it.

4. **Click the Download button. (See Figure 5-2.)**

   A screen pops up and shows it's downloading your file and asks for a location to save it.

   If this screen doesn't automatically pop up, you see a message that says `If the download doesn't start automatically click here` at the bottom of the screen. Click the Here link, and you should then get the Open or Save screen.

5. **Click Save and you can choose the location to save it to.**

   The file is loaded to that location as a Zip file. To open it, unzip the file as you normally do and then click the prezi to open it.

Download button

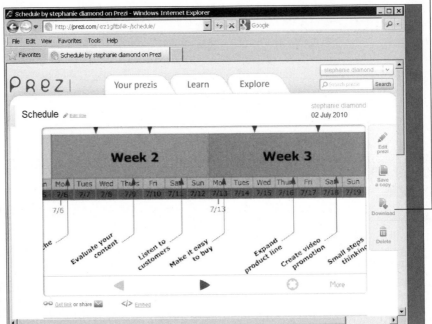

Figure 5-2:
Click the
Download
button to
download a
prezi to
your PC.

Save during online revisions

One of the cardinal rules of using digital information is to remember to back it up. You never know when something might go wrong with your Internet connection, causing you to lose your work. Having to retype a text document is stressful, but redoing a complete presentation can be crazy-making.

As a long time computer user, I've trained myself to click the Save button every few minutes when I'm working in my word processor or other work application. So that you won't lose your changes, the developers at Prezi have instituted an Auto Save feature while you work on the Prezi canvas that ensures your changes will be saved at regular intervals. This is a great feature, but I recommend that you take the initiative to frequently click the Save Now? link while working to be certain that you don't lose anything.

To save a prezi, take the following steps:

1. **Go to the Your Prezis tab (http://prezi.com/your) and click a prezi to open it.**

2. **Click the Edit button and revise your prezi by adding and changing items.**

   When you have worked for a few minutes, the Save Now? link appears in the upper-right corner of the screen.

3. **Click the Save Now? link every few minutes while you work. (See Figure 5-3.)**

4. **When you're ready to close your prezi, click the Save Now? link again before you click Exit to be sure it's saved.**

As an added benefit, Prezi automatically saves your work if you click Exit without saving. The next time you open that prezi, you'll see the newly revised version.

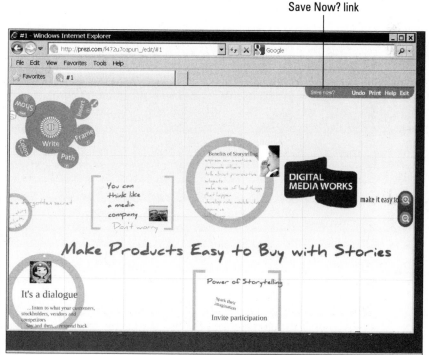

Figure 5-3:
Click the
Save Now?
link in the
upper-right
corner to
save your
work in
progress.

Save a copy

Prezi also allows you to save a duplicate copy of a prezi. By saving a copy of your presentation in its original state, you can be assured you won't lose it. If you are working with a group, you will also be able to see your copy before it was changed by someone in the group (if you gave them the ability to edit your prezi).

To duplicate a prezi, do the following:

1. **Go to the Your Prezis tab (`http://prezi.com/your`) and click to open the prezi you want to duplicate.**

   The screen opens up to showing your prezi.

2. **Click the Save a Copy button on the right side of the screen. (See Figure 5-4.)**

   A new copy of that prezi with the new name is placed on the Your Prezis page along with your other prezis. To edit it, simply click to open it as you would any other prezi.

Save a Copy button

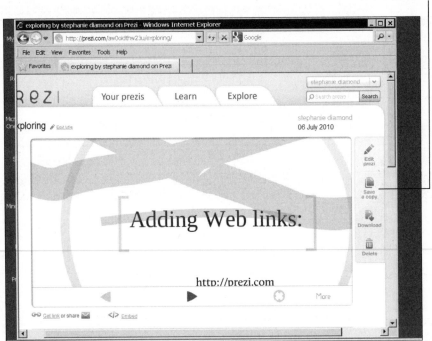

Figure 5-4:
Duplicating
a prezi with
the Save a
Copy button.

Delete

Do you find yourself saving too many versions of a presentation? Or have you found that your prezi is just not saying what you want it to say? If so, sometimes the best thing to do is just to delete it and start over.

To delete a prezi do the following:

1. **Go to the Your Prezis tab (`http://prezi.com/your`) and click to open the prezi you want to delete.**

2. **Locate the Delete button on the right side of the screen and click it.**

A screen pops up, asking whether you really want to delete the prezi.

3. **Click the Delete button. (See Figure 5-5.)**

You are returned to the Your Prezis tab, and that prezi disappears from the page.

Delete button

Figure 5-5: Click the Delete button to delete a prezi.

After you delete a prezi, there is no way to retrieve it, so make sure you really want to delete it. If you have sent links to coeditors, they won't be able to access it, either.

Setting Up Prezi to Share the Work

Once you've created a prezi you're excited about, you'll want to share it with colleagues and friends. Because it's an online application, your prezi is already converted to a digital format that can be sent in a variety of ways. You can show your presentation to your own private circle of colleagues and friends, or you can publish it to be viewed by any online user.

Obviously, proprietary company information or personal information should remain under wraps and kept private. But there are lots of ways of publishing your prezi and making it public. If you have ideas and concepts that you'd like to share, prezis can be sent in e-mails, viewed on social networks, downloaded to desktops, and displayed in the Prezi Explore tab. The next few sections describe these options in detail.

Making your presentation public

If you have a Free license, your prezis are automatically made public. If you have an Enjoy or Pro license, you have the choice to keep it private or make your prezi public. This lets others view your prezi in a variety of ways. If you're ready to share it with others, use the following steps:

1. **Click to open a prezi from the Your Prezis tab (`http://prezi.com/ your`).**

   Your prezi opens, and below the screen are the three radio buttons.

2. **Select the Public radio button if you want to make it public but don't want to allow reuse. (See Figure 5-6.)**

   Your prezi is now published to a URL, and you can continue to edit it. The next time you revise your presentation, it will be updated at this URL.

Public radio button

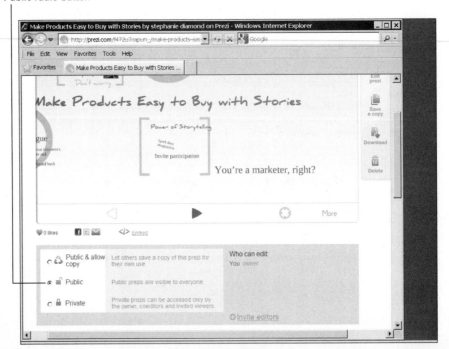

Figure 5-6:
Select the
Publish
radio but-
ton to make
your prezi
public.

It's important to note that you can make your presentation public at any time during its creation or after its implementation if you are an Enjoy or Pro user. If you don't select the Public radio button, your prezi remains private. You can always come back and publish it later.

Allowing reuse of your presentation

Regardless of which license you own, anytime you open your prezi, you're given the option of selecting the Allow Reuse check box. If you select this check box, you allow others to take the contents of your prezi — your graphics, ideas, path, and anything else you have in your presentation — to use as a template for their own presentations. Unless you have some proprietary materials or items of a confidential nature, you may want to consider doing this.

The benefits of allowing reuse of your prezi are

- **Any original graphics you've created get wide distribution and acknowledgment.** If you're a designer or an artist, this may help show off your portfolio.

- **New ideas you have developed are reused and repeated by others.** This is a great way to get your ideas heard around the world.

- **Clever use of path and movement may be copied and used by the Prezi community.** You may gain expertise status among those in the Prezi community.

To let others reuse your presentation, follow these steps:

1. **Click to open a prezi from the Your Prezis tab (`http://prezi.com/your`).**

   Your prezi opens, and below the screen are three radio buttons.

2. **Select the Public and Allow Copy radio button if you want to allow reuse. (See Figure 5-7.)**

   It now shows up when users do a search for prezis in the Explore tab that can be reused as the basis for their new presentations. You can find other people's reusable prezis on the Explore page when you search by selecting the Show Only Reusable check box.

Publi & Allow Copy radio button

Figure 5-7:
Select the
Public and
Allow Copy
radio button
to let others
use your
prezi.

Prezi recommends that people who reuse a prezi provide attribution to the creator of the prezi on their presentation, so remember to do so if you reuse someone else's prezi.

Keeping your prezi private

The third radio button in the privacy settings area is the Private button. If you have either the Enjoy or Pro accounts, you can choose to keep your prezi private. There several good reasons to do this, including the following:

- ✔ You are working on a presentation that is not yet ready for prime-time viewing.

- ✔ You are Mind Mapping or creating something just for yourself.

- ✔ Your prezi contains proprietary information that should not be seen.

- ✔ You will only be sharing your prezi with a select group of family or friends.

Use Prezi as a tool in whatever way it makes sense to you. Remember that first and foremost it's a whiteboard. Don't feel obligated to make every prezi a finished product. You can create drafts and delete them whenever you want.

Sharing Prezis

E-mailing links to public prezis is easy because Prezi has a built-in e-mailer. All you have to do is click the appropriate link on the Prezi screen and you will be sending a public prezi. You can also send a private link via your own e-mail service or other internal sharing program. In this section I describe the process in detail.

Sending a private prezi

To send a private prezi using your own e-mail program, follow these steps:

1. **To open your private prezi, click it from the Your Prezis tab (`http://prezi.com/your`).**

2. **Click the Get link button on the lower-left side of the Prezi screen.**

   A screen pops up with your view-only link. (See Figure 5-8.)

3. **Highlight the link and hit Ctrl+C to copy it.**

   If you wish to revoke the private link you sent previously and generate a new one, you can click the Reset Share Link button below the URL presented to you.

4. **Close the pop-up screen by clicking the Close button.**

5. **Open your own e-mail program or other sharing network and hit Ctrl+V to paste it into the message box.**

   Send it as you normally would. Only those who receive this link from you can access it.

Sending a link to a public prezi via e-mail

Prezi makes it easy to e-mail with a built-in form. To send a public prezi in an e-mail, follow these steps:

1. **Open an existing prezi by clicking from the Your Prezis tab (`http://prezi.com/your`).**

2. **Click the Share downward arrow button below the screen.**

   A screen pops up with a link to set up an e-mail. (See Figure 5-9.)

3. **Type in your information and click the Click the Send Invitation button.**

   A message that the e-mail has been sent successfully appears.

4. **Close the pop-up screen by clicking the Close button.**

   Your e-mail is now off to your chosen recipients.

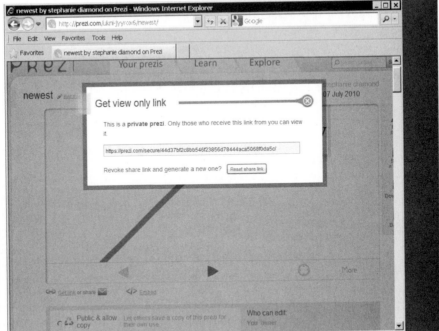

Figure 5-8:
Sending a
private prezi
via a link
defined for
you.

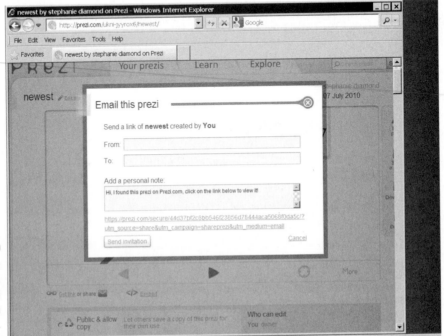

Figure 5-9:
Sending a
public prezi
via a built-in
e-mail form.

Collaborating with Coeditors

When your work has an online component, you'll likely interact with a variety of groups throughout your day. Some of those you connect with are inside your organization, and some are outside; some are in your time zone, and some aren't. Working with coeditors helps you easily stay connected and collaborate with all the parties who have an interest in your work. The advantages of collaborating online include the following:

- ✔ **Quick and easy sharing of new versions of your presentation with all the editors:** You can virtually let each person on your staff submit ideas. This enriches the ideas as a whole and fosters buy in from everyone. The list of people approved for editing is right on the Prezi screen under the Who Can Edit title. There is also a Remove link if you want to revoke editing rights.

- ✔ **Solving the disadvantage of having collaborators in different time zones:** By having the presentation hosted online and available at any time of the day or night, collaborators can contribute at their convenience.

- ✔ **Ability to send a view-only presentation via e-mail for others when the chief stakeholders have finished:** If you haven't participated in the building of a presentation, it's often hard to see exactly what the creator had in mind. If your viewer sets up timing intervals as instructed, you can sequence your prezi in a way you couldn't if you were sending one-dimensional slides in your absence. (See Chapter 3 for more information on timing intervals.)

- ✔ **Save money and time wasted travelling to meeting sites or hosting local meetings.** Most importantly, by collaborating online you always enhance the one nonrenewable commodity you have: time.

Inviting coeditors

By sharing a prezi, you're able to communicate a wealth of important information in addition to sharing your favorite recipe for chocolate chip cookies. What better way to spread your message than to send a brilliantly conceived prezi?

To invite coeditors, go to the Your Prezi tab (http://prezi.com/your), click to open a prezi, and follow these steps:

1. **In the center of the Prezi screen is a grey box. Click the Invite Editors link on the lower right of that grey box.**

   A screen pops up with a link to your editable prezi.

2. **Highlight the link and hit Ctrl+C to copy it. (See Figure 5-10.)**

   If you wish to revoke the share link you sent previously and generate a new one you can click the Reset Share Link button below the URL presented to you.

4. **Close the pop-up screen by clicking the Close button.**

5. **Open your e-mail program or other sharing program and hit Ctrl+V to paste it into the message box.**

   Send it as you normally would. When your collaborator receives the e-mail and clicks on the link, he will be added as a coeditor and be able to edit your prezi.

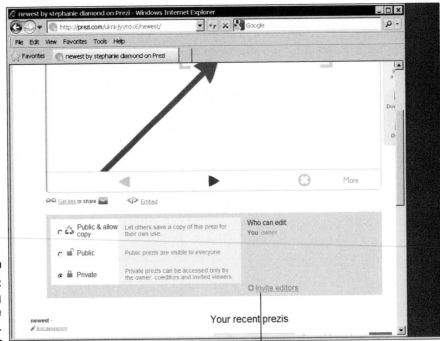

Figure 5-10:
Clicking the Invite Editors link.

Invite Editors link

When several people are working on a presentation in the same timeframe, it's a good idea to save a copy of your most recent version to your desktop in case something gets changed that you want to refer to.

Embedding a prezi on a Web page

You never have to worry about how to figure out how to display prezis on the Web. Because Prezi is hosted online, it's easy to embed a prezi on a Web page.

To share your prezi with your collaboration group by embedding it in a Web page, follow these steps:

1. **Open an existing prezi by clicking it from the Your Prezis tab (`http://prezi.com/your`).**

2. **Click the Embed button below the screen.**

   A screen pops up with the embed code you need. You can also choose to change the height and width in pixels.

3. **Highlight the code and hit Ctrl+C to copy it. (See Figure 5-11)**

4. **Close the pop-up screen by clicking the Close button.**

5. **Go to the HTML source code of your Web site and hit Ctrl+V to paste it in.**

   When viewers come to your Web site they will see your prezi.

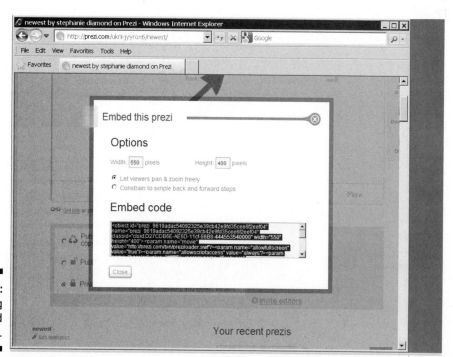

Figure 5-11: Highlighting the embed code.

Publishing to a social media site

Social media networks like Facebook and Twitter were created to foster con-nections developed around the sharing of thoughts and ideas. The power of these networks is that you can direct your friends and followers to a link anywhere on the Web. Links to Twitter and Facebook are built right into the Prezi interface. Spreading ideas can't be easier than that.

To share your prezi on a social network, follow these steps:

1. **Open an existing public prezi by clicking it from the Your Prezis tab (`http://prezi.com/your`).**

2. **If your prezi isn't public, click the Public radio button to make it public. Otherwise, you won't see the social network links.**

   Under the Prezi screen are social network links to Twitter and Facebook. (See Figure 5-12.)

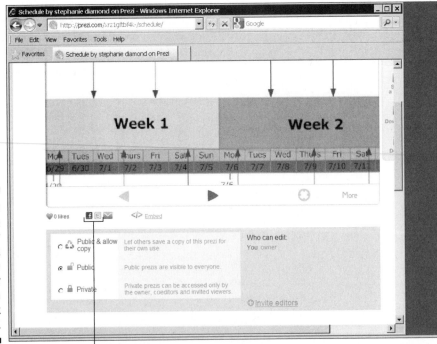

Figure 5-12: Click the Twitter or Facebook link to share it on your social media network account.

Links to Facebook and Twitter

3a. To share the prezi on Twitter, click the Twitter link.

If you're already signed into Twitter, your home page appears with the What's Happening? box containing a message that says `Currently reading` with the assigned URL of your page. You can edit that tweet as you like. If you aren't signed into Twitter, a screen pops up with buttons asking you to choose either Allow or Deny, and you can click Allow.

3b. To share the prezi on Facebook, click the Facebook link.

If you're already logged into Facebook, a Post to Profile screen pops up with the name of the Prezi and the URL to your page. If you aren't already logged in to Facebook, the screen pops up and asks you to supply your password.

4a. On Twitter, click the Tweet button to send.

4b. On Facebook, type your message into the text box and click Share.

Rating and Commenting on Public Prezis

Most people like to be acknowledged for a job well done. You have the opportunity to do just that on the Prezi site. If you choose to make your prezi public, you'll be able to solicit Likes and comments from the Prezi community. You'll also be able to let people know what you think about their presentations.

On the Explore page, you can find all sorts of presentations on a wide variety of topics that authors have submitted for approval and comment from the general public. You get to spread your ideas and get feedback from other prezi creators.

Checking out the Explore tab

The Explore tab is loaded with prezis created by users around the world. Here you can find almost every topic imaginable, and you can also find prezis that you can reuse for your own presentations.

To find interesting prezis that other people in the Prezi community have created, follow these steps:

1. Click the Explore tab at the top of the Prezi site.

The Explore page appears. There you see a collection of prezis people have submitted for consideration. (See Figure 5-13.) You can click one that looks interesting, or you can choose other pages to view.

2. Click a presentation and it pops up in Show mode.

On the right side, below the presentation, is a More link that you can click to select whether you want to set timing intervals to Autoplay the presentation and/or view it in a Full Screen mode. When you choose timing intervals, the presentation advances on its own based on the Path the author has predetermined.

3. **If you choose to advance through the presentation manually, click the right-pointing arrow at the bottom of the viewing screen.**

   If you want to see an overview of the canvas at any time, click the cut out circle icon to the right of the right-facing arrow.

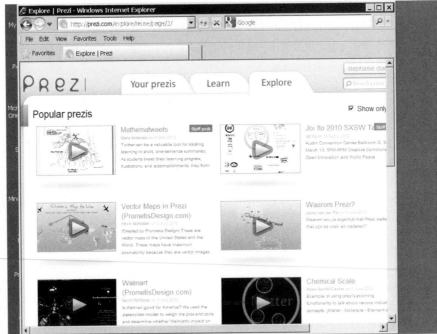

Figure 5-13:
The Explore tab displays presentations created by the Prezi community.

Sharing your opinion

One of the great virtues of the Web is that you can share opinions on just about anything. Prezi gives you the option to let others know you like their prezi by adding Likes.

The good news about these Likes is that you can also receive them from others for your presentation. To show your appreciation and give your fellow users a boost, follow these steps:

1. **Click the Explore tab and click a prezi on which you wish to share an opinion.**

   The prezi show screen opens.

2. **To show you like a prezi, click the Like button on the left side of the prezi Show screen. (See Figure 5-14.)**

   To determine how many people like the prezi, look at the number of Likes displayed next to the Like button.

3. **To enter specific comments about a prezi, type your message in the Add Your Comment box under the last comment and click the Add a Comment button.**

   Once clicked, your name appears below next to your comment along with a list of other people's comments. Next to their comments are Reply buttons, which you can click to add a response to another person's comment.

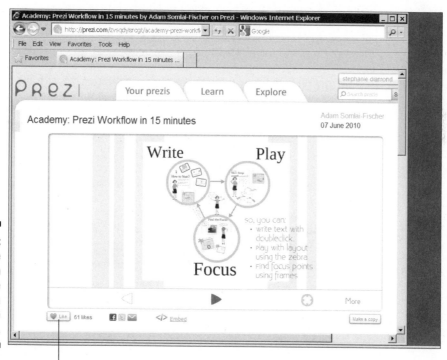

Figure 5-14:
Click the Like button to praise the author of a well-done prezi.

Like button

Delivering Prezis to an Audience

It's been confirmed over and over that public speaking terrifies most people. Perhaps you've heard the saying that when being asked to speak at a funeral, people would rather be "in the casket than delivering the eulogy."

The good news is that prezis are so unique that with a small amount of effort they make most presenters look good. Instead of potentially falling asleep, your audience will be roused by the interesting movement and cool use of graphics. The following sections help you look at how to use the hardware tools of the trade to make your prezi an eye-opener.

Using a projector to simplify the delivery

Giving a presentation with added equipment can be a scary proposition. You never know when a calamity will strike. Either your Internet connection can fail or your equipment will balk. To be safe, it's best to download your prezi ahead of time and have it waiting for you as you set up your projector.

Each projector has its own functions and capabilities. Most have an external video port and require a VGA or DVI cable to connect your laptop or PC. Check ahead to make sure the projector is in good working order. If you're using a Mac, make sure to bring your own connector cable — they aren't usually available on location. You might have to run out to buy one if you haven't planned ahead. Don't let this happen to you.

The best way to use a projector to deliver your prezi is in the following sequence:

1. **Open an existing prezi by clicking it on the Your Prezis tab (`http://prezi.com/your`).**

2. **Click the Download button to the right of the Prezi screen.**

   A screen opens that gives you the option to download as a portable prezi. If you're using Prezi Desktop, you can select the Download for Prezi Desktop option so that you can edit the prezi after downloading it.

   If the file download screen doesn't automatically pop up, you see a message that says `If the download doesn't start automatically click here` at the bottom of the screen. Click the Here link, and you should then get the Open or Save screen.

3. **Click Save and choose the location to save it to.**

   You can save it to the location of your choice or to the desktop, where it will be easy to find when you're setting up your presentation.

The file is loaded to that location as a Zip file. Unzip the file to gain access to the prezi file.

4. **To close the pop-up screen, click the X in the upper-right corner.**

5. **When you set up your project on location, click to open your downloaded prezi file.**

   Resize your prezi to a full screen before you project it.

6. **Plug in the cables and turn on your projector.**

   You can now focus and readjust the position of the projector so that the presentation is centered and ready to show.

Navigating with Smart Zooming

When presenting, you want to have control of your canvas and determine the way your story unfolds. With Smart Zooming, you can focus in closely for specific details and move out to give a wider angle view. This is how you can show the big picture and the details.

The controls allow you to zoom in closer or zoom out. An element of drama is created when you move in close or rotate an object. The Prezi software itself helps you zoom. It has predetermined calculations that find the optimum focus from where you are at any time.

You don't need to create a Path before you use the Smart Zooming feature. A Path adds your specific direction to the presentation, but just clicking an object makes it zoom. For live presentations, I recommend that you set up a path first. I include stepwise instructions in the "Autoplay your prezi with timing intervals" section, later in this chapter, and a fuller description of the Path tool in Chapter 3.

The best thing to do is to experiment with zooming until you get a sense of how it creates movement. Then you'll be comfortable enough to zoom in or out during a live presentation and respond to your audience.

To experiment with Smart Zooming, open a prezi and try any of the following:

✔ To get started, you can view the entire presentation in a big picture way by clicking Ctrl+spacebar. This causes the screen to zoom out to display the entire presentation as one screen. This action orients the audience as to the space being used. If you've used a metaphor for your presentation, your metaphor will become visible.

✔ Click the + sign on the right side of the screen to zoom in or click the – sign to zoom out. (See Figure 5-15.)

✔ Click an object on the screen to zoom in on that object.

✔ If you've rotated an object, you see it perform a rotation when you click it.

✔ Click the Show bubble to remove the menu and experiment by clicking objects in Show mode.

Figure 5-15: Click the + button on the right side to zoom in and the – button to zoom out.

Zoom in and out

Presenting from a browser

It's easy to present from a browser. When you open a prezi online from the Explore tab, you're already using your chosen browser to display it. The tricky part comes in when you have to add a projector or a remote control clicker and present live from the Web. A Web connection can be notoriously fickle.

When you present using a projector, I recommend you first download the prezi onto your desktop. This ensures that even if your Internet connection has issues, you can still present.

If you must present live from a browser, consider these recommendations from Prezi:

✔ **The projector you're using may not let you use keyboard shortcuts if you have your prezi set to Full Screen mode.** It's recommended that you use the Full Screen mode in your browser instead and then go into Show mode by clicking the Show bubble to present.

✔ **Make your browser small before plugging in the projector in case you can't resize it later.**

✔ **To edit your presentation live, type M on the keyboard to hide the Prezi Bubble menu.** You can use keyboard shortcuts to edit as long as your prezi is in Full Screen mode from your browser, not from Prezi itself.

After taking those caveats into account, to present from a browser, click to open your prezi and proceed to present in Show mode.

Setting up a Path

The function of the Path tool is to allow you to set up the way you move from one screen to another during a presentation. You can give careful thought about what should be emphasized and focus on it.

For example, to highlight something specific, you might want to zoom in close on an object and then zoom out so that the audience can see how that object fits into the whole presentation. You do this by presetting the screens with a numbered path. You can see the numbers when you are in Path mode and you can revise it until it's perfect.

For setting up remote controls and timing intervals, you need to have a Path set up first. (For instructions on how to set up a Path, see section on "Path bubble" in Chapter 3.)

Using remote clickers

When it comes to presenting, anything that can make you seem more polished and professional is a welcome addition. With the development of great wireless devices, you may want to consider using a wireless remote control clicker to do your presentation. That way you can advance or reverse the screens with one click.

With a clicker, you can engage your audience more effectively by looking at them instead of your keyboard. It's a good idea to practice a bit before you get up in front of a group, but after you become comfortable, you'll probably find that you want to use it all the time.

If you don't already own one, consider getting a remote clicker that has a built-in USB receiver and doesn't require any software to be installed. Also, remember that before you set up your remote you'll need to set up a Path before you present.

Also, if your clicker is programmable, you can set it up to move around your prezi in Show mode by using the keys in Table 5-1.

Table 5-1:	Moving Around Your Prezi With a Programmable Clicker
To Do This	**Use This Directional Arrow**
Move to the next path number	Right-arrow key
Move back to the previous path number	Left-arrow key
Zoom in	Up-arrow key
Zoom out	Down-arrow key

Due to the technical nature of remotes, it's unlikely that you'll be able to present in your browser's Full Screen mode when using a clicker. Check this out before you present so there are no surprises.

Autoplaying your prezi with timing intervals

One of the features that sets Prezi apart from other presentation software is the ability to create an Autoplay sequence by setting the timing intervals. You can send a prezi to others and have them view it exactly as you would if you were there by having them set up the timing intervals you suggest. You need to have a Path set up before you Autoplay your prezi. The Path ensures that your prezi will be received exactly as you planned it.

To Autoplay your prezi, take the following steps:

1. **Go to the Your Prezis tab (http://prezi.com/your) and click a prezi to open it.**

2. **Click the Edit Prezi button on the right side of the screen.**

3. **Click the Show bubble from the Prezi Bubble menu.**

   In Show mode, a right-arrow button appears in the bottom-right corner of the screen.

4. **Hold down the right-arrow button, and the timing interval choices pop up. (See Figure 5-16.)**

   The choices are 4 seconds, 10 seconds, or 20 seconds. These refer to the number of seconds each screen will display before moving to the next screen when you Autoplay it.

5. **Click to choose the timing interval you prefer.**

   After you've chosen your interval, the prezi begins Autoplaying. If you need to stop the presentation at any point, click Previous, which is the arrow facing left; or click Next, the arrow facing right.

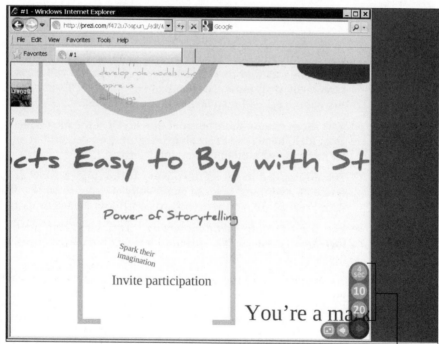

Figure 5-16:
Hold down the right-facing arrow button in the bottom-left corner to choose a timing interval.

Choose timing interval

Collaborating Using Prezi Share

You've seen various ways to share prezis to get feedback and work with teammates. For example, you can send prezis via private e-mail messages to individual co-editors for review, and then collect everyone's responses together, make updates, and then send the resulting prezi around for final approvals. This works fine for most projects. But what about high priority plans that just can't wait?

In today's online environment, things change constantly and you need to respond to them immediately. If your business plan or marketing presentation is even slightly out-of-date, you risk losing an important deal. So what can a 24/7 company like yours do?

You can use Prezi Share to work with colleagues *in real-time*. Working collaboratively in real time on the same prezi canvas makes everything faster and easier. Some benefits of working in real-time on prezis are as follows:

- ✔ **You get buy-in or uncover differences immediately:** When everyone is working together on the same prezi canvas you will know who is in agreement, disgruntled, or just plain confused. This not only strengthens your prezi — it also helps achieve consensus.

- ✔ **New ideas can be incorporated quickly:** If someone comes up with a great idea during the Prezi Share session, you can grab it and build on it. No more losing momentum on innovations.

- ✔ **You don't need to set up third-party technologies:** Most groups have to set up an additional layer of technology in order to work collaboratively. With Prezi Share, you are ready to go with no delays or glitches.

- ✔ **You don't need to spend money on travel when staff needs to work together:** This is a big savings. No one wants to incur travel costs when they can avoid it.

- ✔ **You can speed up the business cycle and get to market faster with your product:** Instant feedback means you can beat the competition without breaking a sweat.

- ✔ **Neither snow nor rain or force majeure will stop your team from working together:** Even if you experience one of the ever-present climate-related catastrophes you can all still work together as planned.

For a more detailed look at Prezi Share go to http://www.dummies.com/store/product/Prezi-For-Dummies.productCd-0470625864.html.

Chapter 6

Engaging the Prezi Community

In This Chapter

▶ Discovering new ideas for prezis

▶ Finding out about online resources

▶ Interacting with the Prezi community

*P*rograms that use graphical interfaces have been highly valued since the advent of the Mac. Following this tradition, Prezi gives you the unlimited capabilities that some of the best design programs have to offer. You aren't limited by a slide motif or held back by the type and size of graphics you can work with.

Prezis are being created everywhere. People are excited by the range of options they are presented with. You can find original prezis created on a wide range of topics from every corner of the globe.

In this chapter, I introduce you to the active Prezi community, both at the Prezi Web site and on social media sites. There are lots of ways to find and interact with Prezi users. This chapter also looks at ways for you to develop your own striking prezis by copying and reusing the great content contributed by other users in the community.

Scouting for New Ideas

After you have signed up at Prezi.com, one of the first things you can do is dive right in and participate online. You can find a wealth of ideas about what you can do with Prezi by looking in the online Explore page at Prezi.com to see what others have done. The Prezi community is very active and loves to find unique ways to use prezis both as educational and business tools.

The Explore tab is the place where users from around the world have uploaded prezis they want to share with others. Prezis here range from very serious topics to those done just for fun. You can find prezis about historical events, personal journals, and everything in between. You can find lots of food for thought here. If you have a Free license, your prezi will automatically be made public and will go into the Explore area. If you own an Enjoy or Pro license, you have the option to keep your prezi private — you can decide to make it public at any time.

Don't forget that you can share other people's great prezis (if they have allowed copy for reuse) in addition to your own. If you see a prezi that you want to share with others or comment on from your blog, you can embed it as you would your own prezi. You can find more on this topic in Chapter 5.

Viewing prezis on the Explore page

On the Explore page, some prezis are designated *Public and Allow Copy* by their owners. This means that you can copy that prezi to your account and reuse all the graphics and text as the basis of your own presentation. This is incredibly useful. I wish all online programs had this feature. It's really a collection of templates at your disposal. You can pick and choose just the right one or combine several together.

If you're pressed for time, or if you want to take advantage of a unique path idea or some original graphics uploaded by a professional designer or photographer, reusable prezis are the way to go. You can use them as a starting point for your own creation. No more starting out with a blank sheet of paper or digital canvas! Everyone knows the feeling of staring at a blank sheet with beads of sweat forming. Now you can postpone that feeling until you start to rehearse.

Keep in mind, though, that not all of the prezis you see on the Explore page can be copied for reuse — only the ones designated as such by their creators. To determine whether a presentation is available for reuse, start by clicking the Explore tab on Prezi.com. Here you can see all the presentations submitted by the Prezi community that have been made public.

To search for reusable prezis, from this area do one or more of the following:

- ✔ **If you want to explore all possible prezis regardless of topic, select the Show Only Reusable check box in the upper-right corner of the screen and click the Search button.** This action returns all the prezis that are available to be copied regardless of topic.

- ✔ **To get a list of reusable prezis related to a specific topic, type in a search term for a specific topic and select the Show Only Reusable check box.**

- ✔ **To see whether a specific prezi you like is reusable, click to open it and look in the lower-right corner for the Make a Copy button. (See Figure 6-1.)** If you see this button, click it. It takes you back to the Your Prezis page, and you can see that a copy of that prezi with the name "Copy of" followed by the title of the original presentation. Now you can begin to evaluate what you want to use for your new prezi.

It's common courtesy to acknowledge the original creator of the prezi if you use his or her content. Don't forget to credit the creator's name at the end of your own prezi.

Determining what makes a good prezi

Everyone has a different opinion about what makes a presentation valuable. When you're creating something, it's helpful to be aware of what other users think is a well-done example. Good examples are instructional — they help you better understand how to create your own great prezis.

There are two quick ways that you can determine what the Prezi community values in a presentation. The first is to look at what individual community members acknowledge by looking at the number of Likes next to the Like button in the Explore area. This designation is given to prezis that people admire. If a prezi is popular with the community, it will have a high number of Likes. There may also be a long list of the names of the people who have commented to express their approval.

Make a Copy button

Figure 6-1: An example of the Make a Copy button on a reusable prezi.

Figure 6-2 shows a popular prezi with many Likes.

The second way to find valued presentations is to look at the prezis that Prezi itself has chosen to feature. Prezi adds top presentations as "Prezi team picks" in the Explore tab. A new one is chosen each week. You can tell a prezi is featured because it has blue brackets around it in the Explore area. (See Figure 6-3.)

Some of the criteria the Prezi team uses to judge submitted prezis include the following:

✔ How well the prezi uses the nonlinear canvas

✔ How it visualizes the points in question with movement

✔ How it shows relationships of items to one another

✔ How well it tells the story

In addition, Prezi looks at user feedback from the Explore tab and Twitter and Facebook accounts. They also check around the Web to see whether great prezis have been featured at conferences and meetings. They want to bring the very best thinking from everyone who uses Prezi.

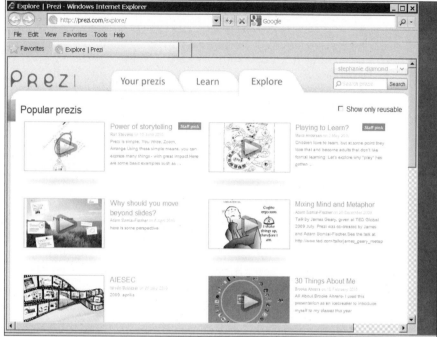

Figure 6-3:
A pre-
sentation
featured by
the Prezi
team.

Checking Out Prezi's Online Resources

Even though Prezi is powerful, it's not very complex. Creating your first prezi might seem a bit intimidating, but after a few minutes working with the canvas, you'll find getting started isn't very difficult. All the functions are labeled in the Bubble menu. The key is to jump right in and start working directly on the canvas.

Still, if you want additional help, or if you want to get off to a quick start, Prezi offers training materials in four places: the Prezi Academy, Live from the Prezi Universe, the online Manual (all on the Learn tab of the Prezi site), and in the Quick Help guide that you can access from the Help link in the upper-right corner of any prezi.

These four sources are discussed in more detail in the following four sections.

The best way to overcome any apprehension you might have about trying Prezi is to open one up, double-click the canvas, and start typing in some text. Then start moving, resizing, and rotating that text with the Zebra tool. You'll see how easily you can create something interesting. To find out more about creating your first prezi, check out Chapter 2.

Prezi Academy

The Prezi Academy is the place where you can find examples and tutorials. The material is grouped into lessons for Basic, Advanced, and Expert. (See Figure 6-4.)

You can start with just the basics and quickly build up to a more sophisticated presentation. You really don't need a lot of practice to create something unique. You're working on several dimensions at once, so unlike a slide show, you have lots of choices.

To become familiar and experiment with these new dimensions, try any of the following:

- **Rotating:** Type in some text and use the Transformation Zebra to rotate the words.
- **Movement:** Add several items on the canvas and then designate a path in the order you want to show the objects.
- **Zooming:** From the edit canvas, click the + and – buttons on the center right of the screen to practice zooming in and out.
- **Flash animation:** Use the Load File button from the Insert menu to add a Flash animation to your prezi and watch it instantly work.
- **Video:** Use the Load File button from the Insert menu to add a video to enhance what you're presenting.
- **Autoplaying with timing intervals:** In Show mode, click the right-arrow button in the lower-right corner of the screen and set a timing interval of 4 seconds, 10 seconds, or 20 seconds per slide when the show is Autoplaying.

Live from the Prezi Universe

In the Prezi Universe section of the Prezi.com Learn tab, you find tips, tricks, and examples of prezis by well-known presenters. (See Figure 6-4.) This is one place to go to find out what's new with the Prezi community. Among the interesting features are interviews with Prezi authors and their accompanying prezis given at major shows and conferences.

Manual

Under the heading Manual on the right side of the Learn page is an Open button. If you click it, you're taken to a page where you find Prezi's online manual. (See Figure 6-5.) It is broken into sections so that you can access the information easily. Topics include Getting started, Editing your prezi, and Presenting and managing.

Figure 6-4:
Prezi
Academy
and Prezi
Universe on
the Learn
page.

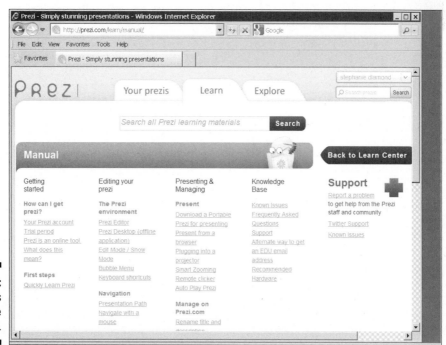

Figure 6-5:
Prezi's
online
manual.

Quick Help

When you're just getting started or need a quick refresher, you might not want to stop to read the online manual. If this is the case, you can access quick Prezi instructions by clicking the Help link in the upper right of the screen inside your prezi. (See Figure 6-6.) The menu offers some quick tips about such things as adding text and moving objects with the Transformation Zebra.

At the bottom of the menu is a link that takes you to the "Getting Started Video" located on the Learn page. The video is about 2 minutes long and shows you the basic Prezi functions you need to know to start building prezis of your very own.

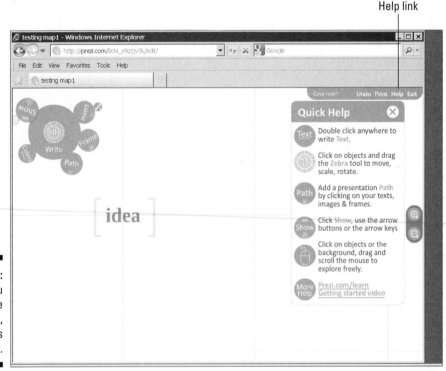

Figure 6-6:
When you click the Help link, you get this box.

Sharing Your Questions and Answers

As you create your presentations, you may have questions about functionality or how to do something that's not covered by the Quick Help available from the Help link inside your Prezi. You can find information in several places online, but here are the best places to get Prezi info:

✔ **Prezi's two Twitter accounts:**

- http://twitter.com/PreziSupport: On this account, users tweet about real-time questions and issues they're having. (See Figure 6-7.) Often the community will have a ready answer even before the Prezi team gets to answer it.

    You should consider the support account your first resource for questions. If you have a quick question you need answered immediately, this is the place to go. If you have a problem that's more complex, however, you will usually find answers on the online forum detailed in the section "Participating in the forum," later in this chapter.

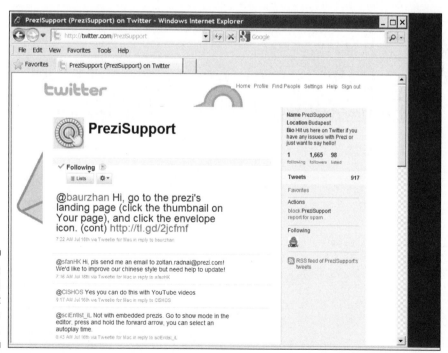

Figure 6-7:
The Prezi
Support
account on
Twitter.

- `http://twitter.com/Prezi`: This account is for Prezi to share information with the community and for followers to exchange new ideas. Here you can read about important updates, new developments, and examples shared by others. You can also find notes about service maintenance. (See Figure 6-8.)

✔ **The Prezi Get Satisfaction forum at `http://community.prezi.com/Prezi`:** This is the main place to get complex questions answered. Here you can add a topic of your own or speak to one the following available topics:

  - Ask a Question

    The Ask a Question text box is especially useful because it's constructed to give you potential answers to your question immediately. The words in the box are matched to previously answered questions. A list of these answers is presented to you in the event that they address your question. If they don't, you can continue on to post your question.

  - Frequently Asked Questions

  - Ideas Under Consideration

  - Common Problems

  - Recent Praise

Figure 6-8:
The Prezi
company
news
account on
Twitter.

You can access the forum by going to the Learn tab and clicking the Report a Problem link in the support area on the right side of the page. You need to register first.

To register and participate, go to the right column of the screen and click the I'm a Customer button. (You might have to scroll down to find the button.) You can sign in on the resulting screen. (See Figure 6-9.) You can register directly with the Get Satisfaction community or you can use one of your current social media or e-mail accounts.

✔ **Prezi's active Facebook community at `www.facebook.com/pages/ Prezi/52193296770`:** Here people from around the world share what they're doing with Prezi and invite discussions. (See Figure 6-10.)

✔ **The Prezi blog at `http://blog.prezi.com`:** Here great presentations are highlighted, and you can find out more about thought leaders from around the globe who are using Prezi to change minds. You can find out about new features here and make comments. (See Figure 6-11.)

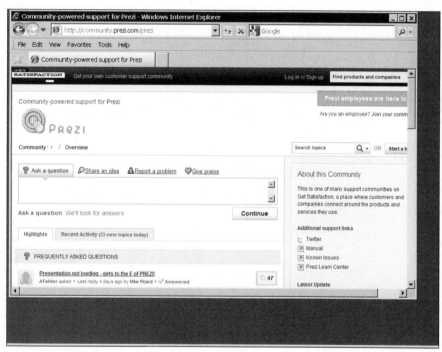

Figure 6-9: The Prezi online forum.

Figure 6-10:
The Prezi
group on
Facebook.

Figure 6-11:
The Prezi
blog.

Additionally, the fastest way to look at prezi screen shots on Flickr is to go to `http://prezi.com/blog` and click the Explore on Flickr link on the right side. Here people have uploaded interesting screen shots and photos related to their Prezis. (See Figure 6-12.)

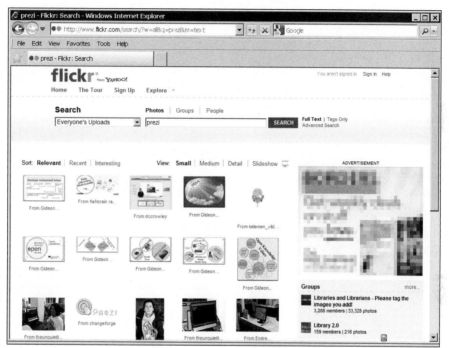

Figure 6-12: Prezis on Flickr.

Part III
Creating Show-Stopping Prezis

The 5th Wave   By Rich Tennant

"Nifty chart, Frank, but not entirely necessary."

In this part . . .

Did you know that neuroscience can help you make better presentations? (Neuro *what*?) The study of the brain as it relates to how people view and understand information plays an important role in developing show-stopping Prezis. And it's easy! Using a picture along with numbers and words can make your ideas quickly understood. Using Prezi to highlight those ideas takes it even further.

This part takes a closer look at how to develop an outstanding Prezi using visuals and emotions. I show you how using graphics can enhance the value of your message and how design professionals can use Prezi to showcase their custom work.

Chapter 7

Making Great Presentations

Great presentations are developed by careful thought and hard work. When you start a new presentation, you should begin with the expectation that you can make it a great one. When you look back at most of the inspiring presentations you've seen, you'll notice that they all have a few things in common. These are the sorts of things I discuss in this chapter: the methods that help you create a firm foundation upon which to build a great prezi.

In this chapter, I show you the key elements that go into making a great presentation and how you can apply them to your next prezi. I discuss how the human mind processes visual information and how storytelling and design factors can support your vision.

Understanding How the Mind Watches a Presentation

To understand the best way to deliver a presentation, it's a good idea to first take a brief look at how the human mind processes visual information. Contrary to what you might imagine, your eyes focus only on a small amount of information at one time. You see about seven to nine letters' worth of space depending on the size of the image or letters. The reason you're not aware of this limited scope is that your eyes are constantly moving and fixing on the next set of letters or images.

What's most important to know is that human eyes take a few seconds to compensate for visual differences. This leads to a crucial presentation rule:

When presenting, you need to give the audience time to see and focus on what you've projected on the screen.

That makes the pace of your prezi a key element in the overall presentation. You have movement, rotation, and focus to think about. You want to make sure that you don't overwhelm the viewers' ability to take in the information you want them to process. Just because you have the capability to keep things constantly moving doesn't mean that you should.

In his seminal book, *The Back of the Napkin,* Dan Roam presents six ways that people actually see things. They are

- ✔ Seeing the whole picture
- ✔ Seeing objects
- ✔ Seeing quantities
- ✔ Seeing position in space
- ✔ Seeing position in time
- ✔ Seeing influence and cause and effect

This breakdown is helpful because it gives you a structured way to take advantage of all of Prezi's tools. Table 7-1 shows you how to use the tools available in Prezi to make the most of your audience's visual understanding.

Table 7-1	Prezi Focus Points Based on How People See
To Do This	*Use These Prezi Tools:*
See the whole picture.	Zoom out to show the big picture in relation to the details.
See objects.	Zoom in to focus in on the details of an object during your narrative.
See quantities.	Use the Frames tool to pick out a container to group things.
See position in space.	Pan the canvas to show relationships.
See position in time.	Set up timing interval in Show mode to advance views in a definitive way.
See influence and cause and effect.	Use the Path tool to create a sequence of items that explains cause and effect.

Avoiding visual mistakes

The Internet has put the world's information at our fingertips. The downside to this is that people find themselves handling too many things at once. The behavior is called *multitasking,* a concept that didn't exist in the last century. Current research indicates that doing more than one thing at a time makes people duller and less able to understand each individual item they're attending to. This is also true when you're delivering your prezi. You can overdo the visual stimulation. If you're asking your viewers to take in too much information at once, you're limiting their ability to understand what you're presenting.

Understanding this principle helps you create a prezi that isn't cluttered and confusing to watch. Prezi puts a wide variety of tools at your command. You don't need to be a great artist to create a prezi that really stands out. Because everything looks so great and is easy to input, the temptation is to load up your prezi with every great visual you can grab. If you do this, your presentation will be too much for your audience to visually handle.

To avoid overload when creating your prezi, remember to evaluate your use of the following:

- **Flash animations:** Don't have too many in one presentation. It will affect the pacing.
- **Rotation:** Use for drama, but don't waste the movement by rotating things too often.
- **Pace:** Don't plan to fly through a lot of screens too quickly. Keep the pacing stimulating but not enough to induce motion sickness.
- **Zooming:** Too much zooming in and out makes people lose their focus on your content.
- **Repeating elements:** When you repeat, you call something to people's attention. Don't repeat unimportant elements just for the fun of it.
- **White space:** The lack of something on the screen (negative space) is as important as the space you do use. As always, less is more.

Benefitting from the Prezi style

If you're new to Prezi and you're trying not to overload your presentations with information, you might be tempted to go to the opposite extreme. That is, you may constrain your presentation to the limits imposed by slide programs. The only way to break out of this trap is to be aware of constraints that are holding you back.

To be sure you're freeing yourself to take advantage of Prezi's tools, don't constrain yourself to the following:

- ✔ **One slide at a time:** You don't need to have each idea as a separate view: You can group things together and show the big picture and the details. Use movement and zooming to traverse the canvas and keep things lively.

- ✔ **Static images:** You can incorporate video and audio as well as a variety of different design styles that you can show off in different ways. You don't need to put content dead center on the screen and play it.

- ✔ **Communication of ideas with long text bullets:** You can break up content into keywords and individual phrases.

- ✔ **Building one slide to develop an idea:** You don't have to stay on one screen and build content on it. You can move about and add things from opposite sides of the canvas if necessary.

- ✔ **Noninteraction with slides:** Zooming allows you to command the canvas and nest ideas. You can zoom into something that starts out as a tiny element on the screen to show how ideas fit together.

Recognizing your presentation style

Understanding the type of presentation you're giving is critical to taking advantage of its benefits. In his book, *Advanced Presentations by Design,* Dr. Andrew Abela divides presentations into two design styles:

- ✔ **The Ballroom:** This style follows an entertainment model. The action is projected outward from the presenter to the audience with no expectation that questions will be taken during the talk. Most often the speaker stands on a stage or at a podium to deliver her presentation. Like a Broadway show, the audience follows the story from start to finish without interruptions.

- ✔ **The Conference Room:** This follows a business model. The interaction is usually two-way, and the speaker aims to persuade the audience in some way. This type of presentation usually takes place around a table or in some interactive environment where people can trade ideas.

By understanding at the outset which presentation you're giving, you can design a prezi that will be appropriate and successful. Prezis can easily accommodate either style effectively. In a post on his blog (http://extremepresentation.typepad.com/blog), Dr. Abela makes this very point: "I think Prezi is one technology that can actually bridge the gap between Ballroom and Conference room styles."

Interestingly, most people are inclined to give a Ballroom-style talk no matter where they present. That's because they're used to watching movies and TV and think they have to produce a presentation like the ones they see.

Double-check your style choice when you're planning a presentation. Most people are called on to present a Conference Room–style talk. If you focus on that fact, your presentation will improve instantly! The pressure will be off you to produce a mini-movie, and you can focus on how to interactively persuade your audience. Understanding this helps you focus more clearly on what you need to include.

Creating the Presentation Partnership

Presenting can be a lonely task until you realize that you have a partner: your audience. Right from the outset, you should understand that you aren't in this alone. The audience for your presentation is hoping that you will provide a memorable experience. Whether it's a business discussion or a big conference, your audience wants you to succeed.

This is true for two reasons. First, audience members want to spend their time profitably. Second, they don't want to see someone fail in front of them. Bad presentations make people uncomfortable. They would rather be smiling and enjoying themselves. Both reasons are selfish, and that's a good thing. Understanding this frees you to prepare with the understanding that the audience is rooting for you. Any of your supposed imperfections are incidental to their happiness. They're looking at you with a lens all their own.

When establishing a partnership, you want to encourage a dialogue. Presenting with traditional slides makes that difficult. The presenter has to scroll back and then back again to find the material under discussion. With Prezi, you can forget the hassle of trying to find your place. You instantly zoom to the material under discussion. Prezi also fosters understanding because it shows both the big picture and the details. You'll be surprised at the interactions you can generate when using Prezi.

Understanding the context for your presentation

The success of your presentation is only a matter of interpretation, subject to the mood and experience of your audience, the lens through which they see the world. Are their budgets being cut? Are they under stress that makes them feel pessimistic about the future? Understanding the forces at work on your audience will go a long way to making your prezi relevant.

To understand the context, investigate the following:

- ✔ **Corporate or group culture:** If you're going to speak to an outside group, talk to people who work there. Understand what is expected of the group and how they are rewarded. If you're speaking before a group that doesn't prize individual contributions, don't expect them to engage in a spirited question and answer session. If you can't learn about the company first hand, speak to others who know the company and research about it online.

- ✔ **Prevailing attitudes about the problem under discussion:** Have audience members already made up their mind about this issue? Is there a movement in the company to quash the very ideas you're presenting? Obviously, it would be invaluable to know that in advance. Find out whether others have already presented on this topic and how they were received.

- ✔ **Economic climate:** What are the major financial factors affecting your audience? If the group members are concerned about keeping their jobs, anything out of the box that you suggest will seem risky. Be aware if the audience is under some budget constraints. You will be viewed very differently in an atmosphere of fear.

- ✔ **Health and family concerns:** If you're speaking to a small group, the health or well-being of team members and their families may be a factor. Ask your host whether there's a topic you should avoid or be sensitive to.

- ✔ **Demographics:** Is there a predominant demographic group in your audience? You'll want to know what norms are appropriate for that group. If you come in with solutions that appeal to an older audience, make sure you're not addressing twenty-somethings.

Letting your audience understand the context from which you speak is also key to making your presentation successful. Share with them the relevant experience or skills that give you the credibility to speak about your topic.

Gaining the audience's trust

If you're presenting online, you aren't subject to the same kind of evaluation that you would be if your presentation were in person. The audience can't judge your body language or wardrobe.

If you're presenting in person, *you* are the most important visual you have. According to author Nick Souter in his book, *Persuasive Presentations,* people judge you by the following:

- ✔ Credibility of your words — 7%
- ✔ How you speak — 38%
- ✔ Body language — 55%

Be aware of these factors and come prepared. Practice making confident gestures. If you signal to the audience members that you don't feel you should be presenting, they will agree.

Establishing the promise: What's in it for me?

People attend your presentations with their own agendas. Some want to be there, some are required to attend and plan to get other work done, and some just want to come in out of the rain. With this in mind, you want to serve the ones who want to be there, but you also want to try and impact those who just showed up without much reason or expectation.

When a person decides to attend a presentation, the first question she usually asks herself is "What's in it for me?" If she does choose to use up some of her valuable time, there needs to be a payoff. Think about the value you're delivering to your audience as you create your presentation.

To make an impact effectively, it helps to understand the expectations of your audience. They usually want one or more of the following:

- ✔ To learn something new
- ✔ To get actionable how-to information
- ✔ To get a recommendation
- ✔ To meet a resource for future information
- ✔ To be entertained
- ✔ To be inspired
- ✔ To share a common experience

If you try to accomplish a few of these things, your audience members will be more responsive. They will gladly exchange their attention for something of value.

Tapping into audience learning styles

I'm sure you know that people learn differently. Everyone has a dominant learning style. If you remember to satisfy each of the learning styles, you're more likely to reach everyone in your audience.

To meet the needs of these groups, follow these tips to accommodate the different learning styles:

- **Visual learners:** This group prefers to see things in their mind's eye. They imagine what ideas look like. Remember to provide diagrams, pictures, maps, colors, and a visual explanation for your topic. Prezis really excel here.

- **Auditory learners:** This group prefers hearing what you're saying and listens to the words very carefully. They enjoy asking questions. If you add sounds and or music to your presentation, you will engage these learners. Don't hesitate to add audio to your prezi.

- **Kinesthetic learners:** This group prefers to learn things by doing. These learners want to experience something before they can assimilate it. If you can do a demonstration or make your prezi interactive, you'll engage this group effectively.

Notice that these styles are not mutually exclusive. Try to add something to your presentation that appeals to each group.

Acknowledging internal clocks

Aside from thinking about learning styles, also consider how the time of day affects your audience. Everyone has an internal clock. Some people work best in the early morning, and some late at night. It's not possible to accommodate everyone's internal clock. But, you can be aware of how hungry or sleepy your audience might be feeling.

If you're doing a talk right after lunch, you might find a few people nodding off. You might want to make coffee available. You also might want to include some upbeat music. Give it some thought. These factors are unrelated to how interesting your talk is, but they affect response. Don't take it personally; be prepared instead. And be aware if you're feeling tired or hungry as well.

Using simplicity to make your presentation powerful

The power of simplicity cannot be overestimated. When people are confused, they generally stop paying attention. There's an old saying in sales: "A confused mind always says no." If you make your presentation overly complex, you're defeating yourself before you start.

In his book, *The Laws of Simplicity,* John Maeda presents ten laws of simplicity. Here are five that I think are important for presentations:

✔ **"Simplicity is about subtracting the obvious and adding the meaningful."** Focus on what matters and leave out the rest.

✔ **"Organization makes a system of many appear fewer."** It's helpful to let the audience know how your talk is structured before you get into it. Take the time to create a clear structure. It will help you as well.

✔ **"Savings in time feel like simplicity."** Don't drone on just to fill time. If you don't have something important to say, cut to questions or involve the audience in some way.

✔ **"Knowledge makes everything simpler."** Don't assume the audience knows everything. If you use acronyms or difficult concepts, explain them and move on.

✔ **"Some things can never be made simple."** If you're dealing with complex material, do your best to structure and explain, but understand that not everything can be simplified.

Researching for Content

A great presentation is supported by facts, and the Internet is the place to look for facts. You can also use the Web as a brainstorming tool to find information to put in your presentation. The world of online searching is easy when you know a few tricks. One way to efficiently look for information about your subject is to use Google search. By constructing your search criteria correctly, you can find information that closely matches what you need.

Google allows you to add prefixes and wildcards to your searches to limit the information returned. (See Figure 7-1.) For example, if you want to search for the term *Prezi* but you want to narrow the results to only those pages in which *Prezi* appears in the title of the page, you would type the following into the Search box:

```
intitle: Prezi
```

To define your Google searches more effectively, then, you can add any of the following prefixes to your searches:

✔ `intitle`: Use this construction to find your topic in the titles of Google's Web pages. (See Figure 7-1.) This is for one-word searches.

✔ `filetype`: This prefix gives you the specified document type, such as a PDF.

✔ `allintitle`: This prefix returns all matching keywords in the titles of Google's Web pages. So if you're searching for more than one word in the title, use this construction.

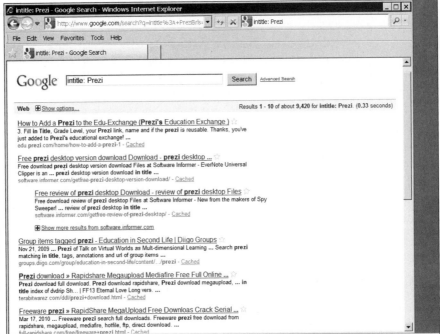

Figure 7-1:
A search
for Prezi in
the titles of
Google's
Web pages.

✔ wildcard: Use an * at the end of a topic to return all possible endings. For example, work* returns all instances of *work, workers, working,* and so on.

✔ inurl: Matches keywords in the URL

✔ allinurl: Brings back the results that have your specified keywords in an URL. That means that if you've specified two keywords, both must be in the URL or it won't be in the search results.

Google Alerts

Google Alerts is a great way to let information come to you. By setting up an alert with keywords that match your topic of interest, you get the latest information available (from blog posts to articles) sent to your e-mail account in real time. In this way, you may find information that you weren't looking for but that is valuable to uncover.

If you already have a Gmail account, you can set up an alert by going to www. google.com/alerts, typing in a phrase that relates to your presentation, and clicking the Create an Alert button. (See Figure 7-2.) Then, when you check your Gmail account, you'll find the alerts waiting for you.

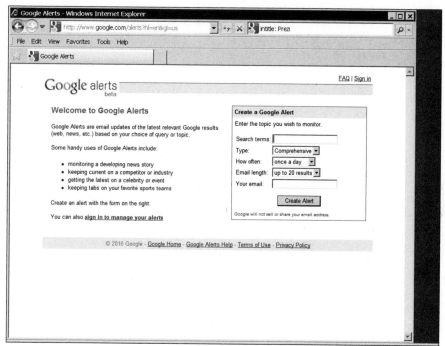

Figure 7-2:
Signing up
a Google
alert.

Talking to experts

If you want information, go to the source: Talk to an expert. Yesterdays' jour-
nalists would be envious of the ease with which great sources can be found
today. The Internet makes it easy to identify experts in your field. The great
news is that many experts are eager to share their expertise and have listed
themselves in a variety of directories. Check them out when you need quot-
able sources.

Some well-known directory sources for experts are

- http://experts.com
- http://expertclick.com
- http://www.refdesk.com/expert.html
- https://profnet.prnewswire.com

Finding influencers

Another way to enhance the value of the information you present is to examine content from *influencers*. Online influencers are defined as people who, through their writings, teachings or celebrity status, impact the opinions of many others. They may write an influential blog or host an online radio show. By looking at their take on your topic, you can get a better understanding about how it might be viewed by your potential audience members.

Try the following online sites to find influencers:

- **Technorati (`http://technorati.com`):** A blog directory that "grades" influencers.
- **Google Blogs (`http://blogsearch.google.com`):** Google's blog search
- **Boardreader (`http://boardreader.com`):** This search engine allows you to search topics in boards and forums.
- **Alltop (`http://alltop.com`):** A collection of top blogs on a great many subjects.
- **Twitter Search (`http://search.Twitter.com`):** A search of tweets for specific topics.

Discovering Stories That Connect with Your Audience

The topic of storytelling has exploded online with the advent of social media networks and tools that let people tell their stories to millions of people. Everyone has a story to tell, and not everyone has heard it yet, so some people spend a lot of time and effort on sharing their stories with others. People who like social networks say they're an unparalleled way to keep in touch. Others think they're a way to over-share with people who would rather not know.

But these tools are more than just a way to let people know about your favorite song. Social networking is a way to spread ideas and change lives. You're thrust into the storytelling arena when you're creating a presentation. You can use it to make your voice be heard.

Devising the plot

Start by creating your plot. The plot explains how the action in your presentation unfolds. This sequence of events carries your reader to the end. In their popular book, *Made to Stick*, Dan Heath and Chip Heath wondered how many plots actually exist. After investigating and boiling it all down, they came to believe that there were really only three types of stories:

- **The Challenge plot:** Fighting against the odds. The focus is on the struggle.

- **The Connection plot:** People who help others regardless of the differences between them. The focus is on the dissimilarities.

- **The Creativity plot:** Someone innovates in a unique way not seen before, and the innovation causes people to change their way of thinking. The focus is on the creative solution.

I think these are very useful designations when you're trying to devise your business story. Rather than deal with all the complicated designations for plots, choose one of these three and you'll have what you need for a great prezi. No need to get too complex.

Finding the hero of your story

Every story needs a hero. You know that instinctively. When you were watching TV or playing video games as a kid, you picked someone to root for. Before you start outlining the parts of your presentation, you need to decide who will be the hero. Think carefully about what you want to champion and who would serve that purpose. The hero will drive the story, so your presentation will stand or fall on the strength of the journey and the hook you create to grab your audience.

When you think about a hero, remember that in a business story the hero could be the brand itself, a plan that you want to implement, or you on your own struggle to get an idea accepted. It can be useful to deconstruct business presentations that you admire to see how they follow these conventions.

A great example of an effective use of stories is employed by Rubbermaid, the company whose product line includes laundry hampers and closet shelving. The Rubbermaid blog details "Adventures in Organization" (http://blog.rubbermaid.com).

Each post tells the story of someone who is moving, cleaning out a garage, or otherwise organizing their life. Who is the hero of each story? It's the customer or professional organizer who suffers until she finds the container or the closet product that saves the day! It makes using the products seem fun. Making the customer the hero helps you relate to the story.

Creating the hook to capture attention

As you likely already know, simply reading what's on the screen turns everyone off. So what can you do to really capture attention?

Fiction writers use the term *hook* to refer to something dramatic that happens early in the story that makes everyone sit up and pay attention. For example, in the blockbuster movie *Jaws* (1975), the hook comes when Brody says to Quint, "You're gonna need a bigger boat." Instantly, the viewers are aware that something very bad is going to happen and their attention is riveted.

You can use this same device in your presentation to make it memorable. Your hook doesn't have to be a car chase or the appearance of a shark, but it should be something that causes your audience to want more.

There are ways to think about creating hooks that makes them easier to uncover. When you want to create a hook, look at the following:

- ✔ **Controversy:** Look at current issues and see how your talk might relate to a disagreement about ideas.

- ✔ **News stories:** Focus on the story of a person who exemplifies what you're speaking about.

- ✔ **Humorous incidents:** Think about a funny story you've heard about your topic. Don't just tell a joke that's not connected to your content.

- ✔ **Quotes:** Find a quote by a famous person that relates to your topic or how you feel about your presentation.

- ✔ **Places of interest:** If there is a place locally or around the globe that has a situation related to your talk, bring in that example.

- ✔ **Person who has influenced you:** If you've been impacted by a mentor or family member, talk about how that relates to your actions.

Don't think that these ideas only apply to Ballroom-style presentations. When you are trying to persuade your colleagues in a Conference Room–style setting, one of these devices just might sway them to your side.

Remember, it's not enough to just cite an example. You have to turn it into something meaningful with emotional content. Screenwriter Robert McKee says that storytelling is the "uniting of an idea and an emotion." The emotion is what makes it memorable. Just repeating a bunch of facts won't make an impact.

Using a Five-Point Plan to Construct Your Story

The traditional storytelling structure used by Aristotle in ancient Greece is still in use today because of its powerful ability to persuade. Aristotle said that in order to effectively persuade, you need a presenter that has/does the following:

- **Ethos:** Is credible and speaks with authority
- **Pathos:** Makes an effective appeal to emotions
- **Logos:** Makes a logical presentation of the facts

You need to structure your presentation it in a way that is easy to follow and makes the audience care what happens.

Screenwriters and novelists know how to put a story together. Sometimes they start with a great ending and work backward, or start with an inciting incident and move forward from there. At the conclusion of their story, they always have a well-thought-out beginning, middle, and end to their stories. To make it easy and effective, you should borrow fiction writers' methods. Your business story moves forward based on how you structure this framework.

You can create a classic structure by using the following parts for your presentation:

- **Part 1. Problem**
- **Part 2. Constraints**
- **Part 3. How to solve problem?**
- **Part 4. Answer**
- **Part 5. Call to action**

These components can make up a one page summary. It can be on a Mind Map, a whiteboard, or a wall with sticky notes. Use whatever you're comfortable with. I also like to have a portable version that I can take with me and add as I think of things. If you like creating a Mind Map for your ideas, I present a method in Chapter 10.

If you want to take an idea through the structure, here's how you do it:

- **Part 1. Problem:** At the beginning of your prezi, you want to give necessary information about the issue you confront. The audience meets the hero, and you use a hook that will capture your audience's imagination. You lay out the problem and provide enough information for the audience to get involved. The audience members don't need to know everything immediately. Draw them in. Make sure you're clear about the purpose for telling your story. What do you want the audience to learn and experience?

✔ **Part 2. Constraints:** You need to overcome several things that are standing in the way of implementing a solution. Demonstrate conflicts using visuals. This is where your research comes in. Build credibility by adding facts and figures as necessary. Don't stop the flow by adding unnecessary information just to show you know it. This won't impress anyone and it may annoy them.

✔ **Part 3. Question:** Frame the question you need to answer to overcome these constraints. Be clear about what really needs to be done. Show why this really is the right question to ask. If the audience members feel you aren't getting to the heart of the matter, they'll lose interest.

✔ **Part 4. Answer:** Outline the solution to the problem and show how its implementation will improve things. The hero succeeds, the company gets larger, and/or the world is a better place.

✔ **Part 5. Call to action:** At the conclusion, you want your audience to do something specific as a result of hearing your presentation. Specifically state what that is.

The key in creating this one-pager is to lay out the structure and then go with it! Prezi is a digital storytelling tool that offers no real constraints. When you have your structure, you can build an amazingly interesting presentation. For more ideas, check out the Prezi blog at `http://prezi.com/blog` to view great presentations that have been given by influentials from around the world. *Influentials* are people who have a large followings online. They may command an important position in industry or government, have a well-read blog or a large Twitter following.

In the following sections, I break down the parts of the structure in more detail.

Understanding the problem

It isn't unusual for a presentation to miss its mark because it doesn't get to the heart of the matter. You don't want to be guilty of this. A key thing you can do to make sure your business presentation really hits the target is to determine whether the situation about which you're presenting is really the problem.

It could just be the symptom of a bigger problem. By uncovering it and presenting a solution, you're doing more to enhance your position in your company than if you just take your assignment at face value. In his book, *Breakthrough Thinking*, Nick Souter talks about finding the "problems behind the problem."

He suggests the best way to uncover this is to do the following:

1. **Create three columns, on paper or digitally, labeled as follows and in the following order:**

   "Root cause of the problem" in the leftmost column, "Problem behind the problem" in the center column, and "Problem" in the right column.

2. **Fill in the sheet starting at the last column and work backward from right to left.**

   Start with the Problem column. Write down a problem. Then in the next column, moving right to left, you'd look at what you think is actually causing that problem. Finally, see if you can uncover a root cause and fill in that column.

   By looking at a more fundamental root cause, you can redefine the problem and refine the topic of your presentation.

Look at the following example:

1. **Problem:** Tech support calls are eating into the profits because each one lasts so long. (This is the problem as you initially define it.)

2. **Problem behind the problem:** Customer service representatives are not properly trained to support technical questions that arise and start from scratch every time they answer a call.

3. **Root cause of the problem:** Customer service has not defined what the top problems are and how they can be solved quickly by putting the answers online and training the reps to answer them quickly.

Obviously, in this example, the problem you listed was merely a symptom of an underlying one. If you do this before you start outlining your presentation, you'll be sure you're working on presenting the true business problem.

Recognizing the constraints

Next, you need to look at what conflicts are holding the hero back from accomplishing her mission.

Consider the following possibilities:

✔ **Are there budgetary constraints?** Margins may have fallen or resources have been cut back. How has this impacted the hero?

✔ **Is there a group of people who want the idea to fail?** Think about all the things that are preventing the hero from moving forward. Don't forget to show your villains. For example, if you're presenting a geographical issue, the villain could be the lack of water or the unrelenting heat. Find photos that show the impact of the constraints.

> ✔ **If the hero is an idea, are there historical events that have played a part?** Visuals are really important here.
>
> ✔ **Can you create an image or a series of images that show the negative forces?** This is where your facts and figures can come in.

Think broadly and make the story interesting to follow. If you don't arouse some emotion in your audience members, you'll lose them early in the presentation.

Presenting the question

The question you ask is the most important part of the story. If you ask a question that no one cares about, the solution will be superfluous. No one will be interested in finding out the answer. You want to frame your question so that the solution will become obvious. As you pursue the solution, the audience will be rooting for you. For example, if you're using the earlier example about customer service training, you can ask the question, "How can we prepare our staff to be ready to answer tech calls quickly?" In the next section, you go about revealing the answer as the solution to the problem.

Uncovering the answer

This is where the hero reveals his solution and wins the day. Use this section to outline your solution to the problem. Show how putting this solution into action benefits everyone. List as many benefits as you can to persuade and engage the audience.

Delivering a call to action

You've gotten to the end of your presentation. What do you want your audience members to do next? That's your call to action. Do you want them to go to your Web site and sign up for your program? Do you want them to support your plan to take your company public? It's crucial that you have this spelled out for your audience members. If you don't tell them what you want them to do, they'll most likely do nothing. To shake people from autopilot mode, you need to be specific. Detail your call to action at the end of your prezi. Don't be so subtle that your audience misses it.

Putting the Show Together

After you've gotten everything exactly the way you want it, it's time to think about your verbal presentation and what you want to give your audience as a takeaway. You can deliver materials online and off, and you can choose to set up a permanent Web page for your presentation.

Developing your speaking notes

When preparing your talk, you must create your speaking notes. You basically have at least three choices when it comes to notes. You can write everything out in a script, create headline-style points, a list that you will hit in a predetermined order, or develop a topic map. A *topic map* is a form of Mind Map where you develop a nonlinear depiction of the topics to cover and you can go through them in any order you choose. Depending on how you like to present, any of these can work for you.

Here are some tips about making a script work:

- Write the script the way you speak.

- Don't say "... next ... next ... next." These aren't slides.

- Get right to the point.

- Read it out loud as you write it. The way it sounds when spoken is often different than the way it sounds in your head.

- Practice being silent instead of using filler sounds like "um" or "ah."

Here are some tips about making a topic map work:

- Use the paper horizontally so that you have room for everything without turning it over.

- Clearly delineate the structure so that you know the order of the points just by glancing at them.

- If you have subtopics that you want to cover, show that they are within the main points.

Figure 7-3 shows an example of a topic map that clearly shows you how things fit together.

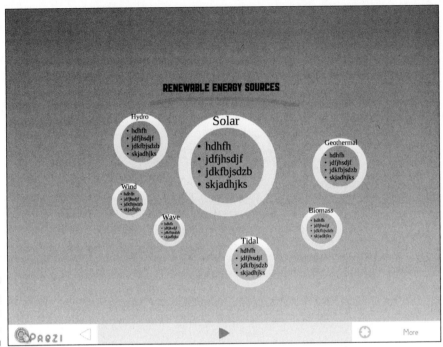

RENEWABLE ENERGY SOURCES

Hydro
• hdhfh
• jdfjhsdjf
• jdkfbjsdzb
• skjadhjks

Solar
• hdhfh
• jdfjhsdjf
• jdkfbjsdzb
• skjadhjks

Geothermal
• hdhfh
• jdfjhsdjf
• jdkfbjsdzb
• skjadhjks

Wind
• hdhfh
• jdfjhsdjf
• jdkfbjsdzb
• skjadhjks

Wave
• hdhfh
• jdfjhsdjf
• jdkfbjsdzb
• skjadhjks

Biomass
• hdhfh
• jdfjhsdjf
• jdkfbjsdzb
• skjadhjks

Tidal
• hdhfh
• jdfjhsdjf
• jdkfbjsdzb
• skjadhjks

PREZI   More

Figure 7-3:
A topic map
in progress.

Supporting online materials

You may find it appropriate to prepare some online materials for people to look at before your presentation. This could be on your Web site, a blog, e-mail, YouTube, the Prezi Explore tab, or a dedicated URL. However, I wouldn't recommend sending a complete portable prezi before the presentation because it won't have the impact your live presentation will. Also, some people feel that if they have everything beforehand they don't need to attend.

You can also choose to supply materials after your presentation. At the end of your prezi, show the URL on the screen where the information is available. You can also send your prezi via e-mail or embed it on your blog or Web site. (See Chapter 5 for more on sharing your prezi.) Always make sure to include your contact information on it.

What you put together very much depends on the nature of the presentation. Keep the following tips in mind:

✔ **Internal audience or client group:** If you're presenting a business case to an internal audience or a client, you may want to have some downloadable intranet charts or figures set up to download and review prior to the meeting. That way, when you do your prezi, you can refer to them without having to linger on them.

✔ **Ballroom group private:** If you're presenting to a Ballroom group at a conference, you can make selected prezi screen shots available as part of the conference from their password-protected portal. You can send the screenshots as a PDF to the conference provider to upload so that it's available to anyone with a password.

✔ **Ballroom group public:** If your meeting is a public one, you can advertise the URL where your materials can be found prior to the meeting.

✔ **Webinar:** You have a variety of options if you have an e-mail list for those attending your webinar. You can do any of the preceding options, and you can provide specific follow-up information. If you've asked permission, the e-mail list can be a way to open up further discussion after the presentation.

Social media networks

If you want to discuss your presentation on a social media network, you can try these options:

✔ **Twitter:** Prior to your presentation, you can create a hash tag for it, such as #PreziConference. *Hash tags* allow tweets to be searched by topic. When they know the hash tag being used, interested followers can find anything said about your presentation by searching for tweets with it. You can arrange for someone to tweet about your presentation in real time if you want. Depending on the profile of the presentation, you may find that audience members are tweeting, too. You can find out more about this in the section "Understanding the Back Channel," later in this chapter.

✔ **Facebook:** You can create a fan page on Facebook dedicated to your presentation. From this page, you can invite your friends and provide information about what's happening. Friends can comment or post photos or other content related to the event.

Preparing to answer questions

Decide how you want to deal with questions. You can take questions at the end only, have a preset time to take questions during the talk, or take them as they come up. You can do whatever makes sense to you; just make sure to let the audience members know what you plan upfront and stick to it. If you've apprised them beforehand, they'll generally adhere to your wishes.

Depending on your venue, you may be confronted with a hostile questioner. It's often true that this person isn't angry because of something you said, but rather he was angry when he arrived.

The anger could be directed at the topic or something tangential to the topic. Generally, the best way to handle this is to understand that you aren't going to convince the person to change his mind. Be polite but move away from his question quickly so that he doesn't disrupt the entire presentation.

Printing Your Show

If you've decided to deliver your prezi as a handout, it's very easy to print it out in its entirety or take selected pages from Acrobat.

To print your prezi in PDF format, take the following steps:

1. **Go to the Your Prezis tab (`http://prezi.com/your`) and click a prezi to open it.**

2. **Click the Edit button on the right side of the screen.**

3. **From the Links menu in the upper-right corner of your Prezi canvas, click Print.**

   When you click this link, a Starting message pops out, and after that, it begins calculating the number of pages that will print based on the Path numbers you have set up.(See Figure 7-4.) If you don't have a path set up, it prints the one main screen.

4. **Click the Click to Save PDF link.**

   The Save File window pops up and asks for a location to save it to. Choose a location, and your PDF is saved there.

5. **Go to the PDF document you just saved and print it out as you normally would print a PDF.**

   If you want to, you can readjust the Path based on how the PDF prints and then reprint it. If you want to take selected page numbers, just print those from the menu.

6. **If you want to create a new PDF with just those pages, open the PDF and choose Document⇨Extract Pages.**

7. **Type in the numbers you want to save and click OK.**

8. **Save the prezi with a new name where prompted and print that newly named document.**

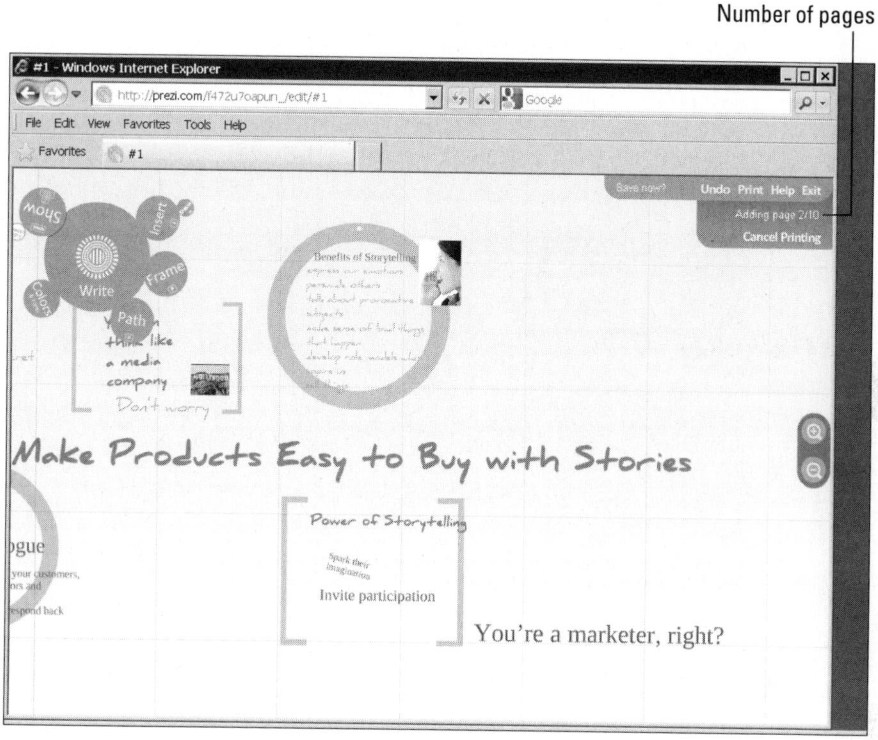

Number of pages

Figure 7-4:
Printing
your prezi.

Understanding the Back Channel

With the advent of social media networks, presenters now have something new to concern themselves with. Attendees may be commenting about their presentation in real time on social media networks like Twitter. Cliff Atkinson talks about this in his book, *The Back Channel*. He defines the *back channel* as

> "A line of communication created by people in an audience to connect with others inside or outside the room with or without the knowledge of the speaker . . ."

This is probably the worst nightmare of speakers who were reluctant to present in front of an audience before they knew they would be critiqued while speaking. The fact that people are now "talking back" can be intimidating. (See Figure 7-5.)

Not all of these real-time messages are adversarial. Plenty of people have tweeted about presentations for the purpose of sharing great ideas. It can be a means of reporting or retorting what's being said. It seems to boil down to whether or not the audience members feel their time is being wasted.

If you're confronted with negative back channel comments, you need to think about whether they are representative of the audience in the room. If the comment reflects only one tweeter's opinion, you may want to ignore it. If you feel it echoes others' sentiments, you may want to ask the audience to vote on how to move forward. These situations are very much decided in the moment. Do what you think is best at the time.

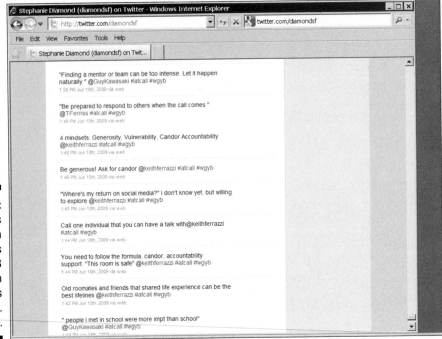

Figure 7-5:
Live tweets
for Keith
Ferrazzi's
#WGYB
book tour on
Authors
Teleseminars.
com.

Chapter 8

Using Graphics to Increase the Value of Your Message

In This Chapter

▶ Making design choices

▶ Supporting your story with visuals.

▶ Discovering visual elements that make a difference

▶ Extending your message with multimedia

▶ Grouping elements to convey meaning

All good designs have a preselected set of elements that help keep the focus on the ideas and off the design itself. If someone is paying attention to the design, they aren't paying attention to your content. Good design supports and helps communicate the message. When it's done well, people notice that the material is presented in a way that makes it easier to understand, but they won't be consciously focusing on the design.

In this chapter, I show you what you can do with graphics to improve message communication. You can use all sorts of graphics. Some are created in Prezi and some in design programs. Take a look at what your options are and then choose from a wide array of elements.

Creating the Best Design

There are several design dimensions to consider when deciding how your prezi will communicate your message. These include the following:

✔ **Text styles:** Choose the fonts that will most effectively communicate the mood and tone as well as the message. The Web has an unlimited number of font styles available for download. You don't need to confine your choices to ones that are available in Prezi. You can use your favorite design program to create text in whatever font you want and upload it to Prezi.

✔ **Consistency:** Select and stick to the specific elements you choose to convey your message. Decide on the fonts and colors you will use and then limit yourself to them. You will have an amateur-looking presentation if you use too many disparate fonts and design elements.

✔ **Contrast:** Make sure that the graphic elements you choose differ in weight, color, and size to distinguish them from one another. If everything looks the same, nothing will make an impact.

✔ **Grouping:** Take care to group items to make their relationship easy to understand. When you group things together, you help your audience understand how things fit together.

✔ **Layering:** Remember that Prezi allows you to zoom in and out to communicate spatial relationships. You aren't dealing with a flat slideshow. Use this to your advantage.

✔ **Balance:** Compose your big picture view so that it doesn't appear to be lopsided or misshapen. When you pull out to the big picture you want your audience to see the major relationships without having to read every word.

✔ **Repetition:** Repeat elements to emphasize important points. Using the Path tool, you can return to elements that you want to want the audience to remember.

✔ **Pacing:** The Path tool is a secret weapon for prezi creators who want to control the pace of their prezis. You can make the action move fast or slow by setting up a Path that meets your needs and the time allotted for the presentation.

Storytelling Using Visuals

Weaving stories for business is not unlike any other kind of storytelling. You need to have a structure. In Chapter 7, you saw how to create a story structure in five parts. After the structure is completed, you need to choose graphics that will support the narrative and move the message along. Consider these story elements that impact the visuals in the presentation:

✔ **Setting:** Where does the story take place? Is this an important part of the story? Think carefully about this. You have the opportunity to convey a message about place, time, and mood. Visuals that support the setting include photos, colors, custom backgrounds, and maps.

✔ **Point of view:** Who is telling the story? Are you the narrator or do you play a part in the story itself? If you're talking about your own struggle to accomplish something, make the graphics personal to you. Use visuals like hand-drawn images, stock photos, and keywords.

✔ **Theme:** What is the overall message you want your presentation to convey? Make sure your message comes across. Supporting visuals for the theme include keywords, phrases, sound, and video.

✔ **Character's profiles:** What does your protagonist look like? What about the villains? Are there some characteristics you can show to make the characters real to the audience? Consider using photos, animation, custom images, and Prezi's Shape tools for drawing and emphasizing graphics.

✔ **Supporting facts and figures:** What information must you include to support your story? Choices you make in this category are critically important to the overall success of your story. If you overload your presentation with hard-to-read charts and graphs, you will lose your audience's attention. The clever use of graphics styled to convey information without overwhelming the audience will be well-received. You can use the Prezi Frames tool to group information along with charts, diagrams, and other visual maps.

Don't be surprised if you spend a great deal of time selecting and creating just the right graphics. They can make or break your presentation. When you are planning, make sure to leave plenty of time for this activity.

Viewing the Big Picture

With Prezi's unlimited canvas, you can lay out your content in whatever way makes sense to you. You can use a metaphor like a desk with papers on it to show information about a school, as shown in Chapter 2. But what if a metaphor doesn't come to mind? When you're just getting starting with Prezi, you may want to consider using familiar shapes as a layout.

Of course, you don't want to lock yourself into a design that ultimately doesn't work for your media. When you're just getting started, you may want to follow a simple shape, such as a circle or star. Doing this makes effective placement of your information easier. I recommend trying out familiar shapes that allow you to zoom out to the big picture and then in on the details in a way that makes it obvious to everyone how things fits together. As you become a master prezi-maker, you'll develop your own way of creating layouts.

Don't be too rigid about the use of these shapes. I recommend this only so you have a starting point. You don't need to space items perfectly. Remember to rotate and use movement. Take advantage of the free flow of space.

For layouts with familiar shapes, you may want to consider any of the following:

- ✔ **Spokes of a wheel:** An idea in the center of your canvas with ideas around it. (See Figure 8-1.)

- ✔ **View of a layer cake:** Strips of content layered on top of one another in a specific shape.

- ✔ **Venn diagram:** Three overlapping circles.

- ✔ **Circle:** Several elements placed inside to demonstrate ideas flowing sequentially within it.

- ✔ **Decision tree:** Branches of ideas with the topic in the center.

- ✔ **Pyramid:** Layered information in a triangle shape with the thinnest part at the top.

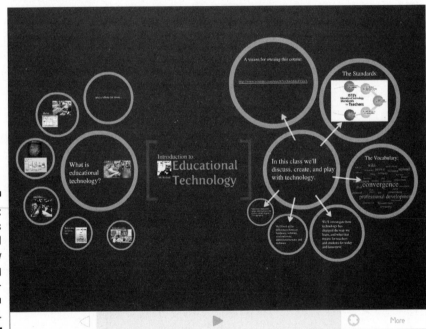

Figure 8-1: The spokes of a wheel show supporting ideas connecting to a main idea.

Looking at the Details

After you've thought about the overall layout of your prezi (see additional information about this in Chapter 2), you're ready think about how to present the details. I've seen prezis that didn't have as much impact as they could have because the details weren't put together effectively. You want to consider each detail and how it might be grouped with others to communicate the message clearly.

Using predetermined designs

When you go to the Colors & Fonts bubble in your Prezi Bubble menu to choose a style, you're presented with predetermined designs. These help you keep everything cohesive. You don't want to have so many fonts and colors that your presentation resembles a ransom note. By choosing a style upfront, you're setting up your palette of elements. You can also vary your palette by uploading stylized fonts from other design programs.

Choosing backgrounds

With Prezi, you have two choices with regard to backgrounds (although you can use them both simultaneously). They are as follows:

- **Background built into the style:** Depending on the background that you choose when you go to the Colors & Fonts bubble, the entire canvas changes to either a white, shaded, or color background.

- **Graphic with background:** Another way to vary your background is to create a graphic with a particular graphic or texture behind it. If you want, you can add a frame to this graphic for emphasis.

Figure 8-2 shows a background created for a specific graphic.

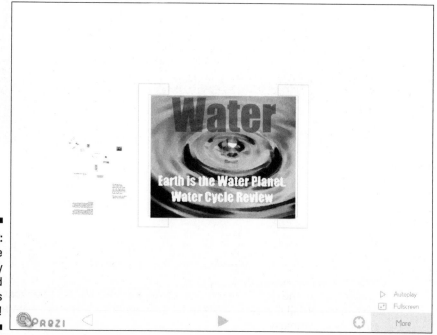

Figure 8-2:
Don't be a drip: Try background graphics today!

Using Single Visual Elements

There are many ways to build a truly creative presentation. Prezi has several built-in design tools (found in the Shapes and Insert sections of the Bubble menu) that you can use to specifically enhance your graphics. These tools are very easy to use and can make an impact with little effort. Following are some examples of how you can use them:

✔ **Highlighter:** You can take anything that you have designated as a title or keyword and use the Highlighter tool to add emphasis. It's as simple as using a regular highlighter pen on a sheet of paper. It's a familiar graphic that business people can relate to. (See Figure 8-3.)

✔ **Rectangle (rectangles as headings):** Using a rectangle as a banner for a title you can create a set of headings that really stand out. On the Web, people expect content to be set off in headings and keywords. With the rectangle, you can create familiar headings bars that look really good with very little effort. (See Figure 8-4.)

✔ **Arrow:** You have lots of flexibility with the prebuilt arrows. You can use them to point to something or indicate a progression of elements. The arrows also come in handy for Mind Maps or other mapping elements indicating direction. (See Figure 8-5.)

Highlighter

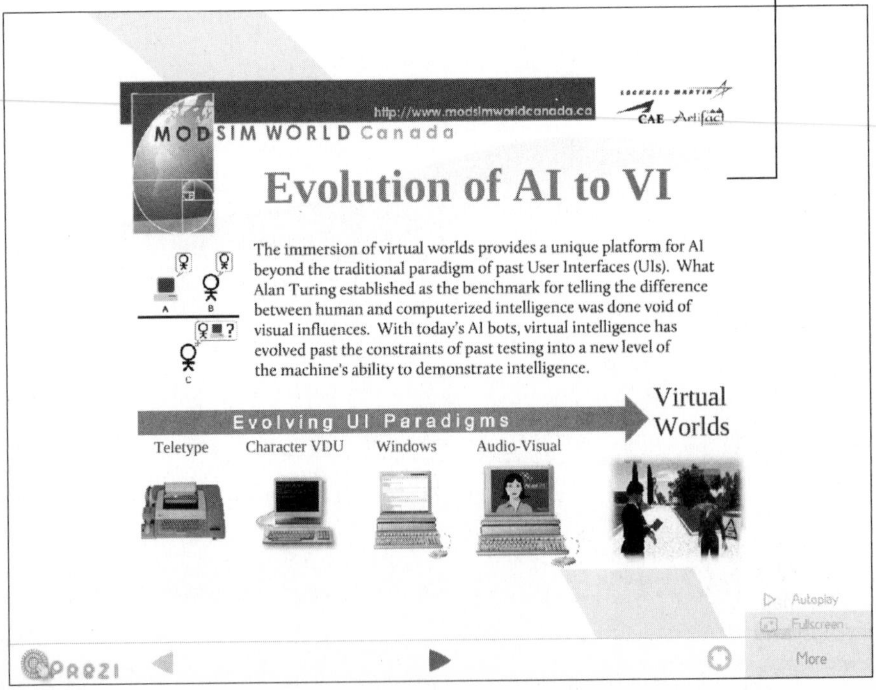

Figure 8-3:
The title is highlighted.

Figure 8-4:
These rectangles make headings pop, and their deliberate placement tells a story.

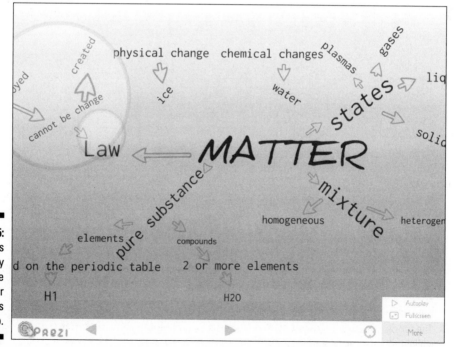

Figure 8-5:
The arrows cleverly lead the viewer through this Mind Map.

✔ **Free form line:** Free form lines can be used for something like circling an item for emphasis or drawing something simple. If you want to draw something complex, you can create it in a design program and use the free form line to enhance it.

✔ **Hand-drawn images:** Clever hand-drawn images always capture attention in business presentations. On the Web today, you can find lots of examples of Web pages with hand-drawn-looking icons. These are actually carefully created to look like they're casually drawn. With Prezi, your drawings have the perfect canvas to set them off. Hand-drawn images need to be created using a drawing program and uploaded to the canvas. Figure 8-6 shows an example of a hand-drawn image that really makes a statement.

Figure 8-6:
This hand-drawn image is demonstrating heat transfer and toasting marshmallows at the same time. Win-win situation.

Presenting Multiple Elements

When introducing graphics with multiple elements, you want to consider how you can make them more effective with zooming and rotation. For example, if you create a grouping of elements to depict a forest you will have trees and plants, along with keywords, and so on. You can show the grouping as one picture or zoom in and out to several elements. Unlike with a single element, you need to focus the Path carefully to ensure that everyone can take in the entire scope and the big picture.

Here are some ways to effectively present multiple elements in Prezi:

✓ **Bulleted lists:** Bulleted lists have gotten a bad name because of their overuse in business presentations. Luckily, they don't have to suffer this fate in Prezi.

In Prezi, you can create bullets by using the built-in text editor. The key is to simply break them up, resize some of the words, and rotate when appropriate. Figure 8-7 shows a good example of how bullets are used to convey the message without anesthetizing your audience.

✓ **Checklists:** When you create a checklist in Prezi, don't feel compelled to create an ordinary-looking one. As long as you have the information you need, you can pan and zoom around the canvas and make things interesting. If you do create a valuable checklist, make sure to have it available online. After the presentation, people may want to use it for their own projects. (See Figure 8-8.)

✓ **Forms:** Forms can be easily uploaded to Prezi in a PDF format. If your forms are complicated, you may want to hand out copies in addition to showing them on the screen. This keeps your presentation flowing and orients the audience members as to how they fit into the big picture. Figure 8-9 shows an example of a form that can be treated this way.

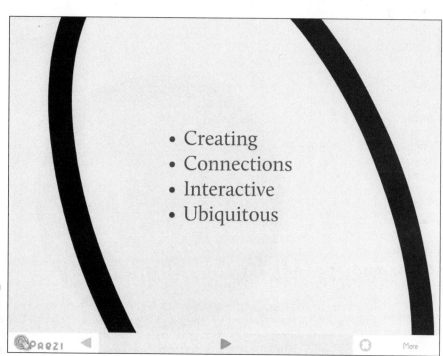

Figure 8-7:
A bulleted
list.

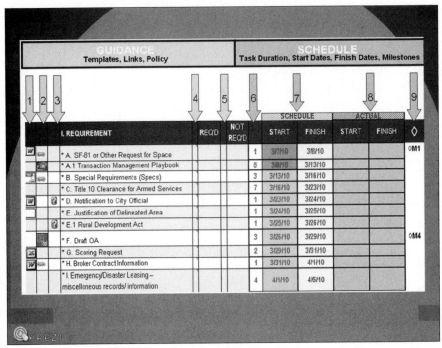

Figure 8-8:
A checklist
in Prezi.

Figure 8-8:
A checklist
in Prezi.

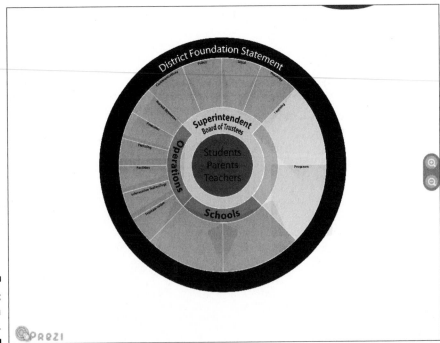

Figure 8-9:
Using a
form.

✔ **Flowcharts:** Flowcharts can really add clarity to a process. You can create them easily in Prezi with shapes and arrows or add a predrawn chart. If you zoom in on them, you can walk your audience through them effectively. Figure 8-10 shows a flowchart that's used to its best advantage.

✔ **Graphs:** When using graphs, you can present them from a big picture view by zooming out and then zooming in on the details, and then repeating as necessary. This is an effective way to give an overall picture of your issue and then to break it down into its parts. Figure 8-11 shows one way a set of graphs has been handled from a big picture view.

✔ **Digital stock images:** Photos can be a great addition to your prezi if they enhance the story. They can be embellished with Prezi drawing tools. Leave them out if they serve no real purpose to move the story line forward.

Stock material is great to use because it lends a professional look to your prezi and it doesn't have to be expensive. The key to using stock material is to choose images that are well-suited to your presentation and not just added as decoration. Typically the online images start at $1 and range up according to size and type. You can join a site and buy credits to be used when you need them.

To find inexpensive stock photos, flash animation, and illustrations for your prezi, try the following popular online sites:

- iStockphoto (www.istockphoto.com)
- Bigstock (www.bigstockphoto.com)
- 123RF (www123rf.com)
- Fotolia (www.fotolia.com)

To find free images, go to Flickr (www.flickr.com) and see whether the photographer has allowed a Creative Commons license to use his photo.

✔ **Sentences and phrases:** People won't read a lot of text on a screen, so don't even try to add it to your presentation. Keywords, phrases, and a short sentence can convey a great deal and are easier to remember.

In Prezi, you probably won't be inclined to pile up lots of text on the screen — it will seem out of place. Text can be broken up and high-lighted more effectively by using movement and pacing. Also consider breaking up words and phrases, resizing them, and using unusual or unexpected fonts like script instead of just Arial and Helvetica. Figure 8-12 shows an effective use of sentences used to move the story along.

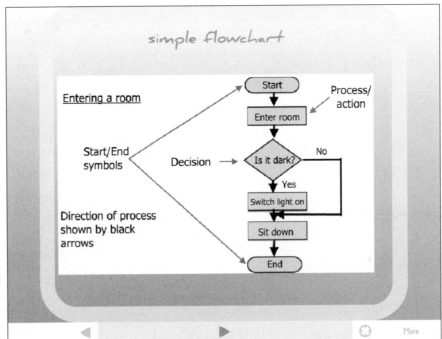

Figure 8-10:
Using a
flowchart.

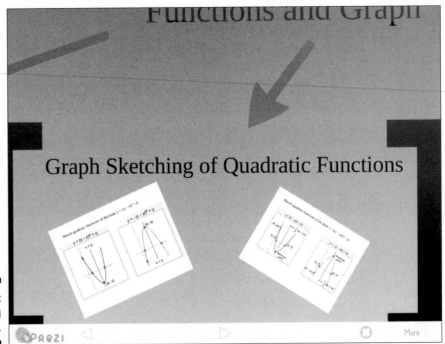

Figure 8-11:
Using
graphs.

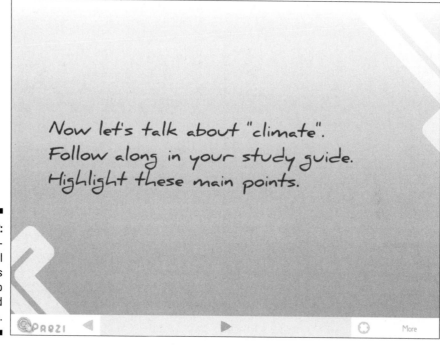

Now let's talk about "climate".
Follow along in your study guide.
Highlight these main points.

Figure 8-12:
These sentences tell the viewers what to expect and what to do.

✔ **Timelines:** You can easily create a timeline with Prezi's built-in tools, or you can add one from another program. The value of timelines in a presentation is that they provide additional context. Consider trying one in your next prezi if applicable.

When you want to provide perspective, timelines are the way to go. They can span centuries or one hour of a day. As a visual tool they excel in communicating a message quickly. Figure 8-13 shows an example of a timeline created in Prezi with a bracket, circles, and an arrow — very simple and very effective.

✔ **Maps:** A map is always a welcome way to help people understand the reality of your issue. You can add them in Prezi to your heart's content.

Maps in Prezi can be shown as a whole and dissected into areas by zooming in and out. You can also convey a message by providing supporting information in a clear and uncomplicated way. Figure 8-14 shows an example of a map with accompanying details told in one big picture look.

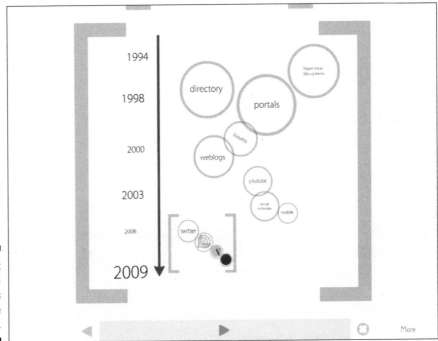

Figure 8-13:
Creating a
timeline is
worth a little
time.

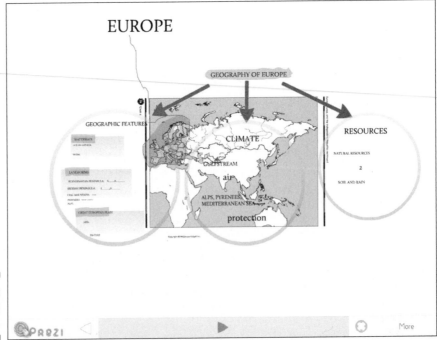

Figure 8-14:
Showing
maps.

One of the great things about using charts and other forms in Prezi is that they don't occupy the whole screen as they generally do on slides. They can have white space around them. This gives you the opportunity to break up the content in interesting ways.

Flash Animation

Adding Flash animation is valuable, but it can be distracting. Should you use it? There are two ways to evaluate using animation in your business presentations. They are as follows:

- ✔ **Clarity:** Ask yourself this: Does your animation serve to make the graphic more understandable? For example, if you want to show a growth curve moving up dramatically, this could be a good use. If you have it just as a novelty, it will be distracting.

- ✔ **Humor:** Humor can be effective in a business presentation. But you need to be sure it is truly a humorous element related to your specific presentation. If you are showing it to make a point or instruct about something it's a good idea. Don't throw in animations gratuitously, hoping people will see the humor. Most often they won't, and it will fall flat. Figure 8-15 shows an example of an animation used to instruct:

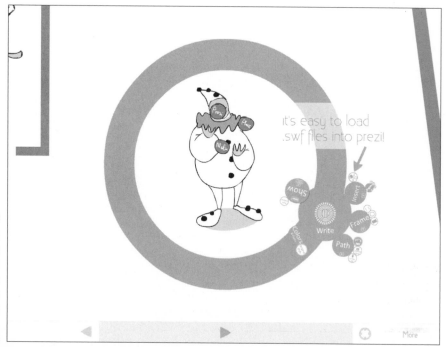

Figure 8-15:
This animated juggler in a Flash file is juggling ideas.

Choosing Frames as Information Containers

Don't overlook the use of Frames as a really compelling way to show off information: Grouping information in your presentation may be a new approach for you, but when you see how useful Frames are, you'll use them more and more.

Here are some ways to get the most from Frames:

- **Grouping:** Grouping is a key function for Frames. You can put items together on a Circle, Bracket, Rectangle, or Hidden Frame, which reinforces their association for the audience. It also helps you reduce panning the canvas, which can cause motion sickness.

- **Seeing the big picture and details:** You can zoom in to grouped objects and zoom back out again using the Path or going directly to them in Show mode.

- **Layering:** You can group elements inside other elements to create a stacked effect. Use layering to avoid providing too many details at once. You want the audience to be able to comfortably absorb the information.

- **Hiding information inside something else:** Here's a very powerful technique: Show an object of some kind with some tiny information inside it and then zoom in dramatically to that layer and show it off. This is different from the big-picture-detail approach because the elements don't necessarily fit together.

The Frame bubble contains the following:

- **Brackets:** Brackets are a common way to group information. Used in Prezi as design elements, they are especially powerful. Figure 8-16 shows an example of a set of information that's grouped effectively and acts as a table of contents for the presentation.

- **Circles:** Everyone loves circles. They're easy to understand and hearken back to early school drawing classes. One of the great things about Prezi circles is that they're always drawn perfectly. All you have to decide is how big or small to make them. Figure 8-17 shows an example of a use of double circles to create boundaries for an idea.

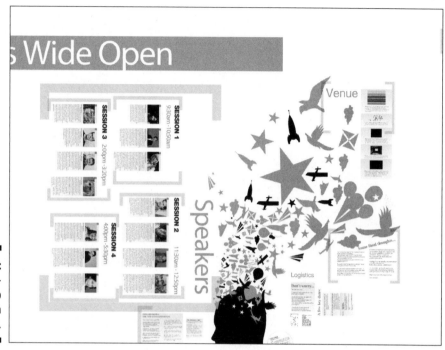

Figure 8-16:
The brackets group information neatly.

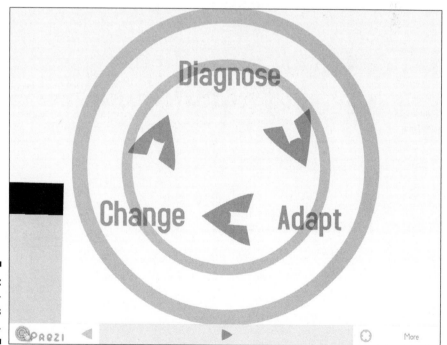

Figure 8-17:
These circles act as containers.

✔ **Rectangles:** As I explain earlier in this chapter, rectangles are very versatile. They can be used with text on top of them as headers or as containers that hold data. Figure 8-18 shows an example of rectangles used to set off topics.

✔ **Hidden Frame:** The Hidden Frame allows you to group information without a visible container around it. This way you don't clutter up the prezi and you can break up your information into sections without a visible bracket or other shape right in the picture.

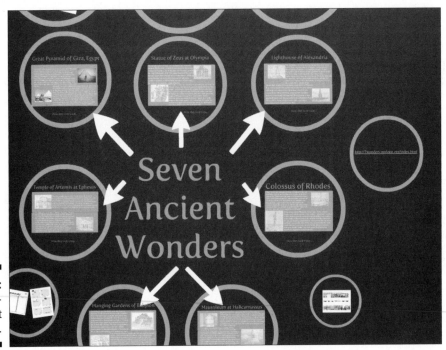

Figure 8-18:
The rectangles present information.

Chapter 9

Helping Designers Use Their Creations

In This Chapter

▶ Using design software to enhance prezis

▶ Protecting your original work

▶ Developing a branded prezi

*T*he field of design has changed dramatically with the advent of software that helps designers work in ways they never could before. Now designers can go down to the pixel level to make repairs and improvements, allowing them to restore and enhance photographs and old artwork. In this way, previously created designs can have a whole new life.

In this chapter, I show you how designers can use their original creations in Prezi. With the click of a mouse, the entire canvas can be filled with graphics that show off your special talents. I look at which design elements are available and how you can use your favorite programs in conjunction with Prezi. You also find out how others have used Prezi to display their design talents. It's all very inspiring. I'm sure you'll want to jump right in.

Understanding the Design Process

Being a designer sets you apart from the crowd. Design skills are valuable in today's graphical interface world. They are called on to create Web sites, logos, and other online graphics. Information design, a subset of design, specifically deals with creating visuals that make understanding information easier. This is not an easy thing to do, but with Prezi, you have a powerful tool at hand.

In her book, *Information Design Workbook,* Kim Baer says that an information designer is easy to spot — she's the person who looks at situations in a slightly different way. Does this sound like you?

Baer says that an information designer is interested in the following:

- Asking questions
- Understanding details
- Respecting the end user
- Seeing the forest for the trees
- Being aware of everyday annoyances
- Imagining what others feel
- Participating and observing at the same time
- Humor

If you're interested in even a few of these things, chances are you are a born designer. Prezi is great for everyone, but designers will take extra delight in being able to use their own elements to outfit a really great presentation. Think back and look into your portfolio to see what you can reuse. You'll be amazed at how single elements really spiff up the canvas.

Evaluating Your Designs

As you're creating your prezi, you can move along in several dimensions. Kurt Hanks and Larry Belliston in their book, *Rapid Viz*, have developed a way to evaluate your presentation designs in a unique way. Their process is particularly useful for prezis because it helps you traverse the layers that you can modify.

Their process has you evaluate your designs along the following continuums:

- Whole to parts
- Known to unknown
- Simple to complex
- Coarse to refined
- Rough to finished
- Vague to clear
- Small to large

Look at your design and see how you can use Prezi's tools to show elements along both ends of the continuum. You can show the big picture and the details, the grouping of objects nested in other objects, and so on. Make sure you move along both extremes so that your prezi is multidimensional. Figure 9-1 shows the use of rough images with smooth text. The juxtaposition has

impact. Include both simple and complex objects. If you really use the continuums, you'll enhance your prezi significantly. When you get the hang of it,
you'll be able to take your prezi to the next level.

Figure 9-1:
An original
design in a
prezi.

Using Design Applications

If you've been designing for any length of time, you probably have favorite
applications in which you consistently produce your work. Prezi accommo-
dates all the major programs. In addition, if you run across something that's
not used in native format, you can convert it to a PDF.

You can upload the following formats for your media:

- ✓ **Any image, stock photo, or personal photo in a JPG, PNG, or GIF
  format:** Maximum size for an uploaded image is 2,880 x 2,880.

- ✓ **Graphics and images you created from drawing software not covered
  in the preceding formats:** Just convert them to a PDF.

- ✓ **Video:** File formats in Flash FLV or F4V are supported.

  For YouTube videos, cut and paste the URL of the video into a text box
  from the Write bubble, and the video will play within Prezi as long as
  you're connected to the Internet.

✔ **Audio:** You need to convert your audio file into an FLV format.

✔ **Images, charts, spreadsheets, graphs, and any content that can be converted to a PDF and uploaded to Prezi:** For example, you can take an Excel spreadsheet and convert it to a PDF and upload it.

Any major design program can work with Prezi. The following list gives you some ideas about working with these types of programs:

✔ **Photoshop:** Professionals and nonprofessionals alike use Photoshop as their primary design program. By adding custom elements created in Photoshop to your prezi, you will have the flexibility to design just about anything your need and upload it. Figure 9-2 shows an example of how one person used a personal design created in Photoshop.

✔ **Adobe Illustrator:** Adobe Illustrator is a well-known drawing program for creating vector images. To use Illustrator graphics, save them as a PDF and upload them to the Prezi canvas. Figure 9-3 shows an example of an Illustrator image used in Prezi.

✔ **Adobe Acrobat:** Acrobat PDF files are used by millions around the Internet. When in doubt, save your creation to a PDF and you'll have no trouble using it in your prezi. Prezi developers have chosen PDF as a supported format because it's easy to use and almost everyone has access to it.

Figure 9-2: Somebody was obviously having some fun in Photoshop.

Figure 9-3:
You can use
Illustrator to
create vec-
tor graphics
like this one
for your
prezi.

✔ **SmartDraw:** If you need to create business graphics, consider SmartDraw. It's a software program that makes it very easy for you to create charts, tables, and a variety of other graphics. It's main feature is that it offers a large selection of professional templates that you can modify to suit your needs. No more using business graphics that look like a kid's finger painting project.

After the graphic is created, you can easily upload it to your canvas in a PDF or in one of the other acceptable formats for Prezi such as JPG. If you want to create a flowchart or other common kinds of business graphics, SmartDraw offers a great many to choose from

Another plus is that there are predefined themes of colors that you can turn to. This means that you don't have to experiment to decide which colors work. The work is done for you.

It's also very easy to change those themes with the click of a mouse button. The biggest benefit of this program is that it cuts your design time by a lot. Not only does it do the job quickly and professionally, but it also makes your prezi look like an expensively designed project in a very short time. Figure 9-4 depicts an example of a chart I created for a training program I designed for my clients.

✔ **Jing (www.jingproject.com) from TechSmith:** Jing is an online pro-gram that allows you to record a video of your screen. The free version of Jing lets you record up to five minutes and save the video as an FLV file, which can be put right into Prezi. If you have something that you want to demonstrate in your presentation, this is a quick and easy way to go.

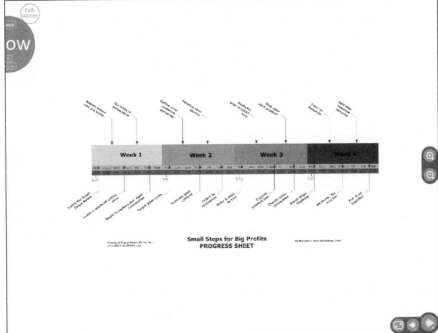

Figure 9-4:
I used
SmartDraw
to create
this prog-
ress sheet
for my prezi.

Protecting Your Original Work

When it comes to copyrights and other legal protections for original design work, the Internet has been uncharted territory. Because it's so easy for people to just cut and paste fabulous artwork into a project, they can forget that someone might own the rights to how that work can be displayed.

Because of this, it's important for you to understand the basics of copyright and licensing on the Web.

Understanding copyrights

Many people think they are automatically authorized to use original media on the Web for commercial purposes, but this isn't true. Custom media that is created by an artist is called original media, and unless specified, you have no right to use it in your projects. People need to check the copyright first. You, of course, are well aware of this. The advent of stock houses online has helped this situation to some extent. A stock house holds a catalog of original media whose rights can be purchased. If someone wants to use an image, he can buy use rights instead of ripping off the artist. The stock houses have the infrastructure in place to make it very easy to get permission and pay for use of original work.

If you are the original creator of some sort of media, your rights fall under the following categories:

✔ Reproduction rights

✔ Derivative rights, the right to create adaptations of original work

✔ Distribution rights, the right to sell a work

✔ Display rights

✔ Performance rights

When you upload a presentation to Prezi, your designs are protected. You have the option to allow reuse of your creations by clicking the Public and Allow Copy radio button below your prezi. Even if you use the free version of Prezi and your design is made public, that doesn't mean it can be reused without your permission. If you do allow reuse, however, you can get wide distribution for your work. The choice is yours.

Creative Commons license

Another option to be aware of is the Creative Commons license. In 2006, Lawrence Lessig and others created this license to help content creators spell out the rights they hold for their creations. This was done to allow digital creators to designate how others can use their work online. The originators of this license felt that traditional copyright laws didn't cover some of the issues that arose in the digital age. Figure 9-5 shows how you get started selecting the right license for your needs. From this screen, you're asked to select the options you want. After you fill in the boxes, an HTML code that displays a banner is returned for you to display in your work. When others see this banner, they can look up online at the Creative Commons Web site what the license covers. You can find this tool at `http://creativecommons.org/choose`.

There are six different types of Creative Commons licenses you can choose from. To understand what each of these licenses contain, you need to first understand the following conditions that apply to your work:

✔ **Attribution:** You must be credited if someone copies, distributes, performs, or uses a derivative of your work.

✔ **Share Alike:** You allow others to distribute a derivative of your work based on the exact license your work holds.

✔ **Non-Commercial:** You allow others to copy, distribute, perform, or use a derivative of your work, but only for noncommercial purposes.

✔ **No Derivative Works:** You allow others to copy, distribute, and perform your work, but don't allow derivative works.

After you decide which conditions apply, you can select which of the six licenses is appropriate. These licenses are explained in detail at the Creative Commons site.

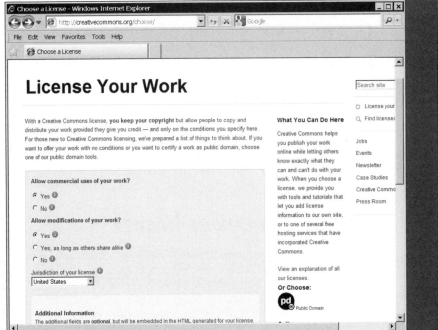

Figure 9-5:
Creative
Commons
license
options to
consider.

Creating a Branded Prezi for Your Company's Use

Branding is a key way to make sure your company is heard among all the noise on the Internet. A brand is a sign, symbol, or other element that identifies you to your customer. When customers see it, they think of something about your company. For example, people need only to see the Swoosh sign on a T-shirt to know the product is from Nike. Nike has effectively paired its symbol with a tagline: "Just do it." When customers think of the Nike brand, they think of taking action, which is great for a sporting goods maker.

Most people don't give much thought to this when they create a presentation that represents their company at a conference or meeting. They usually put their logo on every page and call it a day. With Prezi, you can treat your brand to a better display. You can weave it into the Path and make it a design element that's integrated and memorable.

For example, most companies locate their logo at the top left of every slide. This causes a kind of logo blindness. People don't really see the logo or think about it as part of the presentation. With Prezi, you can make the logo part of the flow of a presentation and zoom in to it. This clearly makes a statement.

Creating your own branded prezi

If you have the need, Prezi designers will create a custom-branded prezi for you for a fee. This means that if you were using the Free version, you won't have the Prezi watermark, and your branded elements will be displayed to your specifications. This is one option. On the other hand, if you want to create your own branded prezi, you can do that, too.

If you have the Enjoy or Pro license, you won't have the Prezi watermark in the lower-left corner of the screen, but if you're presenting from Prezi.com, you can see it.

If you don't need a full branded design created by Prezi, you can create your own branded template. Assuming that your company branding is already created, you can translate that into a prezi that colleagues can use without reinventing the wheel.

So, the great news about developing a branded prezi is that all the essential elements are already digitized. This provides a huge head start. You don't have to worry about how colors will look or whether you've interpreted everything correctly. Most major companies have done all this work when they first published on the Web. All you need to do is check their style guidelines. In their style guidelines, they spell out what and how all elements should be used.

Small companies are also likely to have designed all their branding digitally, whether using a professional or doing it on their own. However, small companies may or may not have style guidelines.

Understanding what goes into your brand's design

Your brand design has been created to communicate what your company stands for. It tells your story in a way that words can't. It evokes feelings and can compel people's loyalty. Above everything else, it's a way to help you develop a relationship with your customer that can't be broken by your competitors. All your brand elements work together. When you're creating your template, you want to make sure you use everything correctly.

Your brand is made up of several design elements, including the following:

- ✔ Name design/logo
- ✔ Tagline
- ✔ Font styles and acceptable sizes
- ✔ Color palette
- ✔ Copyrights and service marks

As you design your template, think about how to integrate these elements into the design without the requisite logo on every screen. Prezis aren't slides, so the use of space isn't limited to a designated rectangle with a title and footer. Make that idea work for you. Go the extra mile and create something unique. It'll be worth your while. Use the elements in a way that make them memorable.

Developing a Prezi template

To get started, collect all the pertinent branding elements listed in the preceding section to develop a template for general use. This doesn't mean that you proscribe exactly what each prezi will look like. It just ensures that the company brand is properly represented. Your legal department will thank you, and the marketing department should, too.

Remember that when you use the Transformation Zebra, your colleagues will be able to take the elements and resize, rotate, and otherwise change them at will. I recommend that you create a short list of the branding guidelines that everyone should know when using the branded elements in Prezi. Upload the list to the canvas as a PDF, and people can delete it after reading it. That way you know that everyone will have at least seen it. Your company may not have strict guidelines, but some companies really want this legal stuff followed. Find out which one your company is and act accordingly.

Depending on your company, some examples of branding guidelines could be

- ✔ Don't resize the logo
- ✔ Don't rotate the tagline
- ✔ Always include the service mark after the product name

Adding a logo and tagline

Here's something you want to remember when adding your logo and your tagline. (See Figure 9-6.) If the logo and tagline are one graphic, you can just add it as proscribed by your company's guidelines. If they're separate elements, you need to position them as necessary. It's easy to forget that the tagline location is just as important as the logo when it comes to branding elements.

The important question then becomes where you place your elements. Given that each prezi created by colleagues will have different screen paths, you want to make it easy to slip it into the overall framework.

Consider the following logo and tagline placement options:

- ✔ Positioned with the opening title
- ✔ As a stand-alone to be dropped anywhere
- ✔ Positioned as an ending screen that includes your Web site URL
- ✔ As an animated graphic if allowed

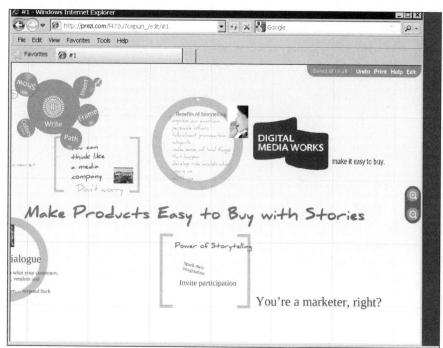

Figure 9-6:
The Digital Media Works logo appears with its tagline in Prezi.

1. **Go to the Your Prezi tab (`http://prezi.com/your`) and click a prezi to open it.**

2. **Click the Edit button on the right side of the screen.**

3. **From the Bubble menu, click Insert.**

   Two smaller bubbles appear.

4. **Click the Load File bubble.**

   A Windows file screen opens, asking you to select the file(s) to upload by Prezi.com.

5. **Pick the file you want and click the Open button.**

   The logo is added to the canvas.

Adding third-party graphics

When other colleagues want to create a new prezi from your branded template, they will most likely need some additional keywords in the company's font. You can assist this effort by adding some key text items (like product names) ahead of time. This will save time for everyone.

Including copyrights and service marks

Don't forget copyrights and service marks. If you want, you can add instructions on how those should be displayed in your document list. You can also make sure they are attached to any product or service name required before you upload them.

Part IV
Using Prezi beyond Presentations

The 5th Wave   By Rich Tennant

"Why don't you try blurring the brimstone and then putting a nice glow effect around the hellfire."

In this part . . .

A new tool is always welcome, especially when it's a multipurpose one. Because Prezi is a digital storytelling application, you can use it to tell all kinds of stories. Don't think you have any stories to tell? How about the one where your company can deliver better service? Or the one about the way your product surpasses the competition? They're all stories worth telling.

In this part, you see how to brainstorm new ideas, create cool business plans, and display your hobbies. You also see how using Prezi as an educational tool enhances the learning process. Don't miss this part of the book if you want to use Prezi in new and exciting ways.

Chapter 10

Brainstorming New Ideas

In This Chapter

▶ Generating new ideas for great presentations

▶ Mind Mapping your thoughts to present more effectively

▶ Selling your ideas using new research about the brain

Do you think you're good at coming up with new ideas for your presentations? If not, take heart. The ability to generate ideas can be learned. It isn't the number of the brain cells you have, but the number of associations you can make with other ideas that determine how innovative you can be.

For this reason, Prezi has been designed to allow you to generate more and better ideas. The tools available in Prezi encourage new ideas because they capitalize on visual imaging techniques.

In this chapter, I show you how you can get new ideas for your presentations and what goes into delivering high-quality prezis. I also give you the latest information about how our brain works to help you make memorable presentations. You presentations will generate more acceptance when you use Prezi to deliver your message.

Generating New Ideas

Creating new ideas takes a bit of creativity and a healthy dose of stick-to-it-ive-ness. Contrary to popular thinking, most ideas aren't developed by a bolt out of the blue. They're a result of the brain's powerful ability to combine things together to develop something unique.

New ideas always have roots in other ideas. Existing ideas function as your mind's jumping-off point. Understand that finding a jumping-off point isn't about stealing ideas — that's when you take someone else's creation outright, without making it your own. A stolen idea is easy to spot and makes your presentation virtually worthless. When creating presentations, it's particularly important to put yourself into the presentation from the idea stage to the unique delivery.

Some people believe that when they create a presentation, they have to invent something completely new. As a result, they put off getting started (see the section "Dealing with presentation procrastination," later in this chapter) or put mental roadblocks in their way. Be mindful of this when you work.

When you think about combining ideas online, think of what's currently known as a *mash up*. Mash ups are products that combine technology and data from two or more other products to create a third new product. An example of this is Zillow.com (www.zillow.com), which uses Google Maps and real estate data to create an application that allows you to find the "value of homes and property for sale online. In the arts, you can find such mash ups as Danger Mouse's *Grey Album* or the book *Pride and Prejudice and Zombies*.

Nonlinear thinking

Prezi was created as a solution to rigid slide programs that adhere to a hierarchical structure. Those programs reflect *linear thinking,* which requires that people follow a step-by-step development of ideas from point A to point B. Think of outlines or flowcharts, which map out thinking in a straight line. Linear thinking has been championed in business because it emphasizes the logical and analytical.

Although this may be a good way to organize collected information, it isn't reflective of how people think. For this reason, there has been a growing recognition of the value of nonlinear thinking. The need for more knowledge workers in the 21st century highlights the need for people who can do both equally well.

Nonlinear thinking reflects free association. You brain supports your ability to combine things together. It makes unlimited numbers of connections. Ideas flow in all directions, and a hierarchy may not present itself until a large amount of information is uncovered. Your mind makes connections as they come to you.

Nonlinear thinking is the way your brain works. For this reason, prezis are a more natural way to foster your creativity. They don't require you to develop a hierarchy and to fill in things in sequence as an outline would. With Prezi, you unleash your ability to make associations and connections at lightning speed.

Understanding your creative style

Before you start generating ideas for your presentation, it's a good idea to figure out what your thinking style is. In his book, *Old Masters and Young*

Geniuses, David W. Galenson talks about artists who approach things conceptually versus those who are more experimental. Both ways are equally powerful. But knowing which style you possess helps you understand how best to approach brainstorming ideas your presentation.

Look at your own style and decide which of the two categories you fall into:

- ✔ **Conceptual:** You work quickly with a flair for drama. You have a clear idea of what you want to do, and you follow it through. If this is your style, you should jot down your ideas and solidify them quickly using Prezi's ability to develop a clear path and movement right away. You'll feel more confident if you don't over-think your prezi and make lots of changes.

- ✔ **Experimental:** You work carefully and quietly. You learn through experience and constantly make changes. If this is your style, you should use Prezi to put all the ideas you can think of and then, over time, rework and refine them. You'll find that your prezis are easier to do because you don't expect to create a full-blown prezi in one session.

Techniques for new ideas

Providing your brain with lots of stimuli increases the chances that you'll come up with more ideas and actually be more creative when problem solving. The exciting thing is that you don't need to confine yourself to materials that relate to your topic to promote stimulation. In fact, you shouldn't limit yourself. You should look at ideas coming from all directions.

Here are some actions you can take to get ideas flowing:

- ✔ **Ask the right questions.** Your ability to meet expectations depends on the questions your presentation will answer. When developing these questions, try to stay away from broad-sweeping ones. It's best to focus on something the mind can relate to. For example, when giving a talk about customer service, rather than posing the question, "What's wrong with our customer service?" you're better off asking a question like "How can we cut our response time to two phone rings?" It's easier to pose several of those types of questions than asking about the global nature of something. Make questions bite-sized.

- ✔ **Combine things together.** Making connections between items enhances idea generation. Thomas Edison knew how to use this principle to great effect. He chose to work on ideas that were already in development in his field so that he could benefit from group advances. He could them improve upon and develop a better version. This helped him move more rapidly toward his goal.

- ✔ **Fail quickly.** Another way to think about this is to take measured risks and test the outcome. You'll get more new ideas faster if you quickly test the ones you have. Even a failure can lead you to a different great idea. Using the feedback you get from failures helps propel you more quickly toward the right answer. Create momentum toward your goal.

- ✔ **Learn from different disciplines.** Be aware of what's happening around you in other fields. You may be able to use a principle at work in one discipline to the benefit of another.

- ✔ **Track the stages of your ideas.** Document and pursue your ideas over time. Ideas you create one year could be much better suited to apply in another. Don't let a good idea fade away.

- ✔ **Use simplicity to strengthen ideas.** Albert Einstein famously said that "everything should be made as simple as possible, but no simpler." Some people have a tendency to complicate an idea to make it seem more important. This makes it harder to understand and to implement. When you present a simple idea that people can take action on immediately, you've given them a little gift.

- ✔ **Look at popular culture.** A look at photos, books, magazines, and paintings helps stimulate the brain, giving it the energy to make connections. Make it a practice to look at things outside your own hobbies and areas of interest. Review various magazines for inspiration. Look at design books even if you aren't a designer. The prolific author Ray Bradbury says that he owes his success to the fact that he is constantly feeding his brain.

- ✔ **Set boundaries.** Contrary to what most people think, new ideas are easier to find if you're working within some boundaries. Boundaries provide something to push against. For example, if you have a limited budget, you have to find ideas that don't require lots of cash. This gives you a jumping-off point. When you have no limits, your ideas can be unfocused or hard to rein in. The idea is to take the limits and overcome them as opposed to being bound by them.

Dealing with presentation procrastination

It's not uncommon to hit a speed bump when you're creating your presentation. There's always a point at which you stop and question whether your ideas are good and your presentation will be accepted. You can begin to lose perspective.

Interestingly enough, this feeling doesn't always relate to the stakes involved. You can feel anxiety and perhaps downright fear no matter how few people you're presenting to or how little your job depends on the outcome. If you acknowledge this feeling and understand that it won't prevent you from being successful, you can usually overcome it and move on.

The key to passing through this procrastination phase is to assure yourself that you've done the following:

- ✔ Successfully completed presentations like this one in the past and you can give successful presentations in the future.

- ✔ Taken the time to understand the material you are presenting so you can speak about it with authority

- ✔ Done the research needed to put together a strong argument

- ✔ Created visuals that assist the audience in understanding and remembering the key ideas

- ✔ Gotten feedback from people you trust

- ✔ Made sure your equipment is in good working order

- ✔ Practiced sufficiently before presenting

After you assure yourself that you've done these things, your fear will subside, and you'll be able to proceed with confidence.

Generating ideas within groups

It has jokingly been said that "A camel is a horse designed by committee." The use of business groups to generate ideas comes in and out of favor depending on the decade. Currently, with the Internet contributing the tools to make collaborating easy, the use of business groups is back in favor.

Social media networks and online communities allow like-minded people to meet virtually and share ideas. The contributions of self-selected volunteers have created a shared encyclopedia. With this new influx of ideas that can be documented and used by others it's easier than ever to extract the best ones from every corner of the globe.

One technique that you might try specifically for generating ideas in a group setting is Edward De Bono's Six Thinking Hats technique. Yes, you do have to put on your proverbial thinking cap, but there's a very sound basis for this technique. It's been in use for 25 years, but don't let that mislead you. It's as powerful now as it was when it was created.

At its core, the Six Thinking Hats technique is really a method for helping everyone in a group to use both right- and left-brained thinking. The key is that it uses *parallel thinking,* which means that it asks everyone to look at something in the same way at the same time. When the technique was developed, the existence of right- and left-brained thinking was unknown. Now that people understand it, it gives even more credence to the technique. See more about that in the section "Mind Mapping Your Thoughts," later in this chapter.

To implement this technique, there are several things you need to know to get started. The first is that the six thinking hats refer to six thinking styles. They are of course imaginary hats. De Bono used colors to name the hats to simplify their use.

For our purposes here, I have greatly abbreviated the details that make up each style. The hats are designated as follows:

- ✔ **The white hat:** Facts and figures
- ✔ **The red hat:** Emotions and feelings
- ✔ **The black hat:** Cautious and careful
- ✔ **The yellow hat:** Speculative-positive
- ✔ **The green hat:** Creative thinking
- ✔ **The blue hat:** Control of thinking

The person running the meeting always wears the blue hat exclusively to set up and implement the process. To start, everyone is asked to put on the same color hat and begin using that thinking style to tackle the problem. The blue hat leader decides when to ask people to switch hats and tries to make sure that all angles of a problem are considered. You might want to give this technique a try if you have lots of clashing styles at work.

Mind Mapping Your Thoughts

Another great breakthrough thinking technique, called Mind Mapping, was developed in the U.K. by Tony Buzan in the 1960s. He primarily created it to help students take notes and memorize material. A Mind Map is a visual thinking tool that allows you to get your ideas out where you can see and manipulate them. It's easier to work with ideas when they are visible to you. You are then free to brainstorm and add new ideas without having to hold everything in your mind at once. When you put your thoughts on paper or canvas, your mind begins to see patterns and make associations you would never find without the visual input.

Mind Maps quickly became a tool that people used to brainstorm, visually depict new ideas, solve problems, and communicate more effectively. Now, almost 50 years later, Mind Mapping is embraced around the world by business leaders, educators, and anyone who wants to be more productive and creative.

Buzan himself has said that his model was based on note-taking techniques used by such great minds as Leonardo DaVinci, Albert Einstein, and Picasso. When you use Prezi for Mind Mapping, you take these techniques one step further by using the power of the software to create your maps.

When creating Mind Maps in Prezi, you are using both your right and left brain to develop maps that move and zoom and bring out your creative side (your right brain) as well as your logical side (your left brain). Most activities don't facilitate the use of both sides at the same time. That's why Mind Maps are so effective. Combining the technique of Mind Mapping with the capabilities of Prezi gives you a distinct advantage over using just one of these approaches.

Benefits of using Mind Maps

Because of the exploding access to information, you're inevitably faced with the issue of information overload. Mind Maps help us by reducing vast amounts of information into keywords and visuals that our mind can assimilate.

Actively working in a map helps stimulate new ideas. Learning studies have shown that people only remember 10 percent of what they read, 70 percent of what they say and write, but 90 percent of what they do. This means that just the act of creating your map helps you remember its contents. This is especially useful for the presentation portion of mapping. You'll feel more confident that you know your material and won't become flustered during a presentation.

If you've been Mind Mapping for a while, using Prezi adds a fresh dimension that stimulates you to be even more creative. If you prefer paper maps for their hand-drawn quality, you'll be surprised to find that Mind Mapping with Prezi can enhance this effect by providing drawing tools that create unequal lines and font sizes.

Mind Maps created with Prezi are even more powerful for the following reasons:

- **By starting with a central sphere and radiating out toward other connections, the Mind Map visually mimics the way your brain works.** Everything you see, hear, taste, and smell creates a connection. When you look at a Mind Map, the center is the starting point, and you create new thoughts out from the center. You can radiate out connections without limits. By focusing your eyes in the center of the map and pulling back out, you can quickly see the scope and concepts that shape your topic. You can determine complexity and depth at a glance. This is a key function of Mind Maps that Prezi makes even more powerful.

- **By capitalizing on the way our memory works — through association and imagination — the Mind Map clarifies your thinking.** In your mind's eye, you see images and make associations with them. Then when you try to remember them, you see the image, not the word itself.

✔ **The Mind Map prevents information overload.** To aid understanding, you can set the Path to zoom out to the big picture and then zoom in again during the show to reinforce how the pieces all fit together. You can then use the Autoplay feature to make sure that whoever sees your presentation sees it in the order you intended it.

✔ **The Mind Map shows the story your map tells.** If you decide to present your map to others, it serves as a guide for you to tell your story. You see the big picture and the details and can explain them to your audience without copious notes. It's much harder to get lost when you follow your map.

✔ **The Mind Map provides a Zoom feature.** With Prezi, you have the ability to manipulate and zoom and interact with all the elements in a way not possible with a static map.

✔ **The Mind Map enhances visual stimulation.** Prezi allows you to take advantage of colors, lines, text, movement, and spatial relationships to enhance the visual stimulation. This is as true for you as the developer of the map as it is for the viewers. Visual stimulation takes place when your eyes focus on something like a color and send a message to your brain. This forms a active connection in your mind that helps you learn.

You can also use Mind Maps in group settings. Using a Mind Map to collect ideas and develop them works well in groups because it allows everyone to participate equally. There is no structure to the ideas, so whatever is offered is accepted. Managers have no advantage over staff in this setting. It also provides a way to get all the ideas out on one sheet of paper for everyone to see. There can be no hidden agendas when the entire map is visible to everyone. This topic is also covered in Chapter 16.

Rules for great Prezi Mind Maps

Creating Mind Maps with Prezi gives you new capabilities and dimensions in which to work. These capabilities enable you to increase the number of ideas you have — ensuring that you'll have more quality ideas, too. In some situations, quantity doesn't equal quality — but when it comes to idea generation, it does. If you've generated many ideas, you can examine each of them to choose the ones with the most promise. If you have only one or two ideas, you're forced to go with one of them whether it's good or bad.

Google now offers a great example of how a digital Mind Map can be used to display a deeper dive into a topic to uncover related information. It's called the Wonder Wheel.

To access the Wonder Wheel, do the following:

1. **Go to www.google.com, enter a search term in the text box, and click the Google Search button.**

   A page of search results will be returned.

2. **Click the Show Options link in the upper-left corner of the results page.**

   An expanded list appears on the left side, and you see a heading called Standard View with the term *Wonder Wheel* under it.

3. **Click the Wonder Wheel link in the center of the page.**

   You see a Mind Map–like image with clickable links. (See Figure 10-1.) You can use these links to drill down to get more information.

To make sure you're starting with a firm foundation, here's what Buzan considers to be some key rules for a good Mind Map:

✔ Always use a central image.

✔ Use keywords instead of sentences to aid memorization.

✔ Use arrows when you want to make connections.

✔ Use color, line, and text to promote creativity.

✔ Use images of varying sizes throughout your map.

✔ Keep your paper or screen in a horizontal position.

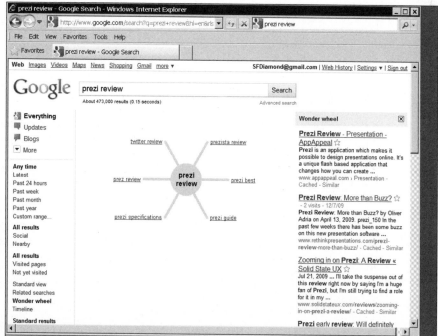

Figure 10-1: An example of a search on the Wonder Wheel.

Using Prezi, you can meet and enhance all these requirements. When you become really comfortable using Prezi to do your Mind Mapping, you can think about which rules to break. To start, however, it's best to stick to the basics.

Creating your first Mind Map

To begin Mind Mapping with Prezi, you have two choices: You can type your ideas directly on the screen or you can begin with pen and paper. If you're brainstorming or trying to solve a problem, the best thing to do is to start a new prezi and work directly in it. You need to be able to input ideas as quickly as they come to you, and there's no benefit to writing them on paper first and transferring them. You can get off to a quicker start by just inputting first and moving things around later.

If you were starting to map for a specific presentation, I would recommend using paper and pen first to think through and gather all the components including graphics, photos, scanned items, and so on.

To get started creating your first Mind Map, use the following steps:

1. **Open a new prezi by clicking the New Prezi button from the Your prezis page (`http://prezi.com/your`).**

   A prompt screen for creating a new prezi appears.

2. **Type a title and description where prompted and then click the New Prezi button.**

   A new prezi opens and is ready for editing.

3. **Begin choosing a style by clicking on the option in the Colors and Fonts bubble.**

   A prezi with the style you chose (including the background and the font styles) appears. If you don't like that style, go back and choose another one by clicking it. In Prezi you can change styles with just the click of a mouse.

   For Mind Maps, I prefer a style with a light background because it doesn't distract from the task of generating ideas. But, you can choose whatever stimulates your creative juices, and you can always change it later if you feel a different style will add impact or clarity.

4. **Double-click anywhere on the screen to start brainstorming.**

   Type your first idea into the text box. When you're brainstorming, it's a good idea to jot down the keywords as they come to you, so begin adding items on the screen as quickly as you think of them.

5. **To add lines radiating from the words, click the Insert bubble and then click the Shapes bubble.**

The Shapes bubble allows you to add free-form circles around your text using the line tool and arrows pointing toward related ideas with the arrow tool.

6. Click the Transformation Zebra tool to scale the sizes of the concepts up and down and rotate them for maximum impact.

You access the Zebra tool by clicking the Write bubble and then clicking the object you want to edit. You see the Transformation Zebra on top of your object. To move the object, click it and drag it where you want it on the canvas. To resize the object, place your cursor on the second inside ring and drag it up or down to increase or decrease the text. To rotate the object, place your cursor on the outer ring and swing it up and down.

7. To review and iterate, you can click the forward-arrow button, which is centered under the prezi.

You can flesh out your ideas and change the scope of your prezi until you feel you have settled on the best way to depict the central ideas and subsets that make up the big picture.

8. Click back to the main Bubble menu and then click the Path bubble.

To choose how to display your ideas, use the Path tool and start by zooming out to show the entire presentation as a shape. (See Figure 10-2.) You can also move in and set a Path number on the words or images on the screen to show major details.

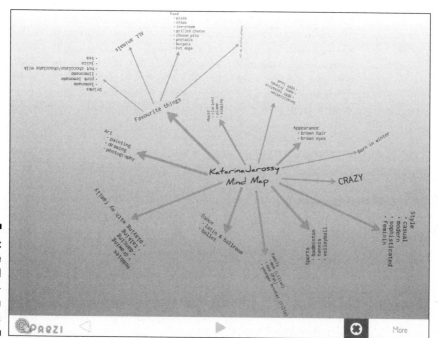

Figure 10-2:
An example of a Mind Map created with Prezi.

Using keywords versus long sentences in Prezi

Tony Buzan, the originator of Mind Mapping, made it a rule that when creating Mind Maps one should use keywords and phrases instead of sentences or paragraphs. He said that keywords are more memorable and make a stronger impact. When you use long passages of text, your audience is apt to lose focus. As you create your Mind Map, bear in mind the ways in which keywords can be used to persuade.

Using keywords to communicate can be evaluated in several ways.

- **Meaning that the words convey:** This is the way people use most often when reading text on a screen or on paper. You can use metaphors and analogies to convey the message right in the map.

- **Size of the words:** Looking at the size of some words in relation to others adjacent to it also conveys meaning. (See Figure 10-3.) You can use all capital letters or all small letters to convey meaning. For example, all capital letters is considered shouting online.

- **Movement of the words:** Using Prezi, you can use spacing and zooming as a way to telegraph a word's importance. Using the unlimited canvas, you can place text very near or far to indicate value. You can also rotate the text on an angle to communicate humor.

- **Increase or decrease the thickness of the arrows and lines:** One capability that's often missing from software that creates Mind Maps is the ability to vary the connections to the words or images. With Prezi, you aren't limited. You can create varying lines by using the Zebra tool to increase the size of the arrow which also increases its thickness. You can also use the Line tool (choose Insert⇨Shapes from the Bubble menu to find the Line tool) to draw thin lines or highlighter-style lines as your connectors.

Interestingly, Prezi gives you so many ways to display text that you can probably bend the keyword rule if you want to supply notes or statistics along with the map. The key is to not let it distract from the map itself. You can also encourage questions because you can place facts and definitions in an easy-to-understand layout, which also aids memorization.

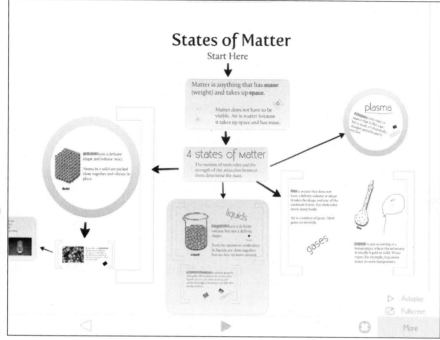

Figure 10-3:
This is a good example of the use of both text and keywords.

Using New Scientific Findings to Visually Sell Your Ideas

The workings of the brain have been the subject of research and popular literature for hundreds of years. Perhaps you've read about Dr. Frankenstein, who got into trouble when he tried to transplant a brain. It's interesting to note that scientists believe that 90 percent of the accumulated information about the brain has been learned in the last 10 years. As scientists become increasingly sophisticated about the way they read the brain with scanners, they discover startling new facts about how people learn and communicate.

One main finding that surprised both educators and scientists is the fact that the brain has the ability to grow and change no matter its age. It is not fixed and unchangeable. This phenomenon is called *plasticity*. This is great news if you've been using slide presentations and fear you can't develop a new mind-set. Other new facts can help you make presentations more effective and memorable. These include ways to present ideas in small pieces, in a specific order, and in specific intervals.

First, before you try to influence the audience's brain, take a quick look at the organ in question. The brain is divided in three functions or brains:

- **Old brain or reptilian (also known as lizard) brain:** This is the part of the brain that reacts without having to reason. It controls your breathing, your blood pressure, and a host of other critical functions. It also responds immediately to perceived threats, giving you those "fight or flight" reactions. If your old brain is on alert, that's where your focus is. Savvy marketers know this when they're trying to sell you something. If they arouse the survival instinct in you, they know they have your attention.

- **Mid brain:** This is where your emotions are processed. It also controls your visual and auditory functions. Blame this part of your brain if you see a big piece of chocolate and impulsively buy it without thought to calories.

- **New brain (the cortex):** This is the place where thinking, reasoning, and planning happens. Most people believe this is the part of the brain they use the most. Of course, salespeople and great presenters know differently.

The following sections explore some of the ways neuroscience (the study of the brain) has taught people to effectively communicate with others.

Chunking your messages

One of the ways in which people learn information is by *chunking* it — by grouping certain items together into smaller pieces, making them easier to remember and understand. (See Figure 10-4.) Studies show that the brain can remember groups of seven items (plus or minus two) relatively easily. That's why you can remember a phone number, a zip code, or your social security number without a great deal of difficulty.

It's a good idea to remember this guideline when you're presenting information. By grouping the information, you make it more memorable and enhance the clarity. By not adding more than five to nine items at a time, you're working with the brain's capacity to store information.

Ordering information presented

I mention earlier in this chapter that information is retained based on the way it is presented to an audience. This is especially important because of how order affects learning. Order affects information retention in the following ways:

✔ **Primacy:** What people see first is what they remember. What you show first in your presentation will have a major impact and is called primacy. Start dramatically and the audience will pay attention.

✔ **Recency:** People also remember what they see last in the presentation. What they see before the presentation ends sticks in their minds. That's why movies often open with a shocking event and have a big finish. It's most likely that audience members will remember what happens first and last, better than specific details along the way.

✔ **Relatedness:** You can also have great resonance with audience members if you touch on something that specifically relates to them and their own situation. Try to learn about your audience and use real-world examples wherever possible.

Knowing these rules, you can take full advantage of the fact that a prezi can operate like a movie with a beginning, a middle, and an end. With Prezi, you can present a show with Autoplay that doesn't require you to be present, but which explains what you want people to see as the big ideas and areas of emphasis.

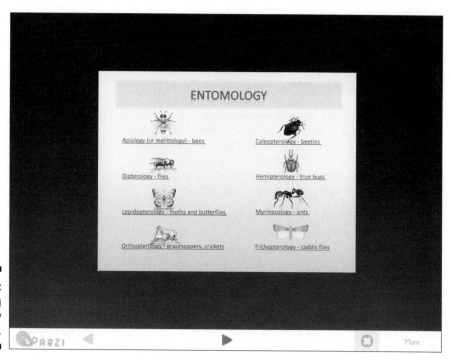

Figure 10-4:
Chunking
to display
items.

Ten-minute transitions

In his book, *Brain Rules,* John Medina discusses the Ten Minute Rule. He asked his college students how long it was before they got restless and started watching the clock. He discovered that while sitting in a classroom or other learning environment, people's attention spans wane after about 10 minutes.

To prevent this lapse of attention, he recommends that you shift your presentation mode approximately every 10 minutes to grab people's attention. This means that every 10 minutes, you need to stop presenting in the format you're using and switch to something else. With Prezi, you have lots of options to change the pace and movement. Experiment and see what works for you.

Here are some ways to change the pace in 10-minute intervals:

- Use the Zoom feature to suddenly pull out to the big picture changing the focus.
- Set up a Frame grouping to rotate at around 10 minutes into the presentation.
- Zoom to repeat something from the beginning.

Creating experiences

People are open to experiences that are memorable and worthy of their time. With this in mind, think about how you can make your prezi an experience. You have video, audio, graphics, and movement to work with.

Another way to be memorable is to create a *discrepant event.* Discrepant events are attention-getting devices used to startle or make the observer confused about what they're seeing. This causes them to pay close attention to what you are saying or doing. Teachers use discrepant events in their classrooms. For instance, science teachers use small experiments to show how something takes an unexpected action like creating a Mentos eruption in a Diet Coke.

Using colors

Color affects people's thinking. Everyone has favorite colors and colors they dislike. Colors can affect mood and command attention. Prezis make great use of color as a way to emphasize ideas and stimulate creativity.

The cortex of the brain is stimulated by the sight of various colors in different ways. Recent studies have shown that people are more creative when they use the color blue in their creative tasks. If you don't think that color matters, think about how easily you identify someone listening to his iPod — it's the white earbuds. The color helps you identify the brand.

Using Prezi, you have the option to use color in a variety of ways:

- ✔ **Uploading graphics:** From the Load File function in the Insert bubble, you can upload colorful images and photos of all types.

- ✔ **Uploading text colors:** You can choose preselected fonts in the styles available to you from the Colors and Fonts bubble. At present, you can't select your own font colors. To work around this, you can cut and paste text with the font and color you want to introduce from other design programs.

- ✔ **Color coding:** Color-code to show that items are part of different groups without having to state it. The grouping of colors does the job.

As with anything color-related, be mindful of those who may be color-blind. This is defined as the inability to see certain colors — usually red and green.

Creating spatial relationships

The brain functions best when it's given unlimited spaces on which to project ideas. That's exactly what Prezi does. It provides you with an unlimited canvas upon which you can freely create. That's one way that Prezi makes creating easier.

Spatial intelligence is a term coined by Professor Howard Gardener as one of the seven types of intelligence that are essential to a well-rounded person. Good spatial intelligence is defined as the ability to think about the world around you in pictures, to create an image and hold it in your mind without any visual reminders. It also means you're able to draw or retain images in your mind with spatial information like maps.

The use of spatial relationships is where using Prezi knocks the ball out of the park. With Prezi, you aren't limited by the boundaries of a static page or a slide. Presentations done with Prezi can use time, space, and movement in a truly unique way. The Frames and Zoom features give you the ability to manipulate time and space. That may constitute a super power.

Developing patterns

Patterns are design features that are repeated. If you look at a piece of fabric with a pattern, you will see that certain items are pictured over and over. When you look at the fabric as a whole, the smaller repeats make up a larger design. Being able to see the big picture of something makes it much easier to understand.

Designers and psychologists refer to a term called the *gestalt* — a unified whole that makes a pattern easier to see. One of the reasons the Prezi canvas makes it easy to see patterns is that you can easily zoom out to the big picture and zoom back in to the details. And you use the same object many times, giving each instance of it different movement. (See Figure 10-5.)

To practice using patterns as a design motif, follow these steps:

1. **Open the prezi from the Your Prezis tab (`http://prezi.com/your`).**

2. **Click the Edit Prezi button.**

   The Prezi canvas opens in Edit mode.

3. **Double-click anywhere on the canvas to open a text box.**

4. **Type in some text to experiment with and click OK.**

   The text box disappears, and the text you typed appears.

5. **Click the Frame bubble from the main Bubble menu and then choose one of the container styles.**

   In this case, choose the Circle style.

6. **Drag the cursor around the text and let go.**

   Next, you want to make it easy to move the circle and text as one entity instead of two separate ones.

7. **Hold the Shift key and drag your cursor around the container and text. Then release the Shift key and mouse button.**

   When you release, there will be a Zebra over the content, and everything in the space you selected with your cursor will move together.

8. **To duplicate this object, copy and paste so that the object is placed on the canvas.**

9. **Create a pattern of repeats and zoom out to view it.**

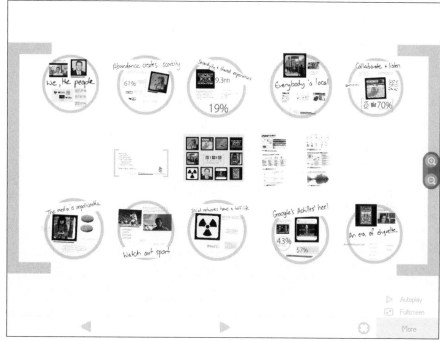

Figure 10-5:
Using a
repeating
pattern.

Applying visuals

Your brain's capacity to process images is amazingly strong. It's the largest system in the brain. In a classroom setting, this ability is downplayed. This causes many people to forget how strong their visual imaginations really are.

When people try to revive this skill as adults, they often feel that the resulting lack of skill means a lack of talent rather than just a weak muscle needing exercise. That is why introducing visual thinking tools to business people is an uphill battle. Using Prezi, you suddenly have all the tools at your fingertips.

No more feeling like you're lacking in talent or inept. Using visuals also draws viewers into the action and engages their creative side.

Some ways to use visual techniques to enhance your presentation are as follows:

- ✔ **Valuation:** Understanding that people associate highly designed presentations with high value.

- ✔ **Metaphors:** A way to enhance visuals is through the use of metaphors. Metaphors describe the characteristics of one thing in comparison to the characteristics of another. Using Prezi, you can enhance the use of metaphors with visuals and create new associations from old ones. Figure 10-6 shows how the words *Be Free* are escaping from the central image.

✔ **Stirring emotions:** Direct marketers and copywriters the world over know the impact that emotions play in persuading others. They employ visuals to stir these emotions and create a positive mood. Interestingly, your brain can relate to a fanciful image with no basis in reality as quickly as it can to one that is real. Knowing this can help you in your quest to use visuals to their greatest effect.

✔ **Music in conjunction with visuals:** Adding music to video can evoke emotions and drive your point home.

✔ **Using static and video images in one presentation:** Remember that the eye processes static images differently than moving ones. By remembering to use both in your prezi, you help the audience process and remember more information.

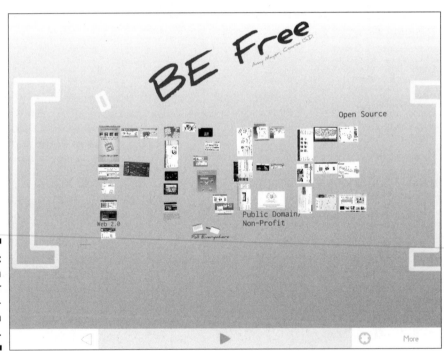

Figure 10-6:
Using a metaphor to communicate a message.

Chapter 11

Presenting Business Plans

· ·

· ·

The goal of most business plans is to explain the big picture of the proposed business and provide enough detail to make investors and others believe it is doable and profitable. As you know, Prezi excels at boiling down complex topics to their essence and presenting them in a visually stimulating way, which makes it a natural choice for creating business plans.

In this chapter, I discuss the visual aspects of creating business plans. Whether you're selling to an internal audience or investors, you need to make the plan inspiring and simple to follow. Telling the story of your business helps sell your vision.

I think of Prezi as being able to produce the ultimate one-page plan, a limitless canvas, capable of including all your information without restrictions.

Introducing a Prezi Business Plan

Anyone who has ever read a formal business plan can agree that it's hard going. Typically such a plan contains figures; tables; and a lot of long, boring explanations. Often they seem to be right out of a business plan book. If you think that's the way it has to be, I would say, not really. Yes, certain sets of figures come into play, but more often than not, a business plan, like most other presentations, is about a person with a vision who wants to persuade others to follow it.

This is not a romantic notion. When you think of investing your hard-earned capital, you think long and hard about whether the people you're betting on will do everything in their power to be successful. You have to believe in the vision. Even if the plan recommends only a slight change, you need to believe that it's worth doing.

If this is the case, then why not rely on the two things that help people understand ideas: stories and pictures? Screenwriter Robert McKee says that stories "unite an idea with an emotion." Isn't that what you want to do? That's why Prezi is the right tool for the job.

A prezi business plan allows you to

- ✔ Crystallize your thinking in a way that a written plan can't.
- ✔ Emphasize simplicity in a way that only visuals can.
- ✔ Help everyone make better decisions because the big picture and the details are visible at once.
- ✔ Communicate your message in exactly the way you want it by sending it with Autoplay.

So who is the audience for this plan? Is it just limited to a select few? A visual plan can be used very effectively with any of the following:

- ✔ Investors, shareholders, boards of directors
- ✔ Bankers
- ✔ Partners and vendors
- ✔ Potential employees and current staff

Developing Visual Concepts That Sell

There are three important things to think about as you begin to develop the visuals for your presentation:

- ✔ **The audience for your plan:** The presentation will be very different if you are presenting to an older audience or a techno-savvy group.

  When I speak to people preparing a presentation, I'm often surprised that they haven't found out much about their audience. They typically have a vague idea of who they'll be presenting to, but nothing concrete. Don't let bad things happen to good presentations. With a bit of effort, you can find out a lot about who will be coming to see you.

  If it's an internal business meeting, you probably know more about your audience than you want to. But what about external meetings with vendors or national conferences? Most national groups have profiles of their members. By speaking personally to a few of the members, you can generally get a feeling for what they're like. Make the effort; it will be worthwhile. Learning about your audience is covered in greater detail in Chapter 7.

✔ **Visual story elements:** Preparing your visuals with your viewers in mind makes it easier to pick just the right elements.

To prepare yourself to tell your business plan story, you should take into account the following comparisons that lend themselves nicely to graphic images and pictures:

- *Big picture of the industry and how you fit into it:* You can show an image of the companies and by comparing your size to theirs show your position in the market.

- *The specific players that impact you now:* A visual of direct competitors can instantly convey what you're up against.

- *Your relationship to potential partnerships:* How to build on it to gain financial strength.

- *How you're different:* A visual about what sets you apart from others can really have an impact. Imagine if you have a visual of your restaurant serving only fresh foods versus your competitor serving some frozen foods. Can you see the icicles hanging off the frozen dinner?

- *How this difference can change the future:* Look at both the short term and the long term.

- *Factors you need to monitor that could affect business success:* Visuals of threats to your success can be shown here.

✔ **The information you must have:** Make sure you have all the info you need and decide whether you need to contact outside experts to fill in the gaps.

If you (or your partners if you have any) are well-versed in your industry, you probably won't need to consult with an expert. But if you feel you're lacking some information, it may be helpful to seek a consultation with someone who can provide you with information you can't get on your own. If it can shorten the time to market, it can be valuable.

You might want to bring in an expert to consult for the following reasons:

- Help you review things you haven't considered

- Gain insights from industry experience you don't possess

- Show you how to test your theories before you create your proposal

- Provide market intelligence not readily available to you

- Help you assess how well suited you are to run your new business

Plan Presentation Logistics

Right up front, you want to know about all the things that impact your presentation. Most likely, they include the following:

- ✔ **Available time:** Depending on the amount of time you have with your audience, you can take your time and go over everything in detail, or you have to just hit the highlights. If you practice a short and long version, you'll be ready for anything that comes your way.

- ✔ **Location:** The place where you show your plan is very important. Much like I discuss in Chapter 7, you need to know what kind of presentation you're giving — Ballroom or Conference Room. I would assume for most business plans you'll be in a conference setting. This means that you should be prepared to explain and defend your choices.

- ✔ **Equipment needed:** When it comes to delivering prezis you have lots of options. You could deliver from a laptop with the presentation on your hard drive. This means a laptop and projector (and remote controls if you prefer.) You can present from an Internet browser, which adds an Internet connection. Obviously, you need to know this well in advance so that you have everything prepared.

- ✔ **Contact numbers of people involved:** With all the flight delays, traffic jams, and unforeseen circumstances possible, you want to have mobile ways to get in touch with your hosts. Get that from the beginning so you can see how responsive they are to your calls.

Collaborating with Team Members

Business plans are usually not the product of one person. When you have such a daunting mission as starting a new business or introducing a new line of products, you're likely to have staff or partners working with you. For this reason, you'll want to invite additional editors to make collaboration easy.

To invite coeditors, go to the Your Prezi tab (`http://prezi.com/your`), click to open a prezi, and follow these steps:

1. **In the center of the prezi screen in the lower-right corner of the grey box, click the Invite Editors link.**

   A screen pops up with a link to your editable prezi.

2. **Highlight the link and press Ctrl+C to copy it. (See Figure 11-1.)**

   If you want to revoke the share link you sent previously and generate a new one, you can click the Reset Share Link button below the URL presented to you.

Figure 11-1:
Inviting
coeditors.

3. **Close the pop-up screen by clicking the X in the upper-right corner.**

4. **Open your e-mail program or other sharing program and press Ctrl+V to paste it into the message box.**

    Send it as you normally would. When your collaborator receives the e-mail and clicks the link, he is added as a coeditor and can edit your prezi.

Covering the Basics

Whether or not you're creating a visual plan, there's some information that everyone will want to know. As you create your plan, make sure you cover the basics:

- ✔ The business model
- ✔ Management team
- ✔ The market analysis and strategy
- ✔ Staff requirements
- ✔ Back office functions
- ✔ Timelines
- ✔ Funding needed

Depending on the purpose of the plan, you'll need to cover some items in greater detail than others.

Understanding the Business Model

Anyone who wants to invest in your new business or sign on as an employee will want to understand your business model. They want to assure themselves that you can establish an ongoing business with profitable cash flow. You also want to supply the emotional content that gives your audience a feeling of comfort about you and your ability to deliver. If an investor is preoccupied with risk, she's not paying attention to the benefits.

If you can make the business model visual, you'll help yourself and your audience immensely. See whether you can break the business model down into its component parts and how it will succeed. Conversely, if you can't show how the business makes money, you may want to rethink it before you go any further.

If you're interested in this topic in more depth, check out the amazing book *Business Model Generation: A Handbook for Visionaries, Game Changers and Challengers*, by Alex Osterwalder and Yves Pigneur. It focuses on how to visually create and depict business models. Their definition of a business model is "[it] describes the rationale of how an organization creates, delivers, and captures value." By thinking about creating and delivering value, you're working at the heart of your business plan.

Making the Numbers Interesting

One of the things you need to devote some time to is presenting the numbers in your plan in an interesting way. (See Figure 11-2.) Not everyone is excited at the prospect of viewing numbers on a screen. Think about using numbers, text, and graphics together in one unit to communicate your numbers.

Following are a few don'ts for creating info graphics:

- Don't make the numbers too small.
- Don't pack the view with too much information.
- Don't present numbers in such as way that they can't be scanned quickly. Make sure there's a definite contrast between the background and the numbers. Also make sure there's enough space between each number them so that they don't all run together.

Figure 11-2:
Presenting
the numbers
in an inter-
esting way.

✔ Don't be inconsistent. Make sure you color-code or otherwise label items in a consistent fashion.

✔ Don't use *chart junk* — decorative but inessential information.

If you want to include a lot of supplementary numerical data, it's a good idea to include the data as attachments so that people who want to delve into the numbers can do so later.

Using Movement to Add Momentum

When creating your presentation, demonstrating your information using movement makes it more memorable and easier to comprehend.

Ways to show movement in Prezi include the following:

✔ **Smart Zooming:** You can zoom in to particular items of interest and then out again to show the big picture. This function is built into Prezi and doesn't require you to do anything except click something. The program determines the correct amount of movement.

✔ **Rotating:** If you place an element at an angle or flip it upside down, the program will straighten it when it focuses in. This gives you the sensation of movement and makes an impact on your viewer.

✔ **Timing:** There's a built-in timing feature that allows you to dictate how long Prezi will display each of your screens in Autoplay. The choices are 4, 10, or 20 seconds.

✔ **Clicking to Web locations from within the program:** Being able to add and click to a Web location from within your business plan is a great way to illustrate what you have or plan to do online. You can remain in Prezi and move right back into the discussion after you've shown the link.

✔ **Using a Path:** Prezi allows you to create a sequence for your elements and then lock that sequence into a Path. This means that when you click the forward arrows to advance the screen, you can determine how and what your viewers will see. If you use the timing intervals, these screens advance on their own. If you want to alter the sequence in any way, all you have to do is change the Path sequence. It's as easy as 1-2-3.

Using Web links

When you're presenting your plan, you'll likely want to show Web links that either illustrate what you plan to do or show work under construction. Prezi makes it very easy to add links that can be accessed within the presentation. It's a smooth transition from the link and then back to the presentation.

To add a Web link, take the following steps:

1. **Double-click anywhere on the canvas.**

   The text box appears.

2. **Type the URL into the box and click OK.**

   Don't forget to include the entire address starting with `http://`, or else the link won't work. (See Figure 11-3.)

3. **To make the link active, save and exit your prezi using the links in the upper-right corner.**

4. **Reopen that prezi, and the link is now active.**

   The link has a line under it denoting an active link. Open the link by clicking it as you would any other Web link.

Sending without a Presenter

You want your business plan to be seen by anyone who can help move it along. That means that you won't always be able to present in person. Prezis can be great for this because Prezi offers lots of alternative ways to share your presentations, including the following:

- ✔ Sharing in a private, secure e-mail so that proprietary information is safe
- ✔ Adding special comments that can be played before or after a presentation

Sending a private prezi via e-mail

When you're working on projects with proprietary information, you want to be as careful as you can when sending it around the Web. Prezi lets you send a unique private URL to avoid having it fall into the wrong hands.

To send a private prezi via e-mail, follow these steps:

1. **To open your private prezi, click it from the Your Prezis tab (`http://prezi.com/your`).**

2. **Click the words Get Link in the lower-left corner of the prezi screen.**

   A screen pops up with your view-only link. (See Figure 11-4.)

3. **Highlight the link and press Ctrl+C to copy it.**

   If you want to revoke the private link you sent previously and generate a new one, you can click the Reset Share Link button below the URL presented to you.

4. **Close the pop-up screen by clicking the X in the upper-right corner.**

5. **Open your e-mail program or other sharing network and press Ctrl+V to paste it into the message box.**

   Send your e-mail as you normally would. Only those who receive this link from you can access it.

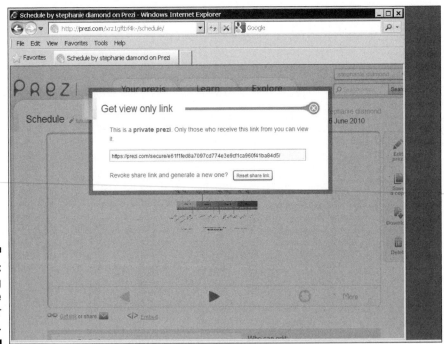

Figure 11-4:
Obtaining a private URL for your prezi.

Designing special comments

When you're sending your plan without a presenter, you may want to think about sending it with special comments. If you have additional information that isn't part of the formal presentation or you have personal comments you want to make, you can add them to the presentation itself.

Special comments take the form of multimedia that you embed in the presentation to be played either at the beginning or the end. Unlike a written e-mail or other document, the embedded comments will be right there every time the presentation is viewed. This is not to be confused with multimedia that's embedded within the presentation and is part of the plan.

- ✓ **Audio Comments:** You may want to have an audio with a photo describing a potential location you've chosen for the business.

- ✓ **Video Comments:** You may have a video of yourself and your team thanking the investor for considering your proposal. The possibilities are endless.

Chapter 12

Educating with Prezi

*Y*ounger audiences are more likely to be first adopters of applications like Prezi because they don't have ingrained thinking that opposes new ways of doing things. Prezi has garnered an enthusiastic response from students and teachers alike. Recognition of its value in classrooms has caused educators to request special Prezi licenses for them and their students.

In this chapter, I look at the ways in which Prezi is being used in schools and universities to make learning more fun. I survey the special Education licenses that have been created to accommodate both students and teachers and then explore the strategies you can use to make students more successful. In addition, I look at how Prezi is being used at major conferences by thought leaders in many different areas.

Using Prezi in Schools and Universities

It's not just the novelty that attracts students and educators to Prezi. The application presents a new way of presenting ideas. In school, presentations are a way of life. Either the teacher is presenting to students or students are asked to present to the class. Finding something to break the monotony of slide presentations is welcomed. Finding a way to use technology in a whole new way is celebrated. Using Prezi, students can capture ideas and rearrange them to create new paradigms. This also facilitates the growth of discussion and new ideas.

Obtaining an Education license

Imagine how cool school would have been if Prezi had been available when you were younger. Well, Prezi developers want to make sure that Prezi is available so that current students don't have to imagine it. Because of an overwhelming request from the education community, Prezi created a special Education license. (See Figure 12-1.)

Teachers and students who request and qualify have the option of using the Edu Enjoy for free (normally $59) or the Edu Pro plan for $59 annually (normally $159).

The plan is as follows:

- **Edu Enjoy:** Cost Free; 30-day free trial. The Enjoy plan gives you 500MB of online storage space to use for your prezis. When you present, you don't see the Prezi watermark on the left side of the screen.. Your prezis remain private unless you make them public.

- **Edu Pro:** Cost $59 annual fee; 30-day free trial. The Edu Pro plan gives you 2,000MB of online storage space. You also get access to the Prezi Desktop software so that you can edit your prezis offline. When you present, you don't see the Prezi watermark. With this plan, your prezis also remain private unless you make them public.

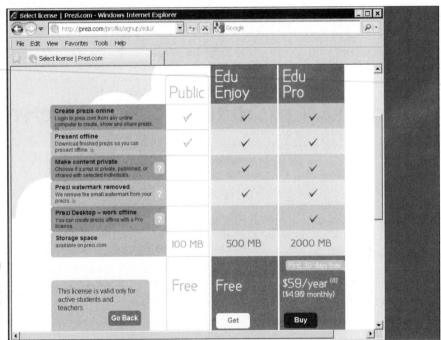

Figure 12-1:
Education subscriptions.

Understanding learning styles in the classroom

For new technology to be deployed in the classroom, it needs to accommodate student's learning types. Prezi works well because it has something for each type of learner. (See Figure 12-2.) Not only does it help the student use both the left and right brain, it engages the three major learning styles:

✔ **Visual learners:** This group prefers to see things in their "mind's eye." They imagine what ideas look like. Remember to provide diagrams, pictures, maps, colors, and a visual explanation for your topic. Prezis really excel here.

✔ **Auditory learners:** This group prefers hearing what you're saying and listens to the words very carefully. They enjoy asking questions. Adding sounds and/or music to your prezi engages them.

✔ **Kinesthetic learners:** This group prefers to learn things by doing. They're the people who want to experience something before they can assimilate it. If you can, do a demonstration or make your Prezi interactive in order to engage this group effectively.

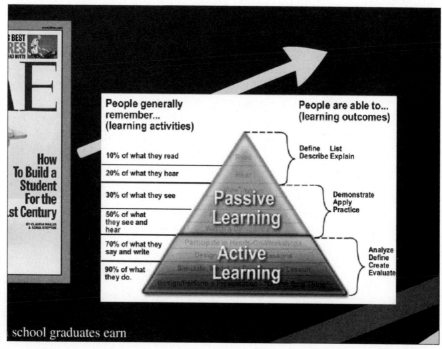

Figure 12-2: Using Prezi in the classroom.

Communicating information

Teachers use lots of techniques to help students pay attention. Following are several that have become popular in recent years:

- ✔ **Chunking:** To make information easier to remember, studies show that the brain can hold seven items (plus or minus two) at any one time — some say even fewer than seven. When using Prezi, remember to group items this way using Frames. It makes your ideas more compelling and memorable.

- ✔ **Ordering of information:** When presenting information, you have three elements that you can use to highlight information:

  - *Primacy:* Primacy refers to what's seen first. Carefully determine what you open your Prezi with. It will be remembered.

  - *Recency:* Recency refers to the information people see last in the presentation. Remember to close with your most important points so the audience will remember them.

  - *Relatedness:* Relatedness refers to anything that makes emotional contact with your audience. You should strive to know your audience well enough to include something that fits that category. If you do, people will be sure to remark about it.

- ✔ **Discrepant events:** Discrepant events are devices used to startle or make the observer confused about what they're seeing. Obviously, this helps them stop and take notice. If you have some humor or topical way to present this, you can make people remember.

- ✔ **Ten-minute transitions:** In his book, *Brain Rules,* John Medina asked his students how long it took them before they got bored. Their answer? Ten minutes. So he coined the term *ten-minute transitions* to alert presenters to the amount of time they should speak without make a transition to gain attention.

Here are some ways to change the pace in ten-minute intervals:

- Use the Zoom feature to suddenly pull out to the big picture changing the focus.

- Set up a Frame grouping to rotate at around 10 minutes.

- Zoom to repeat something from the beginning again.

- Add multimedia after a 10-minute interval.

- Stop and take questions or ask a question.

Thinking Visually in the Classroom

If you're unsure about why visuals work in the classroom, it has been shown by several studies that student's skills improve when visuals are included in the study material.

Improved skills include

- Reading ability
- Writing proficiency
- General test scores
- Problem solving

When you take into account that more than 70 percent of the sensory stimuli people take in is visual, this isn't surprising.

Applying Success Strategies

Students today are faced with economic challenges not seen by recent generations. For this reason, educators need to provide ways to help students understand how to be more successful. With advances in neuroscience and psychology, educators can now teach students using proven strategies that will help them reach their goals.

In the book *The Winner's Brain,* authors Jeff Brown, M. Fenske, and L. Neporent surveyed scientific research and talked with experts around the world to arrive at eight findings, called *Win factors,* which are success strategies that anyone can employ. They are as follows:

- **Self-awareness:** Being able to understand how you fit into the world around you. It makes you aware of your strengths and weaknesses.

- **Motivation:** Being aware of where you want to go and how you can get there. You need to keep your goals in sight at times when your motivation starts to waver.

- **Focus:** Being able to keep distractions at bay. In today's world, the ability to avoid distractions is a key success tool.

- **Emotional balance:** Being aware of how you and others can modify your emotions when situations challenge you.

✔ **Memory:** Knowing how much information to store in memory, but not taking up space with insignificant items. It was said that Albert Einstein did not know his own phone number because he said if he needed it, he could look it up.

✔ **Resilience:** Being able to accept failure and bouncing back no matter what the circumstances. Never giving up.

✔ **Adaptability:** Being able to keep up with changes in your environment and figuring out how to make them work for you.

✔ **Brain care:** This involves a person doing all the things he knows he should do to take care of his body. This includes getting enough sleep, exercise, and eating a healthy diet.

These points are important for both the prezi presenter and her audience. Look at the strategies and see how you can employ them in your life and build them into your prezi. For example, if you have the opportunity to talk about self-awareness, motivation, or resilience in the hero, your story will be strengthened.

Using Prezi in Conferences

When the outcome of your presentation will determine something critical for you, choosing Prezi makes perfect sense. It's no surprise that Prezi shows up at major conferences where the need to communicate effectively is high. Some examples of conferences where Prezi has been used include writer James Geary at TED Oxford and MIT professor, and also Sir Tim Berners-Lee at IdeasLab at the World Economic Forum in Davos, Switzerland. (See Figure 12-3.) These presenters could pick any tool or hire a professional group to create their presentation, and they chose Prezi. Interestingly, the IdeasLab presentation by Berners-Lee followed a *pecha kucha* format. *Pecha kucha* means *chit chat* in Japanese and refers to a presentation format in which a presenter shows 20 images for 20 seconds each.

Prezi developers point out tongue-in-cheek that they have a *pecha kucha* format because you can set your timing interval to 20 seconds using Prezi's built-in timing interval feature.

Figure 12-3:
Prezi at
the World
Economic
Forum 2010.

Getting Attention with Prezi Resumes

Are you graduating or looking for a way to stand out in this tight labor market? Maybe you should consider putting your resume in Prezi. Several Prezi subscribers have reported getting some added attention. You never know what could happen. One way to ensure that you have a resume right for every job vacancy is to create a prezi resume along with your written one. Then you can send whichever is most appropriate. If you're looking for a job online, it may have better resonance with your potential employers.

The key to using Prezi for your resume is to rethink how a static resume would be presented. Clearly, there is some information that every resume must have. But, if you merely transfer your written resume directly into Prezi, you're missing out on the opportunity to display your uniqueness.

To use Prezi for your resume, you need to think about how to present the following in an interesting digital format:

✔ **Chronology:** If you're presenting a chronological resume you can break the content into sections and display them with graphics that are pertinent to each job.

✔ **Functional skills:** If you're doing a functional resume (usually recommended for those with specialty skills or those for whom this is a first job), use text design to highlight your skills. You can create word art or other displays from third-party design software like Photoshop. Make sure you pick graphics that are appropriate for the industry you're in.

✔ **Portfolio samples:** Uploading your custom media is a great way to provide samples of your work product. You can group the samples into one of the Shapes available, like brackets, and put key phrases around them to explain what's important.

✔ **Web links to your writing:** Remember that you can add actual Web links in Prezi itself so that you can show off something you've created or a blog that you write. The viewer can go directly to the link and then back to your presentation.

✔ **Photo:** If it's appropriate you can include a photo of yourself somewhere in the resume. There are conflicting thoughts about whether photos should be sent. Know your audience.

✔ **Education:** Use some flair with this so that it's not the typical boring list of schools.

✔ **Awards, special achievements:** If there's something you're really proud of, include a picture or video of it here.

✔ **Multimedia:** You could shoot a video or record and audio of yourself describing your job goals. If you have some appropriate media that shows off your skills, you may want to include it.

To get the most from creating a resume with Prezi, I recommend that you try to use the following features:

✔ **Zooming in and out:** Remember that using the Smart Zooming feature, you can zoom out to show the total resume and then zoom in to view the details. This zooming can be impressive if you think about how to display the pieces fitting together as a whole. Perhaps you can use a metaphor here.

✔ **Timing intervals:** Prezi allows you to set timing intervals of 4, 10, or 20 seconds per screen. If you ask viewers to set it at that interval, they can play it back in Autoplay exactly as you created it.

✔ **Sharing using password protection:** One of the great features of sending a prezi in an e-mail is that you keep it private it if you are concerned about security.

✔ **Rotating:** This is fun, but keep it to one or two. You don't want to make your resume appear frivolous.

✔ **Printing:** If it makes sense, you can send a printed prezi resume as a PDF along with the digital format. If you are sending a standard resume, you could include some select screens in PDF format from your prezi. That way you have both.

Figure 12-4 shows an example of a resume in Prezi.

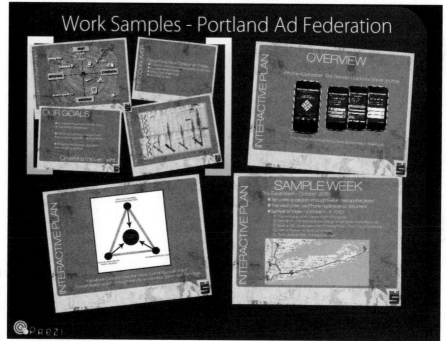

Figure 12-4:
A resume in
Prezi.

Chapter 13

Displaying Your Hobbies and Special Events with Prezi

In This Chapter

▶ Discovering new ways to show off your hobbies

▶ Using themes, styles, and text to set the mood

▶ Communicating emotions with digital mementos

*I*n this chapter, I show you how to use Prezi in ways you may not have thought of before. Hobbies, vacations, club presentations, and more can be made memorable when you use Prezi to communicate your interests. As a digital storytelling tool, Prezi helps you share the fun with family and friends. It creates a permanent record for you to look back on.

The use of text, colors, multimedia, and everyday items can make your collections even more spectacular. When you try using Prezi for more than just business presentations, you'll be hooked.

Exploring Some Uses of the Digital Canvas

Think about Prezi's digital canvas as a big display board for your collections. Or it can be a communication tool to share your favorite events. Don't think individual slides. You aren't limited by anything except your imagination. Here are some of the possible new uses of Prezi:

✓ **Scrapbooks:** Prezi allows you to take scrapbook pages that you've already created and make them come alive! Or you can start from scratch and make a completely new digital scrapbook presentation.

Anything you use for your regular scrapbooking can be used in Prezi. You just have to digitize original artwork, or you can photograph an element like a ribbon or a stamp and then place that image in your prezi. Digital scrapbooking is very common today, but with Prezi you can take it to the next level!

Some great items that you can scrapbook with Prezi include the following:

- *Stamps for inking:* Both homemade and professional

- *Accessories:* Buttons, ribbons, and lace

- *Forms:* Calendars and sheet music

- *Botanicals:* Pressed flowers as well as images and drawings of plants

- *Labels and tags:* Cancelled stamps and hang tags

- *Papers:* Decorative and journal pages

✔ **Recipes:** Grandma's recipes will never be the same after they meet Prezi. You'll almost be able to smell the freshly baked cookies. You have lots of ways to make your recipes more exciting with Prezi by adding multimedia and zooming in on your tempting creations. (See Figure 13-1.)

You can add spice to your presentations by adding any of the following:

- Video of specific cooking techniques used in the recipe.

- A recording of your own voice reading the recipe or making comments about the preparations (Perhaps you'll discover your inner Julia Child.)

- Photos of the stages of cooking and the completed recipe.

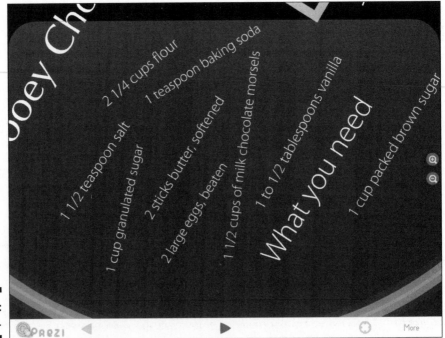

Figure 13-1:
A recipe.

- Fun facts in a decorative font about ingredients and their usage.

- A brief bio of the person who created the recipe.

- A flash animation of a timer ticking down with an audible beep or something fun for your viewer to watch as the presentation unfolds.

TIP

Don't forget that you're able to show movement and progression of time using the Smart Zooming and Transformation Zebra. Also, using Autoplay, you don't have to be present for the recipe to play in Show mode exactly as you planned it.

✔ **Vacations:** Documenting vacations is easy with Prezi. (See Figure 13-2.) You likely want to capture as much of the original items like tickets or maps by scanning them in so you'll have a permanent digital record. This way you won't have to worry about materials that deteriorate over time.

Here are some items to remember to include in your vacation prezi:

- Airline tickets or reservations

- Hotel brochures and napkins with logos

- Photos of places you visited adding special captions

- Video and photos of family and friends

Figure 13-2:
Documenting
a vacation.

- Tickets for amusement parks, movies, and plays

- Maps

- Journal or diary pages

- Special songs or music related to the trip

- Specific dates or statistics

✔ **Hobbies and collections:** Have a collection of cherished items? Prezis are a great way to show off your hobbies. Imagine displaying your favorite pottery collection or classic cars. You can include detailed photos along with information of interest to fellow collectors. (See Figure 13-3.) This is also a good way to keep a record of your valuables for insurance purposes.

Following are some ideas about what you can include:

- Photos of your most prized items

- Statistics about collectors

- Fun facts about the history of your hobby

- Photos of yourself with your collection

- The story about why you started collecting

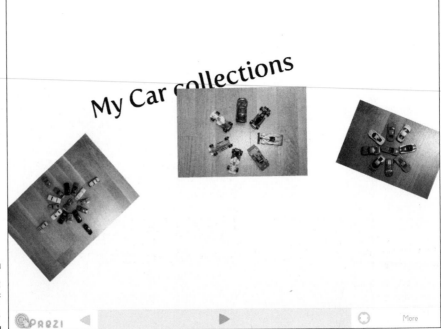

Figure 13-3:
Showing off
a hobby.

✔ **Invitations:** Having a celebration? What better way to communicate " your invitation than with an Autoplaying prezi? (See Figure 13-4.) Entice your guests to enjoy the fun even before they get there using a unique invitation.

Here is some of the information you can include in an entertaining way:

- *What you're celebrating:* Show a humorous photo of the birthday girl or happy couple.

- *A map showing how to get there:* Include a Google map with directions.

- *What to wear:* Cut out and place images of people dressed for the occasion.

- *When it starts and ends:* Use interesting fonts and play with the sizes.

- *What to bring:* Create a hand-drawn image of flowers or other items.

✔ **Photo displays:** Everyone has digital images. Instead of using a common, boring album, why not present your photos in a completely unique way? (See Figure 13-5.) You can use Smart Zooming to focus in on important details and banish the tedious slide-style presentations forever.

Figure 13-4:
A birthday
invitation.

Figure 13-5:
A photo
display.

Choosing a Theme

Before you do any preparation on a hobby or an event, you need to settle on a theme. Choosing the right theme makes your prezi come alive.

Obviously, when you're creating a prezi for a particular event or vacation, you generally know what your theme is. But there's much more to picking a theme than that. If you're presenting an event, it could have a tropical motif, a wilderness setting, or an ocean theme. Give some thought upfront to how you define it. The extra thought will make everything easier as you go along. You can take my example themes and break them down even further into a vintage tropical look or an ocean theme done in an Art Deco style.

Remember, though, that a theme is not a style. The theme *dictates* the style. The style of the prezi is determined by the fonts and colors associated with it.

Selecting a Style

When you select your prezi style from one of those available, you can pick the one that you think most closely supports your theme. There are styles with white backgrounds, colors, and shades. For more information about styles see Chapter 3.

Presently, the number of different font colors available in the Prezi software is limited to black, blue, and red; however, this may be changed by the time you read this. The font styles are varied and can be explored by double-clicking the canvas in Edit mode. You can upload your own stylized fonts by using design software and uploading it to the canvas.

Using Text to Set the Mood

When it comes to displaying text, Prezi is unlike any other presentation software. You have the flexibility to zoom in on a word or phrase. You don't have to limit yourself to the boundaries of a slide, and you can break sentences into pieces so your audience isn't reading too much text on the screen at once. Your screens will pass what's called the *squint test,* meaning you can squint at the screen and still be recognize what it's about. The layout and graphics should be bold enough so that you don't have to be able to read the text to get an understanding.

Here are some ideas for making the text in your prezi more dynamic or attractive:

- ✔ **Word Art:** Using Word Art is a fun way to communicate an idea. It refers to text that is stylized to make words look more like art. Microsoft Office has a Word Art function. You can also find other design applications that will stylize your text. In addition to creating word shapes in your design program, check out Wordle (`www.wordle.net`). Wordle describes itself as an application that creates word clouds. (See Figure 13-6.) A *word cloud* is a group of words presented in a free-form shape. Some of the words are large, some are small, and all are arranged to form an image like a cloud.

  With Wordle, you can create your own word clouds, such as.

  - A collection of text you type in.

  - An RSS feed you have for a blog or other site.

  - Your tags in Delicious at `http://delicious.com`. (Delicious is a bookmarking Web site where people tag articles and posts so that they can be stored and found by others.)

  If you use Wordle to create a word cloud, be sure to credit Wordle.net.

- ✔ **Drop shadows:** Creating text with drop shadows in a hobby prezi is a way to lend some drama to ordinary text. Drop shadows give the text the look of being elevated enough to cast a shadow. (See Figure 13-7.) You can create this effect with most design programs and just upload it to the canvas in one of the approved formats.

Figure 13-6:
A Wordle
created
from my
blog with
Wordle.net.

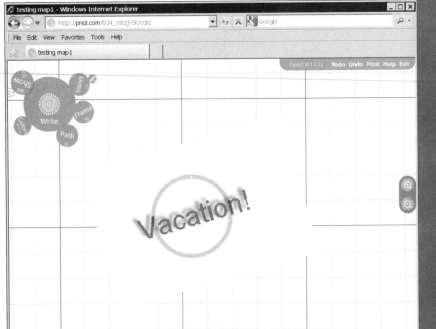

Figure 13-7:
Using drop
shadows
to enhance
text.

✔ **Journaling:** If you use a journal, it would be fun to digitize a page or section and add it to your prezi. If you have a flat-bed scanner, you don't have to remove the page from the journal — just scan it in and go.

Adding Fun Facts

Prezi makes it very easy to display chunks of information in fun and interesting ways. You have several choices when you want to create a display for your fun facts.

What kinds of facts can you use to enliven up your hobby prezi? Here are some ideas:

✔ **Geography:** The terrain of a particular area where you collection was made

✔ **Birthdates:** Famous birthdates

✔ **History:** An event that took place relating to your hobby

✔ **Collector's information:** Little-known facts about how your collection is made

✔ **Videos of ceremonies:** A short clip from a celebration

Following are some examples:

✔ **Nest:** You can take one of the Frames (Brackets, Circles, or Rectangles) and place your fact inside it and then put a larger Frame around it, or group several together in that Frame.

✔ **Rotate:** Once in a container, you can rotate the fact or the Frame itself so that they are not both on the same plane.

✔ **Resize:** Using the Transformation Zebra you can enlarge some of the words in the fact for emphasis.

✔ **Smart Zoom:** You can set up your Path to zoom into your fact and then back out to the larger canvas.

Figure 13-8 shows some neat ways to present facts.

Figure 13-8:
Making
facts more
interesting.

Please step back a little, and see that slides are a side effect of an old unused technology, slide projectors.

Still all presentation software today rely on slides

Please use the bottom right arrow to navigate

Collecting Your Media

I believe it's very important to collect and upload all the materials you think you need to create your prezi. You can upload your materials right to your canvas. Part of this process is to create a worksheet that holds information about where these files are normally stored and who created them. I provide a detailed explanation of this process in Chapter 2. There are two reasons why I recommend this:

- ✔ **Speed and organization:** All the information about how to find and document your materials is stored in one place on one sheet of paper.

- ✔ **Ease of use:** When you're ready to start designing your prezi, you don't have to stop and go looking for something. It's right there on your canvas.

Place all the graphic materials to one side of the Prezi canvas and then move them over as you need them. This method creates a much better flow for the design process.

Demonstrating Movement

You can really use movement to your advantage in a festively themed prezi. You can go far beyond what you would put in a business presentation. Your only limit should be taking care not to induce eye strain.

The type of movement you can introduce in your prezi falls into the following categories:

✔ **Pacing:** Your pacing is controlled either by your live presentation or Autoplay. Pacing for a hobby prezi can be lively and fast. When you're setting up Autoplay, your quickest sequence choice is four seconds. Consider using that unless you have a lot of visuals in each screen to take in.

✔ **Rotation:** With the Transformation Zebra, you can tilt and rotate items to add interest. If you're presenting live, clicking a rotated item causes the screen to zoom in and straighten it. This is a fun effect, but be careful not to overuse it.

✔ **Zooming:** With themed prezis, you want to use Smart Zooming as a primary feature. It can be fun to nest items and then zoom out to each one, revealing another layer. You can do the same by zooming in. Experiment with placement. It's much more interesting if you move to different layers on the canvas.

✔ **Animation and videos:** Including animation in your prezi is a great way to inject some humor. If you can find something that's pertinent to your hobby or event, it will be a surprise addition. Prezis can use an FLV format, and you can find Flash videos at most of the stock photo houses online. A *stock photo* house is an online service where artists, photographers, and videographers catalog and sell their images. Here are a few to check out:

- iStockphoto (www.istockphoto.com)
- Bigstock (www.bigstockphoto.com)
- 123RF (www.123rf.com)
- Fotolia (www.fotolia.com)

Embedding YouTube videos

You can also show off the hobbies you put in YouTube right in your prezi. You must have an Internet connection to play the video live when you are presenting. Note that even if you're using a portable prezi downloaded on your hard drive, you must have an Internet connection. See Chapter 5 for more information on embedding a video.

✔ **Adding Web links:** This is a great feature in Prezi. You can add URLs in your presentation and quickly go right to the Web pages you designate. See Chapter 3 for more information on adding Web links.

Collaborating with Family and Friends

You'll definitely want to share your prezis with family and friends. But how about creating something together? You can have everyone who took the same trip or celebrated at the same event participate in creating a prezi. It's very easy to give friends access to your prezi; it's built right into the software. See Chapter 5 for more information on collaborating with others.

Printing Your Show

You'll appreciate having a printed copy of your prezi hobby to look at when you aren't near a computer. You can store it with your collection or take it with you to show off even if there isn't a digital gadget in sight. You won't have the movement, but you will have the memories.

To print your prezi in PDF format, take the following steps:

1. **Go to the Your Prezis tab (`http://prezi.com/your`) and click a prezi to open it.**

2. **Click the Edit Prezi button.**

   Your prezi is ready to edit.

3. **Click the Print link in the upper-right corner of your Prezi canvas.**

   When you click this link, a message pops out below it that says `Starting` and shows you the number of pages that will print based on the Path numbers you have set up. (See Figure 13-9.) If you don't have a Path set up, Prezi prints the one main screen.

4. **Click the Click to Save PDF link.**

   The Save File window pops up and asks which location you want to save it to. Choose a location, and it's saved there. Then go to the document and print it out as you normally would print a PDF. If you want to, you can readjust the Path based on how the PDF prints and then reprint it.

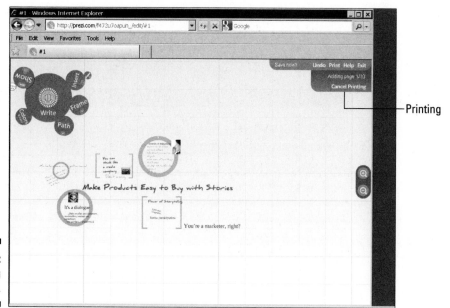

Printing

Figure 13-9:
Printing
your prezi.

Part V
The Part of Tens

By Rich Tennant

"The top line represents our revenue, the middle line is our inventory, and the bottom line shows the rate of my hair loss over the same period."

In this part . . .

At this point, you're probably looking for some final hidden secrets that will give you the edge. That's where this gets intriguing. In this part, I've distilled lots of stuff into lists of ten to tackle specific problems.

There are direct suggestions about how to do things I think will help leverage your special talents. Each chapter has ten points of can't-miss goodness. They include the best ways to fill a blank screen, what to know about visual thinking, how to use Prezi for mind mapping, and, my favorite, the worst things you can do with Prezi. Forgo the special handshake, but don't miss reading this part.

Chapter 14

Ten Ways to Fill a Blank Screen

. . . .

In This Chapter

▶ Planning in analog

▶ Using examples from the Explore tab to spur your thinking

▶ Choosing a layout

▶ Stating the problems you will solve

▶ Creating a timeline of the presentation

. . . .

*F*earing a blank screen is a universal condition. Writers, designers, artists, musicians, and most people faced with a large empty expanse to fill up feel some anxiety. Sportswriter Red Smith was quoted as saying, "Writing is easy. Just stare at a blank sheet of paper until beads of blood form on your forehead."

This chapter helps you avoid forming those beads as you open your prezi and look at the canvas. I provide ten ways to instantly begin to fill the canvas and take the pressure off. After you get started, you'll develop your own tricks.

Planning in Analog

When you start the planning process, take the time to think through all the different phases of the plan by sketching, erasing, and generally scribbling if you want to. Also, involving the sense of touch in your process can help stimulate creative thinking.

Michael J. Gelb, in his book, *Innovate Like Edison,* talks about how Thomas Edison used the visual thinking process to propel his ideas forward. He used what Gelb calls *Kaleidoscope Thinking* to become one of the greatest inventors in history. With a kaleidoscope, you see completely different patterns by simply making one change.

That's how Edison would work. He would take things apart and put them back together with added innovations. This would help him see how to progress. You can do the same by sketching on a writing surface or creating separate elements that you can reassemble. You may do this with an idea map or other tool, but the key is to get the ideas out so you can see them and develop new patterns.

When you have something out on paper, you can transfer it to your prezi canvas. You can start anywhere; the trick is to use the analog planning you've done to make the process of creating something tangible, more comfortable for you.

Setting the Stage

If you're staring at a blank Prezi screen and can't get started, I recommend you try an age-old artist's trick. The trick is to put something down (anything) to break the sight of a screen with nothing on it. Many artists deliberately make a mark with their pencil or draw a faint outline of something tiny in the corner of their canvas just so they've taken action.

If you pause and stare at the screen, you begin to hear that voice in the back of your head telling you how you're probably not up to the task. Or you'll become fearful about finishing on time. To banish these fears, add something to the Prezi canvas immediately.

Begin by adding the title of the presentation (even if you change it later) by double-clicking on the canvas. Put your name down and perhaps your logo or other necessary elements.

Use the Transformation Zebra to move them around and make them large. Just take up space. Now you're ready to continue.

Looking at Examples

If you're looking for something to get you started, you don't have to look any further than the Explore tab found at http://prezi.com/explore. In this gallery, subscribers have placed examples of their work. Any prezi created with a Free account is automatically published in the Explore area. Users with Enjoy or Pro licenses can decide whether to make their prezis public. You can find an amazing array of topics, and you can search for something specific.

One of the great features of the Prezi Explore page is the ability to copy a prezi that has been designated as reusable. This prezi can then become the foundation of your own presentation.

Following are three ways you can benefit from doing this:

- **Reuse graphics.** If someone has granted you the right to use a few clever graphics, that saves you the effort required to find something that really works. It could be something they've hand-drawn or perhaps something they created in third-party design software like Photoshop. When you start using Prezi consistently, you'll find that you focus more on using graphics to tell your story than you did with slide programs. So you'll be on the lookout for storytelling visuals.

- **Reuse movement.** After you have looked at prezis for a while, you'll be able to see what makes a presentation really great. Not only do you need text and graphics to tell an interesting story, but you also need to use movement as well.

  Some people have a knack for being able to create a Path in Prezi that really makes an impact. Not only can you study their work, but you can also reuse the Paths they've created with your own ideas. They may have a method of rotating something or showing a detail within the big picture that you like and can repurpose.

- **Rework ideas.** If you see a prezi on a topic that's related to one you're working on, you can break it down and see how it's presented. Obviously, your prezi will be different based on your own specifics, but it can be instructive to see how the ideas are laid out on the canvas.

Choosing a Potential Layout

Just as you would use metaphors in your writing, you can use visual metaphors in Prezi. Contrary to what you may think, the layout of your prezi in a big-picture view can communicate as much as the details. Built into the Prezi software is the ability to zoom completely out to see the whole and to zoom in to view the details. Remember to take advantage of this feature.

How does this relate to the layout you choose? Everyone in your audience can benefit from seeing how separate ideas fit into a larger context. By using a metaphor to represent the big picture, you instantly help your viewers gain clarity.

For example, suppose you're proposing a new way to meet sales goals. You may want to use a sailing metaphor and show a map of a regatta and the tools to win the race (wind, current, and so on). This metaphor doesn't require you to reach for the cheesy clipart — you can create something thoughtful. The idea is to use your ability to display both the larger context and the individual pieces in Prezi to communicate more effectively.

The benefits of using visual metaphors are as follows:

- ✔ **It enhances emotion.** By invoking emotion with your metaphor, you're helping your ideas to be remembered.
- ✔ **It simplifies an explanation.** Metaphors make ideas easier to understand.
- ✔ **It persuades.** By associating something positive with your idea, you help people to view your idea favorably.
- ✔ **It provides a common language.** Everyone is on the same page and can contribute equally.

Uploading Some Media

Although I don't recommend that you plan your presentation directly in Prezi as you get started, I do think it would be helpful to add some media to the canvas. By this I mean you can upload a couple of graphic elements that you know you want to be included in the presentation. This addition personalizes the canvas and gives you an idea about how the elements will look in the finished presentation.

You have lots of media to choose from, including the following:

- ✔ Story illustrations
- ✔ Word art
- ✔ Custom-designed keywords and phrases
- ✔ Metaphors
- ✔ Mind Maps
- ✔ Flowcharts, graphs, statistics
- ✔ Maps and timelines
- ✔ Personas
- ✔ Photos and stock images
- ✔ Hand-drawn images

> ✔ Animation and video with audio
>
> ✔ Scrapbooking material

You can see that this is quite an extensive list. Just choose one or two things to get yourself started. The key to eliminating a blank screen is to put anything on it that has meaning to you. Then you can proceed to add things with more confidence.

Thinking Up Questions Your Presentation Will Answer

If you're having a hard time staring at the empty screen, one way to get a presentation started is to create a little cheat sheet on the canvas itself. You want to do something that makes you take action. Think of it as putting a sticky note on a physical canvas. You can type in the questions and help clarify in your own mind what the purpose of the presentation is.

The process of thinking about these questions will get you started. The secret to creating your presentation is to use the plans you've created on paper and then to transfer something onto the canvas that has a purpose.

Go to the Write bubble and create a container using the Frames tool (perhaps the Bracket) and write three questions your presentation will answer within the Frame. This helps you focus on the task. Then, as you answer these questions with your content, you can delete them just as you would any sticky note.

Describing the Hero

When starting a presentation, most people give short shrift to the hero of the story. What usually happens is that they spend a lot of time getting their facts and figures together and throw in some thin story line at the end if at all. Don't let this happen to you. Begin by thinking about the ideas and the story line that can make people care about your presentation.

By filling your blank canvas in this way, you move your presentation forward in a useful way. Firstly, it helps you focus on your story. Secondly it makes your presentation stronger.

The difference between a great presentation and a poor one is the ability of the speaker to connect with the audience. Does anyone care about what she's saying? Does it matter to the lives of those listening? Not every presentation lends itself to great drama, but every presentation can evoke emotions.

In a business presentation, there's always supporting information that you'll want to include. The question becomes this: How do you temper that with a story that will make people pay attention?

Is it the pain of losing market share to competitors? How does that translate to something tangible? Are you faced with layoffs if things don't improve? That certainly increases the stakes. Can you tell the story of an employee who will lose his job if the group doesn't rally and fix things? Or it can be something funny or heartwarming. The idea is to break through the boredom to another level of attention.

By forcing yourself to write down some details about the hero on the blank canvas, you're taking steps to make your presentation a strong one. I talk about this more extensively in Chapter 7.

Adding a Quote

Everyone loves a great quote. When trying to fill a blank screen, one option is to pick a quote and put it up on the Prezi canvas. It will help to remove the feeling of inaction, and you'll be on your way.

You have two choices as to what to use. You can put up a quote from the material you will use in your presentation, or you can pick a quote from another source that inspires you when you see it. Either way, the quote is there to serve a distinct purpose. Some people like to have a quote sitting near their work tables, but instead of your work table, you might put it on the canvas to help you over the first hurdle.

Some of the benefits of using quotes are as follows:

- Understanding something that was always a mystery before
- Inspiring others
- Learning about how others see the world
- Amusing people

If nothing comes to mind, you can always type **All things are possible.** That should at least get you on your way.

Using Keywords to Describe the Problem

One of the things you want to use Prezi for is to help you avoid adding big blocks of text. To get started filling in the canvas, you may want to look at your content and see what keywords or phrases come to mind. This is not for search optimization; it's to give your audience major concepts or ideas to pay attention to.

When using Prezi, typing in long sentences is not the best way to present an idea. You want to distill the information so that audience members can see and respond to it emotionally. By developing keywords that have different sizes and formats, you're making them memorable.

To create formatted text in Prezi, you can easily use the Write bubble to place text on the canvas. Then you can use the Transformation Zebra accessed from the Write bubble to move, size, and rotate it. You can also create text in other design programs and add it to the canvas.

After you've started developing the main ideas in your presentation, you'll be on your way to filling the canvas with meaningful content. It will also help you focus on choosing the best visuals for the job.

Some of the benefits of using keywords are as follows:

- ✔ Quickly conveys meaning
- ✔ Is easier to remember
- ✔ Helps you understand the context
- ✔ Aids the presenter in creating better visuals

Creating a Timeline

One helpful thing you can do to fill your blank canvas is to create a timeline. Timelines are great visual tools that can easily be created with Prezi in a variety of ways.

When deciding what the content of the timeline should be, you have two choices:

- ✔ **You can develop a timeline to create the presentation itself.** That might go a long way to making you feel less anxious about the task ahead. You can put in deadlines for each of the steps to complete the presentation and make sure that you've accounted for everything that needs to be done. Then you can work backward and see how much time you can allot to each task. This is always worth doing whether you use a timeline or not.

✔ **The other option is to create a timeline for the information in the presentation.** By constructing a timeline, you can begin to see the story line in context. You may not have thought about your subject along a time continuum. Remember that a timeline can be as short or as long as you need it to be. You're using it to visualize time in a way that makes it tangible. Perhaps just getting the material out of your head and onto a timeline would be valuable. You don't have to include it in the finished presentation. For example, if your presentation is about something that has evolved over several years, the audience might find a timeline useful to understand when things changed.

One of the simplest ways to create a timeline in Prezi is to select the Shapes tool and use the Arrow to draw one long straight line across the canvas. Then you can put items along the line using a highlighter, a Frame tool, or anything that suits your design.

Some benefits of using a timeline are as follows:

✔ Provides a common language with which to plan

✔ Shows the big picture and the details

✔ Shows where along the continuum the major events took place

✔ Demonstrates history and how it relates to events today

Chapter 15

Ten Things You Should Know about Visual Thinking

In This Chapter

▶ Seeing with your eyes and your mind's eye

▶ Understanding that not being artistic is not a deal breaker

▶ Persuading is easier with visuals

*M*ost people didn't grow up with an interest in thinking visually. Visual thinking wasn't discussed in school unless you were studying to be a professional artist. The concept has really come into its own in the past few years because of two things. The first is technology. Tools are available that make it easier for people to express themselves visually. The second is advances in neuroscience. Scientists are finding ways to look at what happens when the human brain encounters information.

This may sound counterintuitive because visual thinking is first and foremost a process. You see something with your mind's eye and can draw a representation of it without requiring any special tools beyond a pencil. But there's much more happening under the surface. This chapter focuses on the importance of visual thinking in your everyday life.

It's the Ability to See with Both the Eyes and the Mind's Eye

People use visuals to represent information. The information can be real or in your mind. When you "see" intangible information (like an idea), the phrase for the experience is that you're seeing it with your mind's eye. Of course, this is an abstract concept. Your mind doesn't have eyes that see inside your head. Interestingly, what scientists know about how humans see is related to information that they've gained in the last ten years about the study of the brain. New advances have permitted scientists to gain great insights about how people process information and factor in emotions.

Following are several major findings:

- ✔ **The main purpose for sight is to alert us to danger.** Sight is a survival mechanism that has been handed down through time to prevent enemies from harming you.

- ✔ **The brain seeks patterns and is dominantly visual.** People see in pictures, never linear outlines.

- ✔ **With the mind's eye, people see associations and make connections.** The brain processes information by making connections and associations to things.

- ✔ **The best way to represent something is to use text, numbers, and visuals together.** This marries linguistic and nonlinguistic skills.

Also be aware that the brain doesn't report what you see accurately. Contrary to what some may think, you don't see a 1:1 representation of the world around you.

According to Carl Purcell in "Drawing With Your Artists Brain," the brain distorts information in at least four ways:

- ✔ It uses previously stored data to build new models.

- ✔ It uses symbols to represent something rather than seeing the actual item.

- ✔ It creates new symbols that aren't exact but are easy to store.

- ✔ It lets surface details represent the whole of the form.

If you understand these facts, you can make your presentation more in tune with the way the mind understands visual representations. For example, use a symbol instead of a sentence to make your idea more memorable.

It Helps People Learn Faster and Remember Better

Most of the school systems around the world are using visual mapping techniques as a way to help students learn faster and remember more. The origins of such tools as Mind Maps were created to help teachers facilitate learning.

People learn faster using visual tools because of the following:

- ✔ Using visual thinking, humans can organize, analyze, and clarify thoughts more effectively.

- ✔ Creating a visual map during lectures instead of reams of notes facilitates understanding and retention.

✔ Using colors on your maps create an emotional impact that makes things memorable.

✔ Using symbols to represent things is a better way to take notes because people are able to remember symbols more easily than blocks of text.

It Includes Sketches, Doodles, Images, Photos, and Other Pictures

When you think about using images to explain your ideas, you probably leap to the conclusion that you need to have a beautifully finished rendering of something that looks exactly as it does in real life. Banish this notion. This is neither required or in some instances even desirable. What you want to do is explain something quickly in a visual form so that others can recognize and understand it.

If you're creating a presentation and you have the time to select great images, that's wonderful. But the need for highly stylized graphics has more to do with people's expectations than anything else. If people are paying to hear you or are part of a big conference, take the time to dress things up. You're sending a message that you respect the audience and want to make your presentation look professional. Does it make your presentation more understandable? Maybe, but it depends on the content.

Your goal should be to communicate the idea in the best way you can. If you're conducting a business meeting and you have a great idea about how to move the desks in the office to enhance productivity, no one cares whether the desks are perfectly drawn. Try to remember this when you work. The focus should be on the idea, not the quality of the drawing.

It Helps with Procrastination and Increases Productivity

Everyone is affected by procrastination to some degree. If it's a big problem, it affects both your work and your home life. People generally put off doing things for all sorts of reasons. Most of the reasons involve fear. You may be procrastinating because of one or more of the following fears:

✔ Fear of failure

✔ Fear of being bored by tasks other people make us do

✔ Fear of being wrong

✔ Fear of things changing for the worse

Fear is aroused in people when they imagine themselves taking an action whose outcome is not assured. It's called the flight-or-flight response. Our ancestors experienced this, too. If they felt threatened, they would either flee the situation or stand and fight to maintain the status quo. Today you're less likely to run into a charging rhino like they did, but the fear still feels the same and you want to escape.

To overcome this flight response, you need to trick yourself into not responding to the fear and avoiding the task. When you use visual thinking techniques, your mind is focusing on something visual that is not threatening. Studies have shown that by using visual thinking to take small steps forward, people can tamp the fear down and move ahead. Sound strange? Let me explain how it works.

Suppose you're afraid of starting to plan a business presentation. Normally, your first response would be to visualize yourself stumbling through it, and you'd feel fear.

If you were to use a visual thinking technique instead, you would find the following:

- ✔ **It's easier to get started.** You would begin by focusing on creating a map of all the ideas you want to cover. In this way, you're making it easier to get started, which is usually a big barrier. So you've gotten past that hurdle.

- ✔ **You don't have to capture ideas in a linear fashion.** Working on the map mimics the way your brain works. You aren't using a hierarchical structure, so the ideas come faster. Unlike an outline, the map doesn't require you to add ideas that way. You can quickly get lots of ideas out to look at.

- ✔ **Organization is quicker.** When you have all the ideas out on the map, you find that it's easier to organize them and see patterns. You can group them and discover a narrative.

- ✔ **It's easier to plan your presentation.** You've gotten to the point where you are able to develop your story line.

Idea mapping helps you move through your procrastination because you don't focus on the fear.

It Affects the Ability to Understand an Environment

You brain works by mapping your environment so that you can interact with it. Such mundane activities as walking into a room and flipping on a light switch would be impossible if you didn't have a way for your brain to organize your surroundings. Researchers have determined that over 70 percent of the information that comes into the brain is visual.

Without conscious thought, you can navigate the world around you. The key to understanding this is that your activities are not linear. Your brain doesn't take things in or get them out in a linear fashion. The Internet has made this type of thinking available by using hyperlinks and graphics. You're free to follow information in your own way instead of in a step-by-step order.

To navigate your environment, you use maps of all kinds. This includes charts, graphs, symbols, maps, timelines, and diagrams. But maps do more than this. They help you make sense of not only the physical world but also your "mental" world. Using your ability to alternate between the concrete (like roads and trees) and the abstract (like a hydraulic system), maps are a mainstay for survival.

Maps help people to

- Find the closest distance between point A and point B
- Simplify data (a lot of information in a small space)
- Find patterns
- Remember information about surroundings
- Understand interdependencies and relationships of items

The next time you need to explain something for a presentation, try using a map of some sort, and you'll find the information easier to understand.

It Helps People Solve Problems

Visual thinking can help you solve problems because it helps your brain work the way it wants to. If you were to follow a typical problem-solving process using visuals, you might do the following:

1. **Brainstorm to get all the ideas out that you can think of.**

   To make it even easier, you may wish to create *artifacts,* which are small units of information on paper or other surfaces with an idea on each (for example, a sticky note for each idea).

2. **Look at all the ideas and begin to organize them.**

   You may begin to see patterns or other ways to classify the ideas.

3. **Build a model or structure to show how things fit together to solve the problem.**

4. **Iterate until you have it in the solution form you want.**

   When you get it into the format you want (for example, as a presentation), you can continue to refine it as you get feedback.

The benefits of using visual techniques to problem solve include the following:

✔ Get ideas out to make them visible to yourself and others.

✔ Make better connections; see patterns.

✔ Access your right and left brain together for more creative output.

✔ When you work in a nonlinear way, you're working the way your brain works.

It Helps People Be More Empathetic

Humans connect with things that they can relate to. If something feels unfamiliar, people are likely to avoid it. When you're trying to stand in someone else's shoes, visual thinking is a very useful tool.

A common tool used in business to help marketers understand their customers is the use of *personas.* A persona is a profile of one of your niche customers. It's rare that a company only has one niche to sell to, but not so rare that they have only identified one.

How does this relate to visual thinking? To create a persona, you begin by culling demographics about the person, their marital status, their income level, and so on. Next you detail psychographics, their motivations for buying. You may also want to pick a photo to represent the customer.

All of this is done to firmly fix your customer in your mind's eye. Similarly, as you plan your presentation, think about how an audience member would receive the information you're presenting. It helps you focus on the facts and not get distracted by cool ideas that have nothing to do with your presentation.

It Helps People Collaborate More Effectively

Prezi makes it easy to collaborate with others. It has a built-in tool to help you set up groups and update them as necessary. As a visual thinking tool, it lets you get all the benefits of using visual thinking in groups.

Visual thinking in groups enhances your ability to do the following:

✔ **Understand each other better using a common language:** When everyone is using the same visual terms to describe something, it becomes easer to clarify and understand another's position.

✔ **Understand your role in relationship to the group:** It's very important for everyone in a group to understand what role they play in relation to others. When people understand how their part of the project enhances the whole, there's a feeling of teamwork and a closer bond. It's the faster way to get everyone on the same page.

✔ **Shortens group meetings:** There are fewer disagreements and misunderstandings when everyone sees the goal clearly mapped out. Timelines and other production tools help everyone get to the finish line.

✔ **Those with a right- or left-brain preference can all participate equally:** Ideas from either group can be added to visual maps with equal value.

It Doesn't Require Artistic Skills

Do you think that you can't be an effective visual thinker because you don't have artistic skills? This section breaks that idea down into its component parts so you can see why it's wrong. Consider the following:

✔ **Visual thinking doesn't require artistic skills.** Visual thinking happens in your brain. Your ability to draw a great sketch has nothing to do with how well you can think visually. It's estimated that 60 percent of the population are visual thinkers. This means that their preferred mode of learning is to visualize. It doesn't mean they're practicing artists.

✔ **You're a better artist than you give yourself credit for.** You may not have the talent of DaVinci, but you can draw better than you think you can. When you were a young child, you had no fear about being able to draw, paint, and be creative. As you got older, you were held to a very high standard. This caused you to stop trying.

Betty Edwards's book, *Drawing on the Right Side of the Brain*, is a classic work. It demonstrates that you can advance your drawing skills quickly. One exercise she uses is the act of drawing something upside down. When you turn an object upside down, you become unable to retreat to what you think you see. You eye perceives the item in a new way. Your drawing of it is usually significantly better than it would be if you drew it right side up. Try it.

If you want to explain something using a picture, you're perfectly capable of making a sketch that would do the job. If you practice, you'll get even better. The main thing is to not be held back by your fears.

Its Use Will Expand Due to the Graphical Internet

In 1994, I started working for AOL. One of the reasons for AOL's instant popularity was its graphical nature. When people signed up for the service, they didn't have to deal with command lines or know anything about the operating system (DOS!). Everything was presented with graphical elements, and features were organized for ease of use. Some programmers pejoratively called it the "Internet with training wheels." That was precisely why it was such a big hit. Not everyone wanted an avocation as a computer programmer.

Thanks to Apple and others, the importance of graphical interfaces has grown to the point where people can create their own great-looking Web sites. With very little experience, they can use tools like WordPress to quickly put up a site. This graphical trend will continue to be an even greater factor in the future. With the advent of tools like the iPad, the need for standard form desktop computers will diminish. Computers will serve as creation and consumption tools in ways you can't even imagine.

Chapter 16

Ten Tips for Mind Mapping with Prezi

In This Chapter

▶ Expanding the scope of and sequences within Mind Maps

▶ Enhancing the visual aspects of your Mind Maps

▶ Improving collaboration using Mind Maps

▶ Discovering better communication through Mind Maps

Mind Mapping is a tool used to encourage visual thinking and creativity. It allows you to see what you're thinking by making your ideas visible. You can use Mind Maps for all types of activities, including solving problems, planning projects, taking meeting notes, and collecting information on your favorite hobby.

A *Mind Map* is a visual thinking tool that allows you to get your ideas out where you can see and manipulate them. It's easier to work with ideas when they're visible to you. You're then free to brainstorm and add new ideas without having to hold everything in your mind at once. When you put your thoughts on paper or canvas, your mind begins to see patterns and make associations you would never find without the visual input.

This wide variety of uses requires Mind Maps to hold lots of complex information. When you use Prezi to create your Mind Maps, you can dramatically increase their effectiveness at presenting such information by taking advantage of Prezi's most powerful features. For example, Prezi enables you to zoom in to examine the detail of a Mind Map and zoom out to view any patterns and get the big picture.

Chapter 10 gives you an overview of creating a Mind Map with Prezi. And in this chapter, I offer you some tips for using prezis to take your Mind Maps to the next level.

Expanding Your Mind Maps' Dimensions

Mind Maps allow you to see the big picture in two dimensions. Prezi enhances the big picture capability by giving you an unlimited canvas on which to develop your big picture. With Prezi, you aren't limited by the length and width of traditional paper, presentation slides, or whiteboards. Use Prezi's scrolling and zooming features to expand the scope of your Mind Map.

Presenting Multiple Layers of Detail

Mind Maps help you see information in chunks and allow you to depict several levels of detail on one screen or sheet of paper. With Prezi, you can drill down to multiple layers of details in a way that incorporates space, movement, and time. Prezi tools help you present the details of your Mind Maps as follows:

- **By offering flexible navigation:** With the Path tool, you can show the details by navigating directly to each one in any order that you like. You can repeat the process for emphasis or change the center of your viewing area and drill down to display other relevant information. In addition to using the Path tool, you can use the zoom feature to show a grouping of details and then zoom in closer to focus on each one.

- **By visually depicting the relationship of details:** The Frames tool gives you three choices of containers that you can put around your details: brackets, circles, and rectangles. By varying the size and angle of these containers, you make a visual statement about its difference or importance to the rest of the material. You can also nest containers so that you instantly see their relationship to other details based on their relative positions in the space. The Zebra tool can also help depict relationships: With it, you can reposition and enlarge the containers, move items to the front and back, and place them at an angle.

Demonstrating Your Nonlinear Thinking

The Mind Maps you create with Prezi can help you capture ideas and information to present in a nonlinear fashion. The unlimited space of the Prezi canvas facilitates the capture.

Start with a central idea, type in lots of other ideas and supporting information, upload media, and let your mind take your map where it wants to go.

When you have all the ideas you want on a page, you can use the Path tool to display them to your audience in sequence or mix them up in some other way. The key idea here is that the Path tool can help you easily rearrange and display your ideas.

Enhancing the Experience with Visuals

Mind Maps use visuals as a way to evoke emotions and boost memorization. With Prezi, you can use visuals of all kinds to greatly enhance the effect. Presenting visuals is where Prezi really excels. Your ability to be creative and make your Mind Map stand out is virtually limitless. Combining unusual elements together can make them unforgettable.

Using the Insert tool, you can add a variety of images. Conversion to a PDF format allows you to use files from other popular design software programs and PowerPoint and Excel. Try videos, stock photos, images, hand-drawn sketches, and Web links — anything you can put into a digital format can be put into a prezi.

Mind Maps haven't traditionally incorporated sound, but you can add audio files to your prezi. Multisensory maps will definitely stimulate your creativity. You can incorporate sound files by uploading them with the Insert tool and using the recommended FLV workaround. Developers are working on creating a direct way to deal with sound — by the time you read this book, it may already be in place.

Adding Dramatic Portrayals of Space

Mind Maps are limited in the way they portray spatial differences. With Prezi, spatial relationships can be demonstrated in several dramatic ways. You aren't limited by the boundaries of a static page. You have the capability to use time, space, and movement as follows:

- **By varying the time between items being presented:** Using the timing interval function, you can vary the screens to display in 4-, 10-, or 20-second intervals. To do this, open your prezi, click the Show bubble and then click and hold the right arrow in the bottom-right corner of the screen. Up pop the three choices for you to select — 4, 10, or 20 seconds per screen. Repetition should also be used to vary timing. Going back to the same item again in your path or showing almost the same item with a minor variation will signal a time shift.

✓ **By changing how items are displayed:** Using the Path tool, click first on the center of the item. (This makes the center area the focus of the path.) Then click the item itself to zoom in on it. This gives you both a wide angle and an in-depth look so you see the same item from different perspectives.

✓ **By moving the distance between items in a group:** With the Zebra tool, you can first zoom in on each item after you have placed them in a random pattern. Just the unequal amount of space will be noted as unique movement.

Extending Understanding through Color

Mind Maps encourage the use of colors. With Prezi, you can use colors for emphasis and understanding. It's recommended that you use at least three different colors in your map to stimulate your brain's cortex (the thinking part). Fewer than three colors appear monotonous to your audience, and limiting your palette in this way won't stimulate your own creativity either.

From the Colors & Fonts bubble , you can choose preselected fonts in one of several styles available with Prezi software. At present, you cannot select your own font colors. To work around this, you can use the Insert tool to upload text images with the font color you want to introduce. You can also add color to your presentation by converting an image from another design program to a PDF.

To make a statement with colors, use the Zebra tool to place the same colors next to one another to form a group or tilt the text. For example, you can tilt every word that is red or make all blue words larger and a uniform size.

Communicating with Keywords

Mind Maps use keywords to enhance memorization. With Prezi, you can also use keywords to emphasize and communicate importance. One of the rules of Mind Mapping is to use keywords to convey major ideas instead of using long sentences or paragraphs. One- or two-word phrases are easier to remember than a page full of notes. Using Prezi, communicating with keywords can be done in the following ways:

✓ **Symbols and meaning:** One easy way to present your message is with the Insert tool. You can upload stylized text using all capital letters or all small letters to convey meaning. These also apply to symbols to help classify thoughts. Symbols replace keywords because of their ability to communicate ideas.

✔ **Visual comparison:** Comparing the size of words in relation to others also conveys meaning. Using the Zebra tool, you can make one phrase larger than the one next to it. By doing this, you're communicating the fact that you place more importance on the larger one.

✔ **Color and font choice:** When you start a prezi, you must choose a style. There are three fonts chosen by the developers corresponding to that choice at the time of this writing; by the time you read this, you may have more font options. These fonts are named Body, referring to body copy; Head, referring to headlines; and Strong, which is text recommended for emphasis. You can use them to suit your own needs or as the developer suggests.

✔ **Tilt or zoom:** The unlimited canvas provides you with a limitless way to communicate emotions. Using the Zebra tool, you can place the text wherever you choose, increase or decrease its size, and rotate it 360 degrees. These options give you a great deal of flexibility to make an impact with each keyword you use. By using the Path tool, you can also zoom right into the words more than once for emphasis.

Viewing Mind Maps to See What's Missing

Mind Maps help you see what's missing. Human minds are hard-wired to want completion. Mind Maps take advantage of the brain's need to fill in the gaps and create a completed whole. They spread ideas or concepts out in front of you with the gaps clearly visible. You find that you feel more comfortable when an idea has something attached to it that explains or completes it. Using the need for closure is a great way to spur thinking.

Another important aspect of Mind Map creation is the need to let your mind rest and then come back to the map with fresh eyes. You can often get a great boost of inspiration by leaving the ideas and coming back to them when your mind is rested. This incubation period is recommended by Buzan and practiced by most good mappers. This enhances the what's-missing factor but also encourages new thoughts. While you're doing other things, your mind is finding and making connections for you.

With Prezi, the added zooming assists you in creating closure. Using the Path tool, you can zoom into ideas that need completion to help yourself or your audience make that connection. You can also enhance the connections by putting boundaries around words using Frames or Shapes. With the Frame tool, you can choose one of three container styles to group the incomplete idea. Or if you prefer, you can use the Line tool from within Shapes and draw a thin or thick line around it.

Recognizing the Patterns in Mind Maps

Mind Maps allow you to see patterns. With Prezi, you can represent those visual patterns more effectively by zooming in and out. Visual processing is done by seeing the parts as a cohesive whole. Calendars and geographic maps are two examples of tools people use to organize information to make it more useful and to get a perspective on how things fit together. With a Mind Map, you're also organizing information in a way that makes it easy to understand and remember.

You make it easy to see patterns in the map when you zoom out to the big picture. Prezi gives you the ability to show these patterns to others. The value of this is that it not only makes the pattern clear; it exposes bad patterns as well.

Use the Path tool to zoom out and then back in when trying to show patterns. You can do this several times throughout the presentation to make the pattern clear and help it stand out. Use the Line tool from within Shapes to draw around the actual pattern for your audience. You can use it to make boundaries clear. With the Insert tool, you can color-code them as well.

Collaborating for Consensus

Mind Maps help you get everyone on the same page. Using Prezi to collaborate on maps makes it easy for everyone to understand their role. Mind Maps are a great collaboration tool for two major reasons:

✔ The first is that they allow people to contribute ideas regardless of their thinking mode. All ideas are welcome, whether they use a right- or left-brain bias.

✔ The second reason is that it makes it very clear who is responsible for which part of the map and how that fits into the whole project. If anyone has an objection or concern, he can voice it as the map is being built.

The ability to use Prezi to play back with timing intervals provides you with a great collaboration tool absent from most mapping software. You can take full advantage of the fact that prezis can operate like a movie with a beginning, a middle, and an end. If your viewer hasn't participated in the building of the Mind Map, it may be hard for her to see exactly what the creator had in mind.

Using the timing intervals, you can have your viewer Autoplay your map in a way you couldn't if you were sending a one or two-dimensional map for others to see in your absence. By setting the timing intervals, you can have your viewer play your map back in the sequence you want — saving time and removing the fear that your presentation will be misunderstood.

Prezi brings out the best in Mind Mapping. It extends the boundaries and gives you capabilities you don't have with other software. As you become more skilled at using Prezi you will see how uploading effective media and movement can bring your ideas to life.

Make sure that you don't clutter up your map just because the capability is there. Like with any tool, prezis can be overdone. Be merciless with your content and remove anything that doesn't support your vision. As with any presentation, less is more.

Chapter 17

Ten Worst Things to Do with Prezi

*U*sing Prezi is an adventure. You get to rethink presentations and let creativity dictate your outcome. Along with this new freedom is the need to explore and find out what works for you.

This chapter looks at some of the mistakes you might make when getting started with Prezi. I've listed some of the things you want to avoid as you go along. There's really no big mistake that you make that can't be corrected. As you become more comfortable with your new tools, you'll quickly see how to avoid them. This list will help prevent you from dragging old habits with you. Out with the old, in with the new!

Keep an Old Mindset

The only requirement you have when you start using Prezi is to open your mind to a new way of thinking about presentations. If you try to shoehorn a previously created slide presentation into a prezi, you will be disappointed.

Slide presentations are flat. They have no dimension or contrasts. When you create presentations in Prezi, you need to break all the pieces apart and think about grouping them in new more effective ways.

Imagine a dense slide that has five bullet points on it. With Prezi, you can take each point and give it its own space, dimension, and timing. This is a very different way of presenting data. You can use Frames as containers to group things instead of showing a list. In these groups can be numbers, words, and graphics. You can make the best use of each type of element.

With Prezi, you can focus your story line in a very precise way. You can zoom in and out when the content dictates it.

For example, Prezi provides you with the ability to demonstrate the following contrasts along a continuum:

✔ Small to large

✔ Close to farther away

✔ Rotated to straight

Prezi also provides a different kind of experience for you as the presenter. You aren't moving in a linear fashion from slide to slide. You have the freedom to move in any order that makes sense to you to make your case. Nothing is stacked up in a row waiting its turn to be seen. This gives you the ability to use comparisons when appropriate and to answer questions more fully.

Lose Track of Your Story

To create an effective presentation, you need to create a story line. Prezi provides you with all the tools you need to develop and show a great story. If you start with something that resembles a story and then you abandon it, your presentation will be weak and confusing. When presenting, it's help-ful to remember the old sales saying, "A confused mind always says no." If you're trying to persuade your audience, clarity is key.

But, you may find the term *story,* as it relates to business, confusing. You don't remember hearing a business *story* — or do you? All the conversations that you exchange with customers, vendors, and colleagues about your work contain stories. It's your job to pull them out and examine them for interest-ing ones worth telling. For example, telling how your tech support personnel saved a client from crashing and losing all their data is a compelling story. This is covered in more detail in Chapter 7.

When you're constructing a story with business content, make sure you follow this seven-point plan:

1. **Devise a plot that demonstrates the problem.**

   Pick a simple plot that doesn't require Sherlock Holmes to solve. Most likely you will choose a challenge plot that requires an overcoming of the odds. Another might be a creativity plot where someone invents a product or innovates a process.

2. **Pick a worthy hero for your story.**

   Luckily for you, you know how the story turns out so you can pick a strong hero. It could be the product, a person, or anything that solves the problem.

3. **Create a hook that is memorable.**

   Don't be lazy about creating a hook for your story. A hook has to be something exciting, puzzling, or otherwise stimulating to the audience. It isn't that hard to create one; you just have to make the effort.

4. **Show the constraints at play.**

   This is where you'll be well versed. In every presentation is a host of reasons why something is being held back — money, people, ideas. Make sure you fully explain these.

5. **Illustrate how the problem can be solved.**

   For your audience to believe your solution, you need to show how using your method to solve it makes the most sense. Be authentic and humble. If you say it's the best solution ever devised, you'll regret it when unforeseen events arise. (Refer to Step 4.)

6. **Present a solution.**

   Finally you get to the solution. If you've done a thorough job of following each of the preceding steps, you should have a winning presentation.

7. **Create a call to action.**

   You gave this presentation for a reason. You want your audience to take some action. It may be to hire you, promote you, or donate money to your cause. Make sure you let the audience members know what you want them to do next.

Use Weak Clipart

Prezi is first and foremost a visual tool. It would be a real waste of a great tool to provide only the weakest of graphic elements. Forget what you've done in the past with graphics that are cheap representations of weak concepts. You can find or create anything visual you want and upload it to Prezi as either a PDF or in one of Prezi's accepted formats. In a section a bit later on, "Neglect to Use the Built-In Design Tools," I discuss the use of the built-in design tools. Here I talk about uploading art from other sources.

For example, you can easily add the following:

- ✔ Video, YouTube videos, and Jing videos
- ✔ Animation
- ✔ Personal and stock photos
- ✔ Word art
- ✔ Charts, graphs, and maps
- ✔ Hand-drawn images
- ✔ Spreadsheets

Omit the Use of Movement

One of Prezi's most popular features is its ability to tell a story using movement. The first time a person sees a prezi, she is immediately attracted to the sense that they're dynamic. Rather than seeing just a flat slide, she's brought in close to items and far away from others. She sees items rotate and pull out for a big picture view.

These tools make prezis come alive with movement:

- ✔ **Smart Zooming:** This is Prezi's special ability to predetermine how close or far to zoom into an item on the canvas. The viewer will see an item zoomed into or out of.

- ✔ **Rotating:** You can tilt or rotate an item on the canvas using the Transformation Zebra. When you are in Show mode and you click that item, the viewer will see the screen zoom in to it and straighten it.

In addition, you can create the sense of a more dimensional presentation using either of the following:

- ✔ **Web links:** You can embed a Web link directly onto Prezi's canvas. When you click that link, the Web page opens up in a browser. When you're finished displaying the page, you can close it and continue on with your presentation.

- ✔ **Grouping of elements:** By grouping elements, you can get different effects when you zoom into them. If you create a Path number by clicking the container, the screen will zoom to the center of the group. If you create a Path number directly on an element in the group, the screen zooms in to the item itself. Remember this when you are considering the movement in your presentation.

In the later section, "Neglect to Use the Built-In Design Tools," I talk about the other major tools that give Prezi its unique personality. That is the creation of a Path and the ability to set timing to it.

Miss Out on Sharing Presentations

Prezis are meant to be shared. Of course, you don't have to share them — you can use them to create Mind Maps or other problem-solving tools— but Prezi makes it easy to send your prezis around the world with the click of a mouse button.

Don't miss out on sharing your prezis using any of the following:

- **Invite editors:** Prezi provides you with the ability to invite editors as you need them. You can collaborate with work teams or friends and family.

- **E-mail:** Prezi also has a built-in tool that allows you to easily send prezis via e-mails. You can also set them up to protect your privacy by keeping them private.

- **Web sites and blogs:** You can embed any public prezi on a Web site or blog by copying the HTML embed code provided when you click the Embed link under your prezi screen. Paste the code into the HTML source code for your blog or site. Then publish it as you normally would.

- **Social networks:** You can use the published URL to put a link in any Tweet or Facebook page you want.

- **Prezi Explore tab:** If you have a Free license, your prezi is public from the start, and it is automatically placed in the Prezi Explore tab. If you have the Enjoy or Pro license, you need to make it public first, and then it shows up in the Explore tab.

Neglect to Use the Built-In Design Tools

Prezi provides lots of built-in design tools in addition to being able to add designs from third-party programs. Make sure to explore and become comfortable with these tools, including the following:

- **Styles:** These styles provide you with the font colors and background styles for your prezi.

- **Write bubble:** From here, you can add text and format it. You just have to double-click on the canvas when the Write bubble is open, and you can add any text you want.

- **Transformation Zebra:** Also accessed from the Write bubble, this tool gives you the ability to move, resize, and rotate any element you place on the canvas.

✔ **Shapes: Arrow, Line, Highlighter:** These are the Shapes tools that allow you to place preformed arrows, free form lines, and highlighting on your canvas.

✔ **Frames: Bracket, Circle, Rectangle, Hidden Frame:** These are the containers that you can put content in to group it more effectively.

Repurpose A Slide Show into Prezi without Making Revisions

You may be tempted to take something you've already created in a slide show program and convert it from a PDF right into a prezi. You may think you'll be saving time and effort. But you'll know immediately upon viewing it that you're missing all the great features that Prezi offers. You'll see a rotating set of slides that completely misses the point.

One of Prezi's greatest strengths is its ability to group and layer content. You can zoom into an image with some text, zoom out to a video, and then zoom back to a group of images. This is something you can't do with a static bunch of slides. Breaking up content and displaying it in a free form way enhances the message communicated.

Forget about the Prezi Community

The Prezi community is very active and likes to share its creations and ideas. You can find a wealth of examples on the Prezi Explore tab, and the numbers grow every day.

The value of the community includes the following:

✔ Being able to study prezis in the Explore tab for ideas about how to handle different topics

✔ Being able to take advantage of the prezis designated for reuse as a foundation to build your own

✔ Visiting the `http://twitter.com/Prezi` account to talk with others about new ideas and ways to develop new prezis

✔ Checking the `http://twitter.com/PreziSupport` account to find out about fixes to problems and new features

✔ Reading the Prezi blog to interact with influential users and explore how Prezis are growing in impact

✔ Sharing prezis on social media sites to develop new networks of interested people

✔ Visiting the Prezi Get Satisfaction tech support site to find out about the latest fixes and updates

Leave Out the Path

Are you afraid you'll lose the plot? Well, in the case of a presentation, I'm sure you've seen it happen. A presenter is moving along in his presentation, and a worried look appears on his face. Suddenly you realize that he has lost his place.

Has he already covered that topic? Is it coming up next? He quickly fumbles with his notes and finds his place. He apologizes and moves on. You breathe a sigh of relief. No one enjoys seeing a presenter in distress.

When you're using Prezi you won't have to worry about losing the story line if you do the following:

✔ **Set up a Path:** Prezi gives you the ability to set up a sequence of steps for your presentation to follow. Each step represents one screen view.

✔ **Add timing intervals:** If you're going to send a Prezi without a presenter, you can ask recipients to set up timing intervals for your prezi. They can set them at 4, 10, or 20 seconds per screen. This way when someone watches your prezi without you, he sees the proper timing.

Fail to Use Prezis for More Than Presentations

Software tools are always open to interpretation. Putting a digital storytelling tool in someone's hands opens up all kinds of great possibilities. Because Prezi is relatively new, people are still discovering clever uses for it.

Some additional business uses include the following:

✔ Business plans

✔ Mind Mapping

✔ Problem solving

✔ Training materials

✔ Resumes

✔ Artist portfolios

Some nonbusiness presentations include the following:

- ✔ Invitations
- ✔ Vacations
- ✔ Recipes
- ✔ Scrapbooking
- ✔ Hobbies and collections
- ✔ Photo albums

Appendix

Resources for Presenters

*P*resenting and persuading are activities that people do every day. Some presentations are more formal than others, but as the writer Robert Louis Stevenson said, "everybody lives by selling something." It may be an idea, a product, the need for a donation, or even the need for some attention. Everyone does it to get by.

Prezi For Dummies has everything you need to use Prezi to persuade and influence. Here in this appendix, I include references to sources for more information that you may find very useful.

With the explosion of digital storytelling on the Web, the nature of online presenting evolves day by day. In this chapter, I include resources that you can check out regularly to keep up-to-date on the evolving world of digital presenting.

Browsing Presentation and Storytelling Sites

Storytelling can take bits of information in your presentation and turn it into a powerful persuasion tool. Pieces of information should never be considered separately. I recommend that you find out as much as you can about how to create an effective business story. In the following list are several helpful blogs, sites, and books about the digital world of presenting and storytelling.

✔ **Presentation Zen Blog (www.presentationzen.com/presentation zen):** Garr Reynolds is well known to presenters around the world who care about great design. Make sure to check out all his different online sites for tips and information about developing and delivering professional presentations.

Check out his book *Presentation Zen* (New Riders).

✔ **Seth Godin (http://sethgodin.typepad.com):** I'm sure if you've been online for any length of time you've run across Seth Godin. He's an amazing resource for creative thinking and doing. If you read his blog, you'll get a never-ending supply of wisdom and good ideas. His thoughts on storytelling and permission marketing are classics. He's also a founder of Squidoo (www.squidoo.com), a site for everyday experts — that's everyone.

Check out his book *All Marketers are Liars* (Penguin).

✔ **Heath Brothers (http://heathbrothers.com):** The Heath Brothers, Chip and Dan, gained great fame for their wonderful book *Made to Stick*. It brought to light the really important concepts about making messages *sticky*. If you're interested in why storytelling is an integral part of presenting, you must read their work.

Check out their book *Made to Stick* (Random House).

✔ **Extreme Presentation Blog (http://extremepresentation.type-pad.com/blog):** This blog written by Dr. Andrew Abela is particularly useful to presenters because it takes a deep dive into creating successful complex presentations. His "Extreme Method" is detailed in his book.

Check out his book *Advanced Presentations by Design* (Pfeiffer).

✔ **Speaking about Presenting Blog (www.speakingaboutpresenting.com):** Olivia Mitchell's site, Speaking about Presenting, is a must-see for new and advanced presenters. She focuses on all the different aspects that go into making presentations memorable. You can find information on every topic related to presentations and becoming a confident speaker.

✔ **Beyond Bullet Points Blog (www.beyondbulletpoints.com/blog):** Although you may think this blog is only about slides, you'd be wrong. Cliff Atkinson provides wonderful presentation information about constructing stories and putting together a first-class presentation. He has also done some work on dealing with the *back channel,* which you'll definitely want to read. The back channel refers to the tweeting that takes place during a presentation. Sometimes the tweeters are watching from another location or they are at the location itself. The comments may be negative or positive, and the speaker needs to decide how to handle them.

Check out his book *The Backchannel* (New Riders).

✔ **Duarte Blog (`http://blog.duarte.com`):** Nancy Duarte's blog and her company focus on the art and science of presentations. She doesn't only focus on slides. She also covers a host of important topics and her book is a must-read if you want to understand what goes into creating compelling presentations.

Check out her book *Slideo:ology* (O'Reilly).

✔ **Other materials to add to your presentation library:**

- *I Hate Presentations* by James Caplin (Wiley)

- *Ideaselling* by Sam Harrison (How Books)

- *The Hero and the Outlaw* by Margaret Mark and Carol S. Pearson (McGraw Hill)

- *The Visual Story* by Bruce Block (Focal Press)

- *Ten Faces of Innovation* by Tom Kelley (Doubleday)

- *Change by Design* by Tim Brown (Harper Business)

Looking at Online Visual Thinking Sites

Understanding how to use visual thinking is key to getting to the essence of your ideas. In the following list I include helpful blogs, Web sites, and books about how you can use visual thinking:

✔ **Digital Roam blog (`www.digitalroam.typepad.com`):** Dan Roam's work is essential for anyone interested in the intersection of business and visual thinking. He provides stories, visuals, and great information about visual thinking and problem solving.

Check out his book *The Back of the Napkin* (Penguin).

✔ **Communication Nation Blog (`http://communicationnation.blogspot.com` or `www.squidoo.com/communicationnation`):** Dave Gray is a major thought leader on the subject of visual thinking. If you look at his blogs, Squidoo sites, his company XPLANE, and other work, he's constantly striving to bring visual thinking to the business community. Don't miss seeing and reading his work.

Check out the book *Game Storming* by Dave Gray, Sunni Brown, and James Macanufo (O'Reilly).

✔ **Viz Think (`www.vizthink.com`):** Viz Think was founded by Dave Gray and others to gather visual thinkers from around the world to share online. It is loaded with great resources, interesting people to communicate with and e-learning that is one of a kind. Check this out for all things visual thinking!

✔ **Periodic Table of Visualization Methods (`www.visual-literacy.org/periodic_table/periodic_table.html`):**

At `www.visual-literacy.org`, you can find a table of visualization methods to use as a reference for techniques you may want to explore. (See Figure A-1.) To see a specific chart, you just have to point your cursor and the map pops up.

Also, the site itself is chock-full of information, videos, and maps about visual thinking culled from university classes.

✔ **Other materials for your visual thinking library:**

• *Visual Explanations* by Edward Tufte (Graphic Press)

• *Rapid Viz* by Kurt Hanks and Larry Belliston (pub)

• *Thinking with a Pencil* by Henning Nelms (Ten Speed Press)

• *Rapid Problem Solving with Post it Notes* by David Straker (Da Capo Press)

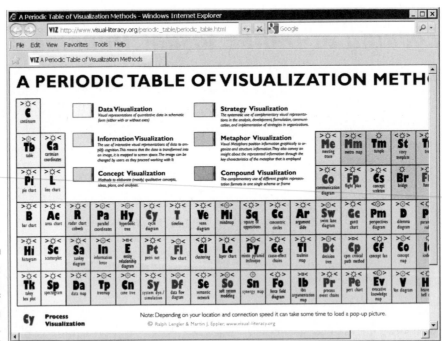

Figure A-1:
The Periodic Table of visualization methods.

Surfing Online Creativity and Innovation Sites

In the following list is information you can reference in blogs, Web sites, and books about how to generate ideas and keep creativity flowing.

- **The 99 Percent (http://the99percent.com):** The tag line for this blog is "It's not about ideas. It's about making ideas happen." For me that's the most important part of developing ideas — getting them out into the world where they can live. This site is called the *think tank* for Behance the company founded by Scott Belsky. You can find great information and visual thinking thought leaders sharing ideas via video, audio, articles, and so on. Don't miss a visit here to see what it's all about. I'm sure you'll stay.

  Check out his book *Making Ideas Happen* (Penguin).

- **Creativity Portal (www.creativity-portal.com):** At this site ,you can find lots of information and hands-on projects that will stimulate your creativity. (See Figure A-2.) Start anywhere on the site and just go where the fun leads you.

Figure A-2: The Creativity Portal site.

✔ **Innovation Tools (www.innovationtools.com):** Innovation Tools bills itself as "the world's largest Web site focused on business innovation, creativity, and brainstorming." Founder Chuck Frey has collected an enormous library of information about all subjects relating to thinking about business and innovation. I recommend that you start here if you're new to this topic and want to grab yourself a full-scale education. (See Figure A-3.)

✔ **Some materials to add to your creativity and innovation library:**

  • *Think Better* by Tim Hurson (McGraw Hill)

  • *What a Great Idea 2.0* by Chic Thompson (Sterling)

  • *Breakthrough Thinking* by Nick Souter (Sterling)

  • *Six Thinking Hats* by Edward DeBono (Back Bay Books)

  • *Business Model Generation* by Alex Osterwald and Yves Pigneur (Wiley)

  • *Innovate Like Edison* by Michael J. Gelb and Sarah Miller Caldicott (Dutton Adult)

Figure A-3:
The
Innovation
Tools site.

Checking Out Sites about Persuasion and the Mind

Check out information from the blogs, Web sites, and books in the following list to find out about advances in persuasion and how they relate to the mind:

✔ **David Rock's Column in Psychology Today (`www.psychologytoday.com/blog/your-brain-work`):** If you're interested in understanding how your mind impacts your performance, start your education by reading David Rock's "Your Brain at Work" column in Psychology Today and then move to his blog and Web sites. He brings a fascinating context to this subject. He's also keen on bringing this information into the area of coaching.

Check out his book *Your Brain at Work* (Harpers).

✔ **Neuromarketing Blog: Where Brain Science and Marketing Meet (`www.neurosciencemarketing.com/blog`):** This site has lots of great information, including how the brain impacts marketing, branding, management, and research. If you're interested in how brain science can me made useable for your everyday life, don't miss this site.

✔ **Martin Lindstrom (`www.martinlindstrom.com`):** Martin Lindstrom calls himself a brand strategist with good cause. His Web site contains all sorts of interesting articles, videos, and information about why people buy your brand. This site is great to check out if you're looking to understand how to make your brand messages resonate with your audience.

Check out his book *Buyology* (Broadway Business).

✔ **Neuromarketing Ning Group (`http://neuromarketing.ning.com`):** If you're interested in social networks, you may want to check out the Ning group Neuromarketing. It was founded by the creators of the online site Salesbrain.net. Patrick Renvoise and Christophe Morin have done a great deal of research and study of this topic. They define *neuromarketing* as the study of "the parts of the brain that decide." Lots of creative information here.

Check out their book *Neuromarketing* (Thomas Nelson).

✔ **Materials to add to your persuasion and the mind library:**

 • *Brain Rules* by John Medina (Pear Press)

 • *Yes: 50 Scientifically Proven Ways to Be Persuasive* by Robert Cialdini (Free Press)

 • *The Winner's Brain* by Jeff Brown, Mark Fenske, and Liz Neporent (Da Capo Press)

Reviewing Mind Mapping Online

In the following list, you can find information about Mind Mapping and innovation gathered in blogs, Web sites, and books:

- **Creative Thinking with Tony Buzan (`www.creativethinkingwith.com/Tony-Buzan.html`):** Tony Buzan is considered the father of Mind Mapping. This site gathers together information about creative thinkers, techniques, and teachers.

  Check out his book *Radiant Thinking* (Plume).

- **Google's Wonder Wheel Step by Step (`www.googlewonderwheel.com/google-wonder-wheel-step-by-step`):** I included the Google Wonder Wheel Step by Step page here to show you how information can be communicated graphically to assist you in creating graphics maps of your own. The Google Wonder Wheel structure is a map that drills down into information until you find what you're looking for. By looking at how this works, I think it will help you understand how visual information maps work. (See Figure A-4.)

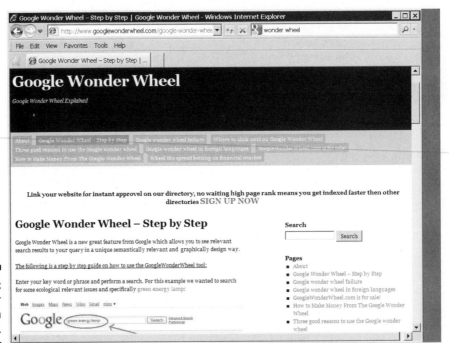

Figure A-4: The Wonder Wheel on Google.com.

✔ **Some materials to add to your Mind Mapping library:**

- *Use Both Sides of Your Brain* by Tony Buzan (Plume)
- *Visual Thinking Tools* by Nancy Margulies (Crown House Publishing)
- *Idea Mapping* by Jamie Nast (Wiley)

Browsing Online about Design and Designers

Are you a professional designer? If so, you can find tons of information to review online. In the following list are some sites and books that relate specifically to information graphics and protecting your work:

✔ **The Infographics Showcase (www.infographicsshowcase.com):** This is a really interesting site that gathers information graphics produced by designers around the world. It's updated frequently, so if you're looking for inspiration, check out this site. (See Figure A-5.)

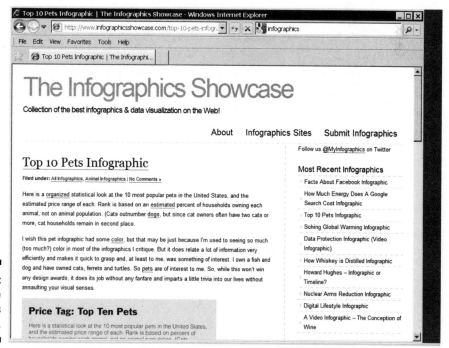

Figure A-5: The Infographics Showcase.

✔ **Infosthetics (`http://infosthetics.com`):** At this site, you can find hundreds of interesting examples of information design about a variety of different topics. It provides a great deal of food for thought.

✔ **Online stock photo sites:** Here are a few great Web sites for obtaining stock photos:

- iStockphoto (`www.istockphoto.com`)

- Bigstock (`www.bigstockphoto.com`)

- 123RF (`www.123rf.com`)

- Fotolia (`www.fotolia.com`)

✔ **Creative Commons (`http://creativecommons.org`):** Creative Commons is the organization that provides licenses that allow you to give people specific rights to reproduce your work. (See Figure A-6.)

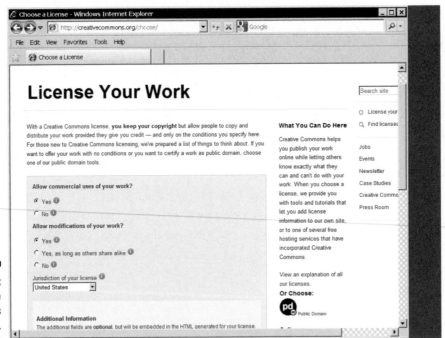

Figure A-6:
The Creative commons site.

✔ **Some materials to add to your design library:**

- *Information Design Workbook* by Kim Baer (Rockport Publishers)

- *Visual Language for Designers* by Connie Malamed (Rockport Publishers)

- *The Path of Least Resistance* by Robert Fritz (Fawcett Books)

- *The War of Art* by Steven Pressfield (Warner Books)

- *Before and After: How to Design Cool Stuff* by John McWade (Peachpit Press)

Surfing Sites for Non-Designers

For information about how to produce great-looking content without professional training, check out the following sites and books:

✔ **About.com(`http://graphicdesign.about.com` or `http://scrapbooking.about.com`):** I recommend that if you're just getting started with online graphics you check out a general information site like About.com. Because of the free-form nature of Prezi, you can start with the graphic design area and also check out the scrapbooking area to grab useful information.

✔ **Some materials to add to your library of books for non-designers:**

- *The Non Designer's Presentation Book* by Robin Williams (Peachpit Press)

- *Design to Sell* by Roger C. Parker (Microsoft)

- *Page Maps* by Becky Fleck (Memory Makers)

- *The New Drawing on the Right Side of the Brain* by Betty Edwards (Tarcher)

Index

• *C* •

Notes

Notes

Notes

Notes

Notes

Business/Accounting & Bookkeeping

Bookkeeping For Dummies
978-0-7645-9848-7

eBay Business
All-in-One For Dummies,
2nd Edition
978-0-470-38536-4

Job Interviews
For Dummies,
3rd Edition
978-0-470-17748-8

Resumes For Dummies,
5th Edition
978-0-470-08037-5

Stock Investing
For Dummies,
3rd Edition
978-0-470-40114-9

Successful Time
Management
For Dummies
978-0-470-29034-7

Computer Hardware

BlackBerry For Dummies,
3rd Edition
978-0-470-45762-7

Computers For Seniors
For Dummies
978-0-470-24055-7

iPhone For Dummies,
2nd Edition
978-0-470-42342-4

Laptops For Dummies,
3rd Edition
978-0-470-27759-1

Macs For Dummies,
10th Edition
978-0-470-27817-8

Cooking & Entertaining

Cooking Basics
For Dummies,
3rd Edition
978-0-7645-7206-7

Wine For Dummies,
4th Edition
978-0-470-04579-4

Diet & Nutrition

Dieting For Dummies,
2nd Edition
978-0-7645-4149-0

Nutrition For Dummies,
4th Edition
978-0-471-79868-2

Weight Training
For Dummies,
3rd Edition
978-0-471-76845-6

Digital Photography

Digital Photography
For Dummies,
6th Edition
978-0-470-25074-7

Photoshop Elements 7
For Dummies
978-0-470-39700-8

Gardening

Gardening Basics
For Dummies
978-0-470-03749-2

Organic Gardening
For Dummies,
2nd Edition
978-0-470-43067-5

Green/Sustainable

Green Building
& Remodeling
For Dummies
978-0-470-17559-0

Green Cleaning
For Dummies
978-0-470-39106-8

Green IT For Dummies
978-0-470-38688-0

Health

Diabetes For Dummies,
3rd Edition
978-0-470-27086-8

Food Allergies
For Dummies
978-0-470-09584-3

Living Gluten-Free
For Dummies
978-0-471-77383-2

Hobbies/General

Chess For Dummies,
2nd Edition
978-0-7645-8404-6

Drawing For Dummies
978-0-7645-5476-6

Knitting For Dummies,
2nd Edition
978-0-470-28747-7

Organizing For Dummies
978-0-7645-5300-4

SuDoku For Dummies
978-0-470-01892-7

Home Improvement

Energy Efficient Homes
For Dummies
978-0-470-37602-7

Home Theater
For Dummies,
3rd Edition
978-0-470-41189-6

Living the Country Lifestyle
All-in-One For Dummies
978-0-470-43061-3

Solar Power Your Home
For Dummies
978-0-470-17569-9

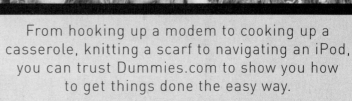
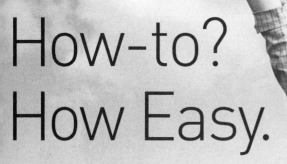

How-to?
How Easy.

From hooking up a modem to cooking up a casserole, knitting a scarf to navigating an iPod, you can trust Dummies.com to show you how to get things done the easy way.

Visit us at Dummies.com

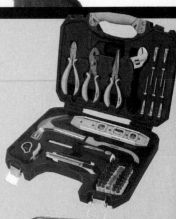